Meditations with
Sri Nisargadatta
Maharaj

English editing by
Suresh Mehta

From the original Marathi transcription by
Dinkar Kshirsagar

YogiImpressions®

YogiImpressions®

MEDITATIONS WITH
SRI NISARGADATTA MAHARAJ
First published in India in 2013 by
Yogi Impressions Books Pvt. Ltd.
1711, Centre 1, World Trade Centre,
Cuffe Parade, Mumbai 400 005, India.
Website: www.yogiimpressions.com

First Edition, June 2014

ISBN 978-93-82742-19-7

Printed at: Uchitha Graphic Printers Pvt. Ltd., Mumbai

CONTENTS

EDITOR'S NOTE

The material presented here is based upon notes taken by Shri Dinkar Kshirsagar while attending the daily gatherings at the residence of Sri Nisargadatta Maharaj. This was done during the period 1977-79, before Maharaj passed away in 1981.

Maharaj used to conduct morning and afternoon talks, mostly in a question-answer form, with the translator sitting next to him. A small group would also join him in meditation at 6:30 in the morning. Additionally, there was a small gathering later in the evening with the conversation being conducted in Marathi. Shri Dinkar usually attended the gatherings on Thursday and Sunday in the evening, as well as on holidays. Marathi being his mother tongue, it was easier for him to directly follow Maharaj's words. He wrote down the poignant Marathi sentences verbatim. As a result, we are fortunate to have a direct and accurate record.

The daily notes are titled *Nirupanas*. The word means 'investigating', 'defining', 'searching', etc. Maharaj says: *'To tell you about your true nature as to what it is and how it is, is the meaning of the word Nirupana'.*

Towards the end of his life, Maharaj preferred to emphasize on the core teaching and not dwell on peripheral topics. He used to say that what was being discussed at that time was different from the earlier dialogs documented in *I Am That.*

These notes were looked at by Maharaj and he encouraged distribution of the same. The sentences are mostly left as spoken, without rearrangement.

I consider the Nirupanas as passages for meditation. That is their purpose and that is where they lead. They may seem to be repetitive, yet there is a different nuance to them almost every time you read them. Consequently, this is not a book one would read perhaps in one sitting. One should rather read a passage at random and meditate on the same. It will tear away all your internal and external covers and leave your innermost core bare, with no support and ultimately no concepts, method or system to cling onto. At its foundation, of course, are the non-dual teachings of Vedanta or similar schools of thought.

Its uniqueness is that here it comes to us from an enlightened master's direct experience expressed spontaneously.

We owe the first attempted translation of these notes to Mrs. Damayantie Doongaji Ph.D., one of the senior disciples. She forwarded hand-written texts to her friend Jean Dunn in the mid-1990s. Jean had already published several books on the teachings by this time. She in turn asked me to take on the task of editing. Subsequently, Shri Dinkar revised the first translation and I re-edited the same through several iterations. I eventually verified it against the Marathi notes – one sentence at a time. My small regret is that it has taken a long time to bring this effort to fruition.

It is difficult to translate the original words (Sanskrit as well as colloquial Marathi) into English, as exact equivalents do not exist. This being the case, readers who are familiar with them will be able to interpret the equivalents with the right contextual meaning. There are plenty of precedents to this, of course. Then again, what we have here is inexpressible in words, as such. It is presented in known languages with their fundamental limitations. Sometimes, they are pointed out or explicit; sometimes they are implied.

Also, many a time the same words are used to express a different meaning or interpretation. For example, the word 'consciousness' has been used as *prana* – the life force; as awareness; as knowingness; as 'self'; or, as the ultimate root of manifestation that is *Brahman*. Hence, the context is very important.

I had the good fortune of attending Maharaj's talks in the summer and monsoon of 1979, when I lived in Mumbai.

During a visit to Sri Ramanasramam in Tiruvannamalai, a year earlier, someone had given me Maharaj's address. Later, when I read an article by Jean Dunn in *The Mountain Path* – the Asramam's magazine, I decided to go visit him.

It is impossible to second-guess how, why, and when things happen.

As I reflect back on those visits, the most poignant feeling that arises is a sense of grace. He did not call himself a Guru. And yet, I believe, if you were 'initiated' you somehow experienced it. It seemed that he did not form an image of you as such. He rarely called people by their names. It was as if we had no names. His mind did not seem to record the meetings.

Somehow, the questions one had and were never verbalized were answered during the flow of the session. It was as if divinity was playing its role but there was no player, so to speak. Once in a while, he would look at you and ask you what the question was. His primary advice was to regularly meditate on the sense 'I am'.

After a few months, when I told him I was going back to USA, his only comment was: 'You have to pass the time somehow'. When I asked if I would see him again, he gave a look that suggested he did not like such questions. Then he said I would see him. It so happened that I had to make a quick trip back to India less than a year-and-a-half later and he graced me with a meeting. Eight months later, he passed away.

A few quotations from the Nirupanas have been presented in an earlier pictorial book *The Wisdom Teachings of Nisargadatta Maharaj*, published by Inner Directions in 2003.

I am grateful to Shri Dinkar for allowing me to edit his painstaking notes and publish the same. I am also thankful to late Damayantie Doongaji for initiating this, and my friends and mentors late Jean Dunn and Saumitra K. Mullarpattan for guidance and encouragement. The latter had asked me to contact Gautam Sachdeva of Yogi Impressions for publishing the same.

I am thankful to him for making it happen. I also must thank him and his team for a careful, thorough and extensive review of the text for syntax, punctuation and consistency.

Gautam's firm has earlier published three books on Maharaj, and he has himself been deeply inspired by the Teaching. He has captured the 'essence' of this book in a short video that can be viewed on YouTube: http://youtu.be/NaIvHDpbFqM or http://tinyurl.com/MaharajBook1

– Suresh N. Mehta
Pleasanton, CA
June 23, 2014

INTRODUCTION

The earliest Indian scriptures, the Vedas, are some of the oldest texts in the history of the world, mostly composed during the Bronze Age. Vedas primarily dealt with the material and non-material aspects of life. As the sages turned their attention inwards to study consciousness, the revelations that they received helped them compose the Upanishads. They are a record of their insights. The foundation of Indian spiritual thought can, largely, be traced to these compositions.

The sages realized that to understand the mind and make it steady, purity of thought and concentration were necessary. Towards this goal, they prescribed certain spiritual practices. These were broadly classified as *Bhakti* yoga (yoga of devotion), *Karma* yoga (yoga of righteous action), and *Jnana* yoga (yoga of self-discovery).

Sri Nisargadatta Maharaj was a jnana yogi. In 1932, his Guru Sri Siddharameshwar Maharaj explained what the true nature of man was and asked him to meditate on the same. Nisargadatta Maharaj followed this very diligently and within three years had an unshakable insight: his Self-realization.

Maharaj spent nearly 50 years sharing his insights with all sincere seekers. People from all over the world came to his residence that was in a narrow lane of Mumbai. Their queries were answered and elaborated upon, appropriate for the enquirer's state of mind. For a Self-realized sage, this process occurs without any deliberation and is spontaneous.

The nature of the human mind is to identify with the body; its name and form, consciously and unconsciously. This identification does not allow us to reach our formless, attribute-less Self – the *Atman* – which is pure consciousness. A jnana yogi contemplates on this after intense study, and realizes the same. This is called the 'direct path'. It may be compared to the path of the bird that flies directly to the top. This is the first part of the spiritual search.

After this, the seeker meditates and gains knowledge of the pure consciousness. He then understands how it rises, sustains and sets. This understanding leads to ultimate liberation.

A realized sage is called *Sadguru* – one who has realized the emergence, sustenance and dissolution of His own consciousness. He in turn introduces it to the seeker and initiates him.

In the absence of a master, the Self as 'pure consciousness' is also called Sadguru.

Maharaj explained *sadhana,* spiritual practice, as follows:

Listening: Paying close attention to the teaching of the Sadguru invariably brings change. This is exemplified in the dialog between Sri Krishna and Arjuna as described in the Gita. Arjuna listened carefully even while fighting a war, and was liberated. There is no need to listen once the change is complete.

Bhajans: The *chitta* (inner mind) is purified by the words and singing of devotional songs. Worldly thoughts are at abeyance at such time. For some people this is the best practice.

Chanting: Silently reciting the name of a chosen deity, or a *mantra* (secret set of words given by a Guru), while paying attention to the breath. A mantra is usually given during the initiation of a seeker. Since mind and breath are closely related, prana – the life force, is thus purified. The mantra gets personified. This leads to dissolution of the mind and results in a state of *samadhi* (yogic inner trance).

The sage Valmiki, who was once a bandit, recited the mantra given to him by Narada, the messenger of the gods. By doing so, he transformed himself and wrote the magnificent epic Ramayana. Purification of prana may lead to spiritual powers that are inherent to pure consciousness. A *jnani* (realized being) generally refrains from using them.

Meditation: For purification of the mind, *dhyana* or meditation, is the best practice. After waking up and before going to bed, meditate for half an hour. This is what Maharaj used to prescribe: Sit steady with the back erect. Contemplate on: 'I am not the body. I am formless. I am self-illumined, pure consciousness'.

Remain aware of pure consciousness without words till you forget yourself while still awake. Do not visualize any deity, or chant any name. Just 'TO BE' and to remain steady with the awareness 'I AM' is the beginning and end of spiritual practice.

Maharaj has given further spiritual advice: 'The search for happiness is the cause of suffering'. The world is a repository of desire and fear. True detachment brings peace. The anxiety of 'what will happen to me?' is removed by detachment.

Our self-image, our ego, is strengthened by aspirations. Hence, one is advised to cast-off personal aspirations. The end of searching is ultimately the advent of Self-realization, which is timeless.

The sense 'I am' is always in the present moment. Eternity is in the present moment. We miss this because our mind wanders between the past and the future. One must understand that nothing exists which one should fear.

Consciousness and the world appear together and disappear together. They are two sides of the same coin. The world exists till the mind exists. The world comes into being with the birth of the body. Realize that the world is within you and not you in the world.

Maharaj says: 'From your point of view, you are born and you will die. From my point of view, the world appears and then disappears'. One cannot change the world, but one can change oneself and become free from desire and fear.

Meeting a Sadguru is the most precious thing in the life of a seeker. The sense of restlessness for the seeker, the divine dissatisfaction, is a benediction from the Guru.

The seeker needs to follow the teaching with love and faith. Do not see the Guru as a physical person. To follow his teaching earnestly is of the greatest importance.

I first met Maharaj on 14th May 1977. Two days later he gave me initiation. I usually visited him on Thursday and Sunday evenings. The first six months were very difficult for me as what I heard was different from my traditional knowledge, and this led to a conflict. Maharaj taught that there was nothing to attain or nothing to lose, but to understand, not intellectually but actually, the rising and dissolution of consciousness and its relationship with the world.

I started to write down important sentences so I could ruminate over them later. These formed the basis of the Nirupanas.

Maharaj was neither a preacher, nor a philosopher, nor a missionary. He spoke from his own direct experience, in his simple language. He used to say that if you take a few sentences and ruminate over them constantly, you will be free.

I was fortunate to be in the holy presence of Maharaj for four years, up to the last day of his physical existence.

May the passages on the following pages lead you to the Truth.

It is inevitable they will.

– Dinkar Kshirsagar

THE
NIRUPANAS

Nirupana 1
Sunday, November 27, 1977

All worldly activities are being done for the sake of entertainment of the consciousness of every living being.

The quality of the fruit depends upon the quality of the seed. Hence, it is important to listen to good things.

What is seen is the reflection of the seer's own consciousness. The pervader (you, as consciousness) and the pervaded (the manifest universe) are not different; they are one and the same. That through which space is created is within us. Mind has neither birth nor death. Mind means the speech (thoughts). The mind becomes silent when the word-flow ceases. The word comes from space, mind comes through the word, and your behavior depends upon your mind. (From this perspective, the first sound-word is OM which symbolizes the manifestation – the first vibration. The mind is formed from the words thereon.) In fact, *you* are not the doer.

You wear clothes but you do not say, 'I am the clothes'. Similarly, learn to say, 'I am not the body'. Your form is of the nature of space.

(In this discourse Maharaj is telling us to go back to our Source. When we get up in the morning, the first to appear is the seed consciousness, just a feeling of our beingness. In a few seconds, this seed consciousness expands and space comes into existence. In this space everything is seen, including our own body. This has been happening every day from our childhood. Since then, we have identified ourselves with the body. This deep-rooted impression cannot be dismissed without the guidance of an enlightened Guru. The Guru asks us to go inwards by saying, 'I am not the body. I am consciousness within the body'.)

Nirupana 2
Thursday, December 1, 1977

Brahman (the manifestation) is eternal. However, even the concept 'I am Lord Vishnu' does not last. What does that mean? Can the meaning be understood through austerities? It can only be understood through right discrimination. (Maharaj points out that Vishnu may be the supreme One, but when He sleeps, He forgets everything including His own name. As long as one regards oneself as a body, even if one is an incarnation, one cannot remain in his true state of being.)

To keep in mind what is heard is meditation.

What was done in childhood was true, what was done in youth was true, and what was done in old age was also true; but finally one must realize that it was altogether false (as it passed away with time).

Liberation means being free. It is freedom from our own concepts, from the bondage of our mind, intellect and imagination. The Self is free from the concept, 'I want to be' and requires no liberation.

One who has recognized the source of mind and intellect remains free from the resulting harassment. They arise out of body-consciousness.

Parabrahman (Absolute) does not belong to any organization. All cults are concepts and all concepts are incomplete.

What is the Guru-word? It is: 'You are not the body, you are consciousness in the body'. Hold onto this.

Time will end, but you will never end. One who says 'I am the body' will never understand this.

When there is no time, there is no world. (This time is not by the clock. Maharaj says time starts with the birth of the person. It is not the child, but it is time that is born. So, the world is there as long as you are.)

You know that 'you are'. That is the misery. Consciousness in the body is the reason why everything is seen. This subtle self-sensation is the Guru. Always remember this. That is meditation. Even if the pure sense of beingness is not held consciously in the mind, it is always there. The experience of time disappears along with the world, just like the ending of a dream. One who witnesses the dissolution of the universe is certainly prior to it. The situation is like that of a sleeping man witnessing a dream.

You will get time for spirituality only when your mind is silent. For this, concentrate on the goal. Krishna says: 'That, through which the world is known, is My nature as well as yours'.

Maya is difficult to grasp. She blocks the path to Self-realization, unless there is devotion to the Guru. Practice non-dual devotion. Catch hold of the knowledge 'I am'. (Here, Guru is not a physical person; it is your pure consciousness. It is also called jnana. The common meaning of maya is delusion. The root-maya is your seed-consciousness.)

By adhering to the Guru's word, you will grow spiritually and be happy in household life as well.

It is said that there are three *gunas* (qualities). Really speaking there is only one guna – *Sattva guna* – pure consciousness. When it takes up doership, it is *Tamo guna*. When it is active, it is *Rajo guna*. The presence of these gunas is known through worldly dealings.

Nirupana 3
A Compilation

(This Nirupana is a collection of sentences compiled over a period of time. They represent a unique self-assertion of an enlightened person. Generally, Maharaj did not talk about himself.)

"My identity is beyond description. I have no use for myself. Others may find me useful depending on their faith. The eternal Truth, Parabrahman, is always with me. The accumulated experience of 81 years is the only obstacle that has come over me. When I am beyond my sense of 'I am', how can I commit a sin or a virtuous act?"

"I have seen the existence-consciousness-bliss (*sat-chit-ananda*) in its naked form; hence I talk like this. Parabrahman – the unmanifest, is guiding Brahman – the manifest. I am not talking to a person as a person. I am talking to pure consciousness, not the body. As you listen while identified to the body-form, you do not understand this."

"I accepted what my Guru taught me; no other advice. Due to maya, I felt that 'I am', which was not prior to maya. When I realized this mistake, I knew I was always there, but without knowingness."

"I am fully aware that the devotee is not different from me. I am not talking to the individual but to consciousness and the love within it. We have an eternal friendship, only if you keep it up. The difference between you and I is gone. The sense of individuality is replaced with a sense of the totality. Now, death has become of the nature of the Absolute."

"My answers to your questions come up spontaneously. I do not think over them."

"My birth is the birth of the world. The Source of my speech is the golden womb (*Hiranya Garbha*) through which the world is created."

"Here, the word is replying to the word. However, I am outside the word. In my identity, there is no light, no darkness, no 'I' nor 'you'. Who will recognize me in my unmanifested state? I can be known when the knower himself is dissolved. When the passions are silent, there is no urge to go outside. I am the witness of 'beingness' and the 'non-beingness'."

"I am giving you the knowledge of my true nature. Listen to the same as if it is your own. By the grace of the Guru, I have undergone Self-realization. As I have known my true nature, the great scholars cannot compete with me in arguments. Rich people, highly educated people and dignitaries come to meet me. I behave with them just as I would with anyone. I know why and how one feels that 'he is'. Therefore I see no difference between big and small. I see no difference between God and the devotee. You will not understand this without discrimination."

"I was convinced that I had attained a lot of knowledge and I was also convinced that I had attained no knowledge at all. All these are seasonal concepts. I have undergone all the yogic experiences. I have washed them off, as there is no real greatness in spiritual powers. You must know that I praise consciousness and condemn it as well. People are bothered by their memories. I have baked myself and I have eaten myself up."

"The sensation of beingness is a matter of experience, but I am beyond that. Some people claim that they have memories of past lives. I do not have even the experience of myself at anytime."

"No specimen of my individuality will be found in the world. I am only the totality. A life of an extra 100 years will be of no use to a person like me. I have disappeared with negation. I have no use of my beingness. I am desireless Parabrahman. You are listening to me while treating yourself as the body, hence this is not affecting you. My saying and your understanding should be reconciled."

"You may not be able to endure what I will say from now on. Therefore I ask you to leave. I have no use of myself. But for you, I will be available anywhere according to your faith. My form will depend upon your concept. You will meet me according to your concept."

The following are the last words of Maharaj before he lost his voice:

"I feel the pain in the body but I have no pain of dying. What has manifested is not 'I'. I am That which is always there and which is prior to manifestation. I am not consciousness; on the contrary, consciousness is a nuisance to me."

Nirupana 4
Thursday, December 22, 1977

Your dream is your own, no one else can watch it. Similarly, your world is your own.

The fact 'I am not the clothes I wear' can be easily understood. The fact 'I am not the body' cannot be understood without the grace of the Guru. The Guru's word, 'I am pure consciousness' is as good as a mantra.

Self-realization never changes. The greater the understanding, the lesser will be the desires. The nature of the Self has no desires.

Jiva (self, identified with the body) is fond of the body. However, do not forget that even when absorbed in the Self, the body should be well looked after. The Guru's word reflects our true nature. After our efforts are over, the true nature shines automatically.

One who has contemplated upon the Self even a little, will not need any gods or deities; in fact, he will not need anything. Such a one will not hurt even the smallest creature.

After realizing your nature you will not ask for anything.

The body has not been created by you, or by your parents, or by God. It has been created spontaneously.

Compared to knowing your true nature, the holy places of the world are nothing. The holy places have their importance through your light alone.

Doubting the Guru-word is the greatest sin.

The light which you see outside arises from your own light. The light of the sun and the moon cannot be compared to the light of your Self. The body pertains to the human being, but the one that acts through the body is not a human being. It is the true nature of the Self. Because of body-consciousness, you think you are someone or the other. This is not so once the Self is realized. You are certainly going to die, but with what identity?

The sense 'I am' is making a small gesture towards you – catch hold of it. It is easy for a man who is disgusted by worldly dealings. The knowledge of beingness is motivating all. The consciousness that gives you the feeling 'you are', is the same as the feet of the Sadguru. Be in touch with it. At least remember the fact that your corpse-like body contains the seed of the Absolute. Contemplate on the flame of the Self. The eternal nature of this flame will be understood on Self-realization.

Keep in mind that this is your own story. Then your worthiness will be as good as that of Brahman. As you do not forget that you are a woman or a man, so also remember 'I am Brahman'. Do not face death by calling yourself as the body. The meditation on the Self is what redeems us. Time will get dissolved into you and not you into time.

'Oh Guru, your true nature is my own Self, I see no difference in them, and that is how I have surrendered to you'. This should be your conviction. This knowledge of beingness is like the missile called *Brahmastra*. It will never fail. Such a person may look ordinary, but he is different. Meditate on the meditator, not on others. It is very fortunate to get to listen to Self-knowledge in this way.

Nirupana 5
Sunday, December 25, 1977

People keep themselves busy because they find it difficult to bear their own consciousness. People look for various entertainments to escape from themselves. The greatest challenge lies in looking at oneself; sitting alone by oneself.

A much greater number of people have died than those who are living now. Where have they gone, the burden of their bodies weighing millions of tons? What must they be doing now? The answer is that they are now as they were before their birth.

The ultimate religion is Self-realization. This is an unbroken and fearless state of being. This state refers to consciousness within the body. The religions based upon the bodily behavior of human beings take them to their downfall. The highest religion means to live with the conviction that we are pure consciousness. Liberation means to be free. Then one is not affected by the bondage of mind, intellect and ego. One who follows this gets freedom from all concepts. Only the religion of one's own Self will last to the end. That through which worldly dealings are known is our true nature. Though fully immersed in mundane activity, one is not affected. Understand this fact, be silent and at peace. All your needs will be taken care of. Krishna says: 'I take the responsibility of sustenance for the one who follows the religion of his own true nature'. For him, all that is required is supplied automatically. Spiritual effort is as easy as it is difficult.

One who holds onto the Guru's word that 'I am the self-luminous Atman' will find it easy. The highest charity is to offer Self-knowledge.

A true *brahmin* is one who knows he is Brahman – pure consciousness. Those who are truly religious get the real reward of Self-knowledge. Prana (vital breath, the life force) does all the dealings; hence, be friends with it. If prana is purified by the Guru-mantra, then it mingles with the universal prana when one dies. Others who do not know take a fall.

Prana represents all the types of speech: *para* – intuition, *pashyanti* – thought-form, *madhyama* – word unspoken, and *vaikari* – word spoken. Madhyama is called the mind and when it speaks it is called vaikari. Thus the mind is not different from prana. Prana is *pranava* – the primordial sound Om. Prana, the life force, does not differentiate between a worm and a human being. It treats each body the same. The jnani does not see prana as an individual form. To him all is one. Prana of a jnani becomes prana of the universe. Where consciousness is stabilized, there is compassion. That is the only thing left with the jnani. When your prana is pleased, you will come to know: 'Who really speaks, is it you or your prana?'

Nirupana 6
Thursday, January 5, 1978

Thoughts come and go the way they came. They linger if there is a need. A jnani has not even the need for himself. How does the household of a jnani work? The One that nourishes the child for nine months in the womb takes care of the jnani. How is the child looked after and protected until he gets the knowingness that he has a body? The answer is, the universal consciousness that he is, does everything. Even if you live for a thousand years, your identification with the body will not go. How can the One who is light and pure existence, be a body? The experience of your beingness, without pronouncing a single word, is true knowledge.

The body is made of five elements. Its essence is the consciousness that resides in the body. Know with certainty that you are not the body. You are without form; you are of the nature of light. You can see light and darkness because of your own light. Om symbolizes the hum of ascent (of breath), the assurance of your beingness. As you get to know your consciousness, you become liberated. If you are not the body, how are you going to act and with whom? That is the unshakable, immovable state. Once it is known that you are of the nature of light, there is no further coming and going. You are of the nature of the self-luminous light by whose virtue you can see things. Yet you believe that 'I am so-and-so, having a body'. When the body falls, prana leaves. No one says that prana is dead. If prana is pure, the mind and intellect are also pure. If prana is satisfied, can one have the experience of misery? The power of prana is the same as the power of life – the vital force. The force of prana is the same as the primordial maya – it is the same as the power of Brahman. If someone becomes great, it is only by the power of prana.

There is love for the word as long as there is ignorance. After knowledge, there is no use of words. After realization, the sense 'I am' is still there but the attitude of the mind is entirely changed.

Continue your chanting of the mantra, keeping its meaning in mind. Think of who should worship whom and why? If you want the Guru's grace, take the word of the Guru as authority.

Nirupana 7
Sunday, January 15, 1978

The movement of prana and the movement of God are not different. Watch your breathing. Without the vital life force, the feeling 'I am' will not be there. Consciousness in the body is the characteristic-guna of prana. (They are not separate.) Once you have realized the Self, it is not at all necessary to put on a special pose. That would be a sign of ignorance. To grow a beard, to look impressive, etc., is tied to body-consciousness. They are not the characteristics of the Self. The concept that you may take for your meditation will be realized and you will have visions accordingly. They are all unreal.

There is no method comparable to listening to such talks. Once you listen to this, liberation is within reach. The manifest principle has movement, but the unmanifest does not. It is without qualities.

As old age comes, childhood and youth go away automatically. It is not necessary to renounce them with purpose. Similarly, your ego should naturally fade away. No experience is lasting. There is no creator of the world, nor is there a sustainer, nor a destroyer. All happens spontaneously. What we know becomes the source of our happiness or sorrow. That which is not known to us cannot be the source of our happiness or sorrow.

Mind is the concept, and concept is the mind. The concept gives birth to whatever it likes. Such is the kingdom of the mind. The Self has no association. When one understands the concept, simultaneously one realizes That which is without concepts. This becomes possible even by listening. What you have learnt from childhood has become the real world for you. 'Jiva', 'jagat' and 'Brahman' (individual soul, the world and the supreme Self) are concepts. The concept creates its own meanings resulting in the three gunas. At the root there is the manifest consciousness. When consciousness becomes active through dealings, the mind is created. The manifest consciousness is the base on which the mind floats.

When we get up from sleep, at that moment we feel 'we are', prior to any words. That is the basic thought. How did this world come into existence? It is like a dreamer creating a dream world without doing anything. We feel the world to be real because we feel our body to be real, and vice-versa. Though the world is immense, there is not an iota of truth in it. The unmanifest became manifest and created the mind. The mind created the world, which appears to be real. The one who goes beyond the manifest and remains in the unmanifest cannot quite say, 'Now, I am unknown to me'. First comes consciousness, then the mind is created through it followed by all the activities. In the absence of consciousness, is it possible to do anything? The feeling 'I am' is a natural concept. That concept is never satisfied. When you try to be one with your consciousness, mind comes in the way. Keep trying. Pay attention to the Source from which consciousness has appeared. This consciousness is untrue.

The listener should watch himself rather than interfering in the affairs of others. He should take the opportunity to see or know what he is. After knowing the meaning of the concept, you will know that the world is a joke. 'Absolutely nothing has happened, I have not seen anybody, nobody has ever seen me'; this will be your conviction.

Whatever desire you do penance with, it projects on your mind and everything appears accordingly. The life force takes shape and then come the visions. If you act with body-consciousness, concepts will proliferate. If you make friendship with your pure consciousness, it will uncover its true nature. When consciousness knows what it is, it vanishes and what remains is *vijnana* – true direct knowledge that has no name. If you behave accordingly, sooner or later you will realize that you never had any experience of the world. Then where is the question of going about in such a world? Till such time that you know this, do all your dealings as you like. Look after the household. Do not run away from it.

When you were born you were in your natural state, before you started hearing words. After what you heard, which you believed was true, you have come to the present state. What has entered your mind so far is behaving in different ways.

The greatest endeavor is to understand oneself. That you must achieve. Then the secret of the whole world will be understood. When you realize yourself, you will understand the world at the same time. You will know what 'you' are. Have the firm conviction that I am what the Guru told me. In worldly dealings you can use your identity as a man or a woman, but do not keep it within you. Everything depends upon who you are going to die as.

Death is only a word. It is never an experience. What will you experience other than Brahman when there is nothing else other than Brahman? You have become the disciple of the mind. Mind is designing you. Mind does not know its source. Your conviction should rest in the Guru's word. 'Guru initiated me' means he told me about my true nature. Believing it to be true, if one behaves with conviction, then the Truth will be known. From other people's point of view, a man is dead. From the point of view of a jnani, he has become free of his delusion. 'I am such and such, a woman or a man', is the delusion.

First the food gets ready, and then the jiva takes birth through that. The nature of the food is the same as that of the jiva. The body is only transformed food. It is the food for consciousness. So long as there is consciousness, there is hunger and thirst.

Either you become determined through the Guru's word, or keep on stumbling in vain. That experience to which you are attracted today is false. It will not last. You may take the best nutrition and stay strong. Yet, when old age comes the hands and feet are sure to shake. Think of that. Surrender to consciousness which says, *Jai Guru, Jai Guru*'. Because you believe that you are the body, such concepts as 'I am a child, I am a youth, I am old' occur to you. 'I am surely here and always will be; the body goes on changing.' This is the discrimination.

Nirupana 8
Thursday, January 19, 1978

Both reading and listening are necessary. But the knowledge received from the Guru should perfectly tally with what is read and heard. 'I am exactly like what I have heard and read and what the Guru has told me': this is the way. That which remains after dismissing one's consciousness is the Truth. Union with God is *yoga*. After the union, both of them get extinguished and the One who witnesses is the supreme Self – the unmanifest state of being.

The body is *prakriti* (nature) and the one who resides in the body is *Purusha* (Self). The one who acts is prakriti, while the Purusha is the passive witness. In other words, prana is the movement and its knower is consciousness. Both the energies have no form. Prakriti and Purusha are not separate. So long as you take yourself as the body, there is no peace. Keep in mind what you have heard and discriminate constantly. One who has realized prakriti and Purusha becomes liberated.

In the body, God is experiencing Himself with the feeling 'I am'. The Guru's word is your beingness; this should be your conviction. Surrender yourself to prana; drop identification with the body. One who knows the power of prana is a jnani. His meditation continues all through the day. Concentrate on the source of the vital energy (*shakti*). This meditation is carried out with that energy. Everlasting peace is the great accomplishment. When both prakriti and Purusha are forgotten, there is real *rest*. By virtue of meditation, the feeling 'I am so-and-so' is lost. To make meditation successful, be faithful to it. Concentrate on the Self with the energy of prana. When this energy is arrested, the consciousness becomes one with it and samadhi ensues. The knowledge received from the books has to be tested with one's own experience.

When we get up from deep sleep, the first to appear is microscopic consciousness. It is the feeling 'I am', before any words. This seed consciousness is the cause of all experiences. In no time, it takes on the form of the universe. But you have to see how this consciousness is unreal. The world appears with your wakefulness. The experience goes away along with the one who experiences. Catch the Source of this knowingness. When an operation is done under anesthesia, there is no pain. If a man dies in that unconscious state, is there any pain of death?

While listening to these talks, you forget yourself and thereby forget the world. You remain in your natural state of being. Is it not a great benefit? Devotion to the Guru rewards you with Self-realization.

Nirupana 9
Sunday, January 22, 1978

Your true nature is not different from Parabrahman. Your self-identity is based upon your body and you consider yourself as male or female. It is a mistake that you call yourself a human being. That which is listening now is your true nature; it is pure consciousness. It is a mistake to call it a body. Your true identity (unmanifest principle) is there prior to your knowledge. Whatever form you take yourself to be will not last. Actually, you have no birth or death. They pertain to the body.

Your consciousness is a result of the activity of the three gunas. It is transient. It is not understood properly because of the three gunas. Your sense of happiness or sorrow is the result of consciousness. But this consciousness will vanish just as fire gets extinguished. The supreme fire is Self-realization.

Does the sun know that its brightness varies? You experience the fact by virtue of your own light. The most important of the three qualities is the quality of knowing (Sattva). You know everything through this quality. Who creates the houses, machines, roads, etc.? Is it not due to someone's consciousness?

You enslave yourself because of your needs. You will be free from this slavery when you realize that consciousness, which is listening, is free and formless. It is your true nature. Recognize That by which you feel you are alive. *To tell you about your true nature as to what it is and how it is, is the meaning of the word Nirupana.*

What you conceive through the mind will not last. Sense of 'me' and 'mine' is the natural characteristic of consciousness. Catch hold of the main guna – Sattva as jnana – the quality of knowingness. Live a life without expectations. Then, automatically, the attachments will fall off. Recognize that you are without requirements. Your true state is spontaneously there. Do not disturb it through the mind.

You have always taken God as your support. That does not mean that you know God. Rama, Krishna and Vishnu are names of bodies. They command great devotion because they had realized the Truth.

A devotee can have visions of the deities if he meditates on them according to what he has heard. What is the source of that vision? He, himself, is the source of it. Whatever you have taken for granted has no value. Worldly dealings are not under your control. They will keep on going. Once you are stabilized in your Self, you will never feel a want of anything.

Brahma, Vishnu and Shiva (God as creator, sustainer and destroyer) are the names of your own Self. Jiva is born as a matter of course along with time. There is desire associated with the jiva. Your knowledge of the world depends upon your consciousness. When someone says, 'I go to the subtle', what does it mean? It, of course, implies consciousness, your sense of 'I am'. It has no shape, no color. It has a taste – the awareness that 'you are'. What is the relationship of this knowledge to you? Does it die when the five-elemental body ceases to be? Think of how you would appear if you were not the body. Keeping in mind what you have heard and pondering over it is the greatest penance. Through the practice of this kind of meditation, you will go on changing continuously and you will reach a stage where there is no further change.

The Truth has no knowledge of Itself (it is unmanifest). Attend to this goal constantly. Drive away body-consciousness from your mind. No matter how much you insist, you cannot be a man or a woman forever. The five elements will merge into the five elements.

Even if you do not understand all this, at least understand That by which you know 'you are'. Once again, meditate on your goal continuously. It will enlighten you. Your mind needs some support. You cannot bear your consciousness without having something else to think over. To meditate on the Self is possible only with the grace of the Guru. Such meditation is unique, not commonly found in the world.

The nature of time is such that it will not allow anything to remain steady. If you cannot focus your attention on the goal (consciousness), call it as 'Guru' and say, 'I am meditating on my Guru'. This is simple. The world is a creation of your own consciousness. Purusha is the passive witness – the seer, and prakriti (the power of prana) is doing everything through the body. Mind, intellect and intuition are all names of the energy of prana. There is no separation between jnana (consciousness) and prana (the life force). They are two sides of the same coin. Hence, if prana is pleased, consciousness is pleased. Meditate on the life force; then meditation on consciousness will take place indirectly.

Both have no form. All activities take place because of these. How can one say that they (jnana and prana) are dead when the body dies?

Your thoughts of 'me and mine' do not allow you to know your Self. Hence, you live in an undignified manner. At least remember what Purusha and prakriti are. Achieve union with prana. Prana is God. It implies movement. In the end, the knower of the movement and the movement itself both merge into that non-qualitative state. For the sage, the occasion of prana leaving the body, the occasion of the great departure, is a celebration.

'Wait for a moment at the door of God. All the four kinds of liberation are there.' The meaning of this quotation is that if for a moment your attention is fixed on your Self, you will be liberated. The Guru liberates you. He initiates you by saying, 'your true nature is like my own'. He gives you the mantra, not taking you as male or female, but as the consciousness that listens.

Jiva is perfect and yet he is moaning with the fear of death. The sage feels compassion for the jiva; for its condition. That is the reason why he sometimes gets angry and impatient.

Nirupana 10
Sunday, January 29, 1978

When you look at the moon, what do you see between your eyes and the moon? The space in between is not seen. Similarly, your own light, through which you look, is also not seen. They are one and the same. Your consciousness is of the nature of space.

The creation in descending order is as follows: First comes the seed consciousness i.e. the feeling 'I am', then space, followed by the other four elements. This is the sequence.

The one who has realized his own consciousness, its cause and its duration, is the knower. He does not act. When the king is seated on the throne, the administration goes on, just because he *is*. Similarly, the knower does not act. Along with birth, the feeling 'I am' arises. Before birth, there was no such feeling. The vital energy carries out all the actions. The knower is beyond the known. (The knower means the supreme Self or the *Paramatman* who is prior to consciousness.) It is the unmanifested state. It is the true nature of everyone. One who has realized this state is called a jnani. The ignorant person takes the feeling 'I am' as the body, the seeker takes it as pure consciousness, but the jnani does not identify with anything. After listening to this, compare it with your present state of being.

There was no concept before birth but an eternal peaceful reality. The concept 'I am' comes through the power of the Sattva guna. Because of ignorance one apparently enjoys body-consciousness. A seeker enjoys it as knowledge. The knower is beyond knowledge. A realized soul is beyond that enjoyment altogether.

Sometimes it is said that a remedy can be an obstacle, yet there is one remedy available to you. Chant your mantra. With faith in the one who has given you the mantra, your consciousness will become stronger. As a result, there will be no weakness in your actions. The greater the faith in the Guru, the earlier the success. If you take your Guru as a human being, your consciousness will harass you. One who follows this faithfully will enjoy liberation in this very body. To surrender means to be without body-consciousness. To offer everything to Brahman means to be without quality. Act with the conviction that the consciousness that sustains the universe is within your body. On your own, you are unable to do anything. All the actions are carried out by the life force. The Guru introduces you to consciousness.

Because of your presence (the pure consciousness) the places of your pilgrimage become holy. There is nothing more sacred than consciousness. When you realize your Self, there will be nothing as holy as you. When you get this conviction, there will be no need for associating with others. One who has pride of his (so-called) enlightenment is ignorant. How can one have any pride when he realizes that nothing has happened?

Love implies our need for beingness. Love is infinite and unlimited. It is consciousness that has arisen in us unknowingly. It is without shape, caste or creed. It is the pure quality of the vital energy. It is the power of this love by which we feel that 'we are'.

A jnani never competes with anyone. Therefore he is beyond criticism. Those who dislike a jnani are unripe due to their body-consciousness. They do not understand what a jnani says. With the grace of the Guru, the understanding could come in an instant. Do not impose body-consciousness on the Guru who is without quality and without form. What you are hearing now is the knowledge of the experience of the Self. It is not hearsay.

Whose is this voice? When was it created and why? It is the voice of prana. It is not your voice. Meditate with your consciousness, not with the body. Only love moves around in the form of the three gunas and the five elements. It is the self-love.

Devotion to the Guru opens your eyes. That which is seen without the eyes is superior. Before the eyes open, the light has got a dark blue shade. As soon as the eyes open, it becomes colorless. Be loyal to the Sadguru. Do not impose your body-consciousness on Him. After recognizing the seed-consciousness, everything becomes an offering to Brahman. (Such a person becomes unattached to worldly affairs.)

Who is talking? Is it you that is talking? The word belongs to space. And you are beyond space.

My Guru used to say no matter how old you are, you are only a child. (The body gets older. Yet consciousness is always in the present moment. It is like a newborn child at all times.)

There are various kinds of practices in the world. To work miracles after getting spiritual powers is also a type of learning. I did not get into that. I only studied the nature of the Self as taught by my Guru. In comparison to the realization of the Self, all else is meaningless. Without faith in the Guru, you will wander about going to various teachers and holy places. If you follow your Guru's word it will not be necessary to go anywhere.

Nirupana 11
Thursday, February 9, 1978

Consciousness can observe only that which undergoes change. That which is eternal cannot be observed by consciousness. Therefore it cannot be known. The concept 'I am so-and-so' is not permanent. One who knows this is everlasting. Concepts and desires appear with the body, and also disappear with the body. All that is known is a concept. However great the knower of the Self may be, what he teaches is still a concept that pleases him.

All your actions are transient. It does not matter how long they last. What is today, not a trace of it will remain tomorrow as nothing is everlasting. What will you do when the mind-flow stops?

The one who knows what 'he is' will never censure anyone. The world is bound by the three gunas. One who knows the gunas, does not censure the gunas. So long as you consider yourself a body with a name, there is no direct knowledge of the Self. Without that one becomes a tattler, who blames things on someone else. All wordy attacks are the result of body-consciousness. The feeling 'I am', which everyone has, is God. So whom will you criticize?

The respect you give to the Guru, the same will be created in you. Guru means jnana (consciousness). Guru means Parabrahman. Atman is the self-luminous knowledge. It is of the nature of God. His very form is this knowledge. The feeling that 'you are' is the soul of the world. Remember this constantly. Put aside what you have learnt from books. As long as you think you are separate, you have to do sadhana (spiritual practice). Whatever happens or does not happen is within God, and by God. You are not concerned with that. To keep this awareness throughout the day is constant meditation on the Self. Whether prana leaves today or 10,000 years from now, there is no gain, no loss for a jnani.

Faith in the Guru and understanding received through the Guru's word cannot be compared with anything else. It is so pure. Consciousness is spotless, formless and prior to intellect. Worldly knowledge is born out of the word. Without your consciousness, would the sun exist as the sun? As you identify yourself with the body, you cannot even imagine the immense consciousness. Everything is transitory. One who knows that is eternal. What you take yourself as, its effects will be felt by you. If you live with the understanding that you are Brahman, the same will be your destiny.

Consciousness as 'I am' is atomic. The moment it comes into being, it becomes self-luminous and creates the immense world. How can you put an end to the things that have been created by your own light?

Nirupana 12
Thursday, February 16, 1978

Your consciousness contains the immense phenomenal world. Yet it appears outside. As it is created from this subtle consciousness, it is untrue. Only Brahman is true.

Hold tight to that knowledge. That is true meditation. As long as you look for personal benefit, you will not get Self-realization. Atman is our true nature. It is the formless consciousness. With the combination of body, prana and Atman, there is the sense 'I am'. Put aside your problems if any and get stabilized in the Self. The body has a form but consciousness within the body has no form. By taking the body as our form, duality is created. It brings the experience of happiness and misery. Worship only consciousness by which all of this is experienced. It is beyond intellect.

The knowledge (jnana) is called the Guru. That means the knowledge that the teacher has is the Guru. Where there is an experience of the Self, there is bliss. We are that bliss. Consciousness is the hum of beingness. To catch hold of it is meditation. People say they are happy, but has anyone of them experienced bliss? Our true nature is neither happiness nor sorrow. The Self, itself, is happiness. To worship the Guru is to worship his word. It means to worship our own consciousness. 'I am' is beyond the mind, it is also beyond the qualities. Its nature is like space. It is the all-pervading firmament of consciousness. It is fearless just as space is fearless. It is stupendous and fathomless. Keep your attention on It. Worship It without bringing in duality. Do not identify with the body. You are the ocean of bliss.

In summary, worship the word of the Guru, 'I am not the body, I am the formless, pure life force or Brahman that vitalizes the body'. There is no limit to happiness where there is no body-consciousness. Consciousness will sustain you in every sense if you have faith in the Guru's word. When your inner urge is devotion to the Guru, death has no effect on you. Consciousness appears in various forms including different types of visions. One who is firmly established in the Guru's teaching has no fear. Because of body-consciousness, the Atman who is of the nature of perfect bliss has to endure misery. Do not take yourself to be an individual. Stay with the awareness of the manifest (totality). Its body is space.

Take the Guru's word to your heart. It will enable you to see and experience clearly the seed within. That seed has become the world. Though it moves about in myriad bodies, it is spotless. Hence, you need not worry about the purification of the body. You do not require rules and regulations of any creed. Your consciousness will slowly crystallize and you will realize your true nature. The concept of death will seem ridiculous. The true religion of a devotee is faith. Strictly observe the Guru's word, 'I have no other form but consciousness'. Then, do what you like. Do not worry. It is a waste of intellect and energy. Spontaneously, everything is happening in God, through God, and by God.

Nirupana 13
Thursday, March 2, 1978

Observe your present life, how and why it has become like this. Know that this is a temporary show. You call upon God but where was God before you came to know 'you are'? Find the source of all this. That which is of the nature of time is not everlasting because time itself is not real. Your intellect also changes with time. The manifest is bound by time. Gods and deities are a result of the power of the word. We are alive by virtue of the word. The pulse itself is the word. Whatever you believe in is true for you. However, it is time-bound and not eternal. The Truth is unmanifested. (Maharaj is saying that the manifestation is a time-bound concept. Our body-mind is part of it. The first word, Om, is the symbol of manifestation.) Meditate on that by which you know 'you are'.

Birth and death are nonsense. Who is born? It is only a sport of the five elements. The vital life force is playing as it pleases, by collecting and mixing the five elements in the form of a body. They have no intelligence. Why would a merciful God create a world like this, where life depends on life? That is why there is no creator. The world is there due to duality. No duality, no world.

People who want to make money should do just that. Search for spiritual knowledge and pursuit of wealth cannot be done at the same time. Spirituality is possible only when you let go of everything. As long as you take yourself as the body, what you say is true for you. It is as true as the body. All activities take place because of the rise of consciousness in the body. The feeling of misery and happiness is there due to the sense 'I am'.

Sleep and awakening come spontaneously. They are not a result of your will. The nature of the dream continues through wakefulness. Where is the profit or loss if there is no individual thought like 'I am so-and-so'? Have you thought of how this sense of 'I am' is created and how long will it last?

Such knowledge should be discussed only with people who have a sense of detachment.

Why are people interested in miracles? Is not the greatest miracle your own beingness? Because of that the immense world is created in an instant.

One may get spiritual powers by performing special practices. The knowledge of the Self has nothing to do with it.

As consciousness, you are prior to space. Before going to sleep, at least say, 'I am of the nature of space'. This knowledge is beyond words. It cannot be acquired through austerities or *japa*. Sri Krishna taught it out of love. Most people get involved in rituals and various methods of search. As a result they may get visions and feel satisfied. Self-knowledge is beyond concepts. It is beyond words. It is eternal. Why and from where have the experiences of the world and of our own self come over us? How were we prior to this experience? This has to be understood. Keep listening until you have no doubt about your identity as to what you are and how you have come into existence. Faith in the Guru and devotion to the Guru spontaneously brings the understanding.

The knowledge once acquired can never be lost. One who knows samadhi does not get involved in mundane dealings. Without faith in the Guru, there is no hope for such knowledge. Krishna taught the ultimate knowledge: how the universe appears and disappears while the unmanifest remains.

This knowledge is not affected by words. When the manifest withdraws into the unmanifest, samadhi ensues. One wants meaning to the words, but this knowledge is beyond words. How the wordless state is, has to be explained in words. All doubts have to be eradicated. Worldly knowledge is of no use. When listened to, this knowledge grows by itself, becomes all-pervading, and in the end merges into the Absolute. It is pleased with devotion to the Guru and the love for the Guru. The listener should be of a pure heart. You get happiness only when you forget yourself. All other activities are entertainment. The love for the Guru is not an ordinary thing. One who goes on repeating the mantra will realize the Truth. Always remember that our consciousness is in accordance with the Guru's word. Keep this firmly in mind. That is meditation. When the meaning of the Guru-word sprouts in a person, he goes beyond everything. He understands how the temporary consciousness merges into the eternal state of his nature (Absolute).

Your body is the food for your consciousness. It is because of the food that you feel 'you are'. With faith in the Guru's words, all will be explained. Simple devotees will get liberated sooner than the intellectuals. If there is fear of death at the last moment, such a devotee calls upon

God, forgets himself and gets dissolved into the universal consciousness. Prana leaves and then there is no rebirth. The intellectual devotee becomes involved in concepts and is born again according to his last concept.

Nirupana 14
Sunday, March 5, 1978

A teacher instructs according to his own concepts. People accept that and become his followers. This is the way various creeds come about. However, the situation is quite different. How can That which has no beginning and no end be conceptualized? Nevertheless, people keep on doing some practices and rituals according to their own concepts. People have to do this, as they cannot keep quiet. Sai Baba of Shirdi was an exception. He was always immersed in the Absolute. He had no concepts. He never gave initiation. He had no disciples. So there was no creed around him.

During this act of the body and prana, the experience of a concept is there in one form or the other. Most people are tied to the body. A rare one recognizes that the body depends upon consciousness. It is because of the nature of time that a person says, 'I am the body' and takes on the doership, followed by miseries and happiness. To think 'I am like this or like that' is external knowledge. To see one's true nature is direct internal knowledge. The ignorance (consciousness) arises and shines, but it is not permanent. It is not steady because of wakefulness and sleep. So long as one is aware of being awake, there is no lasting peace. Dismiss everything that is not you. Here, no action is required.

In the Gita, Arjuna, after getting enlightenment, said to Krishna, 'So long as this consciousness lasts, I shall follow your advice. I shall do what you say'. His samadhi was not broken even while fighting the enemy. His peace remained unadulterated. You will not know this until you achieve Self-realization. When you understand it, there will be no need to know anything else.

Krishna said: 'Your consciousness through all the five senses is protecting you. It is My own manifestation'. Accept consciousness as the Guru and worship it. It sustains all the bodies. It has no form of its own. It is self-luminous. It has come over you uninvited. The bliss from this consciousness has no match in material happiness. It gives sustenance to innumerable beings. It is pleased with love, it is a devotee of love. The flavor of your beingness is the love. (The sense 'I am' is the love.) Remember its worthiness. The scriptures describe its greatness. It dwells in your heart. It will offer you enlightenment, perfection, and you will be bliss yourself. Without it, the tongue does not know taste. When this tiny consciousness leaves, people say the person is dead.

That which is self-sensing, which is your own beingness, is within you. It is blissful. It is inside you. Without it there cannot be any witnessing. It is the holy feet of Sri Guru. It is the life force. It has the flavor of self-love.

Your true state precedes the five elements, the sun and the moon. Scriptures never get tired of praising It. It is microscopic. It nourishes and protects the body. Take refuge at Its feet, as It is your own true nature. This is the Guru's word. It is through this that you will be liberated. After getting liberation, you may behave in any way you like.

When talking to ignorant people, do not contradict them. Do not react. What they believe according to their understanding is correct.

Nirupana 15
Thursday, March 9, 1978

It is true that the association of a sage is beneficial but one should be prepared internally. One should have inner worthiness. The concept of sin and virtue has importance so long as you consider yourself as the body. The effects depend upon your idea about them. What is said at a certain time is true at that time. It ends when that time has gone.

The light of your beingness is of the nature of space. Is space seen in sleep? (In deep sleep there is no consciousness, hence there is no space.) Your consciousness 'I am' is directly within you. You have a great need of your beingness. You take care of yourself so as to preserve it. The reason is that you know you are going to die one day. That which is everlasting need not be taken care of. Are you watching your beingness without making any effort?

It is true that previously you were not known to yourself, but now you know 'you are'. You are the witness of this knowingness. One who witnesses it must be prior to it.

You will not understand all the things you have heard unless you have worthiness. For this you have to practice meditation. The Sadguru introduces you to meditation and consciousness. First what was not, now IS. Who knows that it was not there? Similarly, who knows that it is there? Those who say that one will need many births to be liberated base it upon hearsay. Only an ignorant person keeps traditional faith. Will the jnani do so? You must see what is correct, directly. Keep quiet until you are not aware of your silence. When someone claims that he is liberated, it should be understood that he was liberated in a dream. (Liberation means there is no duality. Then how can one say he is liberated?)

Why did you get up from deep sleep? Why did you see a dream while asleep? Do you have an answer for these questions? The wakefulness that came has brought the world. No waking up means no world. The dream is untrue; similarly, the wakefulness is false. There is no difference between them. They happen spontaneously. Our talk is also happening in a dream. You know that 'you are'. What is the reason for this? Deliberate on this. You must practice japa, meditation and listening. With sharp intellect, one gets liberated in a short period of time just by listening.

Your daily behavior is the result of your impressions.

First think through these things and then remain in a thoughtless state. Do not become a slave of your own thoughts. One who has reached the stage where there is no thought will not have to do anything for his sustenance, for his protection. Whatever experience there is in the world, there is no doer. Everything happens spontaneously. Space is everywhere but consciousness is prior to space. The light of consciousness is space. You will experience its vastness when your body-consciousness goes.

'I am' is the root thought. Without that basic feeling, what can we take ourselves as? What are we in deep sleep or in a trance? When there is no feeling of 'I am', it is called the unmanifest. All worldly dealings of an entire lifetime are based upon the concept 'I am'. However, it has no real existence. This concept is not born of the body. Even if you have no concept that 'you are', you still are. Consciousness is subtle, luminous and self-sensing. It is subtler than space. You will know all this when you become of the nature of consciousness. You accept the body as your uniform but you are not the body.

Yoga means union. Unless Purusha and prakriti unite, there is no knowledge of beingness. A yogi is one who achieves this union. By identifying with the body, you will not understand That which has been created in the body out of this union.

All things are identified with names, which are words. Hence, all dealings are based upon these words. The world is not known without words. The word arises out of prana. The basic word has appeared in various forms. The word is also called the mind. It is the result of impressions received by it. Behavior depends upon the mind. Meditate with the conviction that 'I am not the mind'.

When the atomic consciousness manifests, the vast world is created. This atom is the subtle consciousness. There is no peace until this atom is realized. You believe you are the gross body because you have not realized the subtle. The vast world arises out of ignorance and subsides in ignorance. It is unreal. When you will really say, 'I do not know', you will be in a state of Parabrahman.

The blessing 'May good things happen to you' has meaning only with reference to the body. From deep sleep, the atomic wakefulness has sprouted. Without it there is no world. Both are illusory. It is the root-maya. All existence is in words. Hence, go beyond the words. Understand worldly dealings as unreal, and then you will not suffer from them. Think over why and how all these things have come into existence.

Nirupana 16
Sunday, March 19, 1978

'I am not the body, I am the Self'. If you meditate like this, you will become God. This great mantra is the same as pure consciousness. Do not worship it by giving it a form. The idea that you are the body must go. Then the rest will be fine. You say, 'I forgot to meditate', but the one who says it has not forgotten it.

Just as gold is the source of ornaments, similarly, the sense 'I am' is the source of all words. When consciousness realizes itself, it is called the grace of the Guru. One must be the proof of the Guru's words. The initiation with mantra establishes a special relationship with the Guru. Hence, you must have faith in the Guru. One could die anytime. Then how can he neglect the Guru's words?

Real devotees are illumined by Self-knowledge. Their existence is like that of space. When the stage of the seeker evolves, his behavior also changes. Some behave in a peculiar fashion. Some go about naked, some keep silent, and some become very abusive. As they are Self-realized they do not behave consciously. A Self-realized person has no concern with how the body behaves. His conduct is not governed by any rule of law.

The flavor of your beingness is the holy presence of God. The concern about the individual self can be compared to a snakebite. Sages do not consider themselves as the body, so they are not bitten. The Self is beyond light and darkness. Only the body or the mind gets stained.

Bhagavan means light. The light of Bhagavan is a big void of light. Is there a difference between that light and your own light? When you know your consciousness and become a witness, you will understand that the sky is your light. There is nothing beyond the light of God. The natural quality of God is your own consciousness. As soon as consciousness arises, the five elements are created along with the world. Your sight has the same color as that of space. All the names are of the incarnations of God. Were there any names prior to that? Bhagavan means the manifested consciousness. That by which you know 'you are' is the same as His nature. Embrace it tightly.

In everything all around, there is God and only God. Does this light see any difference between a man and a woman? All this, one and all, in its totality is consciousness. That taste or knowledge of self-existence is Bhagavan. To understand this means to see God in every living being.

Forget that you are a human being. Your light is the light of Bhagavan. In all that appears, what is the underlying luminous Source? It is this light alone. It is present even in a stone but it is prominently expressed in you.

In all things there is only one true quality. It is consciousness. It demonstrates existence. All other knowledge comes about because of knowingness. Paramatman means 'I, myself, am Atman'. He is not a deity. Deities worship Him. It is my own Self. It is the direct, correct knowledge. It is there before a single word is uttered. The one that rises and the one that sets finds his rest in Paramatman. People are awed by the knowledge of Paramatman. How can it even be felt when one has no body? The enlightened devotee says, 'I am not the body'. Then who is it that became enlightened? (When a person becomes realized, he no longer considers himself a body. Then who says, 'I have become realized'? In other words, there is no one who has become enlightened. There is neither knower, nor known. No one is born, no one dies, nothing has happened.)

The experience can be described in many ways but the experiencer cannot be described. When words are silent, there is no sense in enumerating the divine names.

Nirupana 17
Thursday, March 23, 1978

Self-knowledge means having a perfect understanding of what exactly we are. The body, for which all the care is taken, is impermanent and untrue. Whatever can be known is *not* the knowledge of the Self. One who believes that he is going to die is ignorant. He should have the association of *Sat* (that which exists forever), and not that of the body.

Sage means our own pure, ever-present, true nature. There is no personality there. The sage is not a person; he is alone. He signifies a state of permanent *satsang* (holy association). Meanwhile, the course of life keeps changing and its finale is death. What you believe as 'yourself' is not your true companion; it never was and never will be. One who tolerates everything is a sage (jnani). Can he cause pain to others? The actions of the five elements are not his own.

Whatever identity you try to create for yourself in order to be happy is going to be left behind. Your intellect changes with age. You take pride in being so-and-so as a body-form. You feel you are like this or like that. The feeling 'I am suffering from this or that' is ignorance. Be convinced that you are separate from the senses; their experience is not your experience. This is the condition of Brahman. Pure consciousness has never had any experience. Mind is the collection of impressions that have been recorded in it since birth.

What is in the body is of the nature of the rest of the world. When it considers itself as the body, it becomes different from the world. To be one with the world means to have devotion for all beings, as if they are God. One who thinks he is the body has no tolerance, nor patience. Atman means my Self. It is ever free. It has no shape, but It has its own light: the sense 'I am'. It is pure consciousness. When one lives in this state one knows: 'I am not the body, I am the self-luminous consciousness'. What is real does not come and go; only the body falls. Does your body know that you are sitting here? All bodies in the entire universe move about because of the life force. This very life-energy is given various names such as God, *Iswara* and Atman, etc. Actually, consciousness has no name. Names are given for everyday dealings in the practical world. Once consciousness leaves the body, it does not recognize the body. That which is limitless has no knowledge of its own. It has no pride such as 'I am like this or like that'. Millions of beings are born in that consciousness every day. The same consciousness abides in all.

Your memory functions automatically. It is recorded chemically. Anything which you take doership of remains with you as a memory. Your body is a machine that produces vital energy that has the feeling of 'I am'. It carries out all dealings. Was there any experience to guide you before you started learning about things? This chemical 'I am-ness' does everything. That knowledge is not affected by the three gunas. When there was no experience of the body, what were you like? Without ignorance, there can be no knowledge. If the basic ignorance of a child is not there, no knowledge can be acquired later. Knowledge appears because there is ignorance. With the body, when one knows 'I am', it is called *vrutta* (knowingness). Paramatman has no such knowledge of a separate existence. This knowledge-information is called the mind, intellect, beingness, intuition, etc. There is no truth in it. When the meaning of this is grasped, the mind disappears.

Did we come first or did the mind (words) come first? Whatever there is, is because of the root word 'I'. What can that state (prior to words) be called as? Because words in daily dealings are taken to be true, the word body-consciousness has stuck to you. The knower (of the Self) does not consciously experience the knowingness 'I am'. When you become unattached, compassion will flow through you. All undesirable things will vanish. To become unattached means you exist as the Absolute. In such company, others also get peace. Such a one knows how the world is created.

Ego means identification with the body. When that goes, purposeful behavior also vanishes. The worship of such sages uplifts even the deities. God is indebted to the devotee as He becomes free from his body. To get rid of the body while one is alive is the most difficult task. Consciousness in the body is God.

Nirupana 18
Sunday, March 26, 1978

The feeling 'I know a lot' is ignorance. Once it is understood that this is pure ignorance, it does not matter whether one talks a lot or not at all. When you go to sleep, you are sleep itself. You are not separate from the sleep. On waking up, the knowledge 'I am' dawns upon you and instantly creates the world. When you are asleep, you are pure ignorance. What would happen if one day this ignorance does not wake up? Then who would be there to die? Ignorance sleeps and wakes up every day! What is the meaning of the removal of ignorance? You can take any meaning you like. But what is the real situation? You, who are awake, go to sleep. That means the knowledge itself becomes ignorance. You have to understand the true import of this fact. (Here, ignorance implies the Absolute, and knowledge implies the sense 'I am'.)

When Brahman is liberated, Parabrahman stays as He is. That which is the cause of this itch (happiness and misery) is Brahman. When the itch disappears, it is Parabrahman. What I am, here and now, is awakened ignorance. The base for all things is ignorance that is called sleep. Wakefulness is the child of ignorance. If there is ignorance, only then there can be knowledge.

The faith that 'you are' is created in you. It has come uninvited. Faith or devotion means love. It is the love for the Self. The certitude that 'you are' is the pure and holy manifestation of Paramatman. It is jnana. Recognition of the body comes through this faith in the Self. The holy names are for that certitude of the Self.

45

Do not worship the impermanent i.e. the body. The use of this body is to nourish the faith in the Self. The fragrance of 'I am' coming through the body is God. One who believes he is the body faces death.

You have different kinds of beliefs. You become according to what you believe. How very powerful is the effect of beliefs! Be aware of that fact. Your faith that 'you are' is of the nature of the Guru or God. It is in your heart in the form of light (knowingness). The light of the Self never dies. One whose Self-light does not die, will he ever die? He may not live in today's form, that is all. The form is illumined by this light. The sense 'I am' is God. It is called *saguna*-Brahman (the manifest with quality). It is contained in Parabrahman (the Absolute without quality). You are Brahman. The great mantra given to you is the expression of Brahman. It is your own nature. You must invoke It by the mantra. It will surely reveal Itself.

One who wins a big lottery becomes happy. He considers himself a rich man. It took only a moment for this to happen. If this is so, why does not the Guru's mantra bring about such instantaneous change? With faith in the Guru, fear of death vanishes forever. Thereby the fear of birth also vanishes. As you nurse in your heart the faith of your beingness, your conduct will go on changing. The belief that 'I am a meager human being' changes to 'I am Brahman'. Then the work is done. The Guru's word is perfect knowledge. It is the state of Being – it is movement as well. Hold onto it tightly. All other means cannot even come close to it.

Nirupana 19
Thursday, March 30, 1978

'I am without a body and everything is perceived through my own light.' This must be firmly established within. You say you cannot see your own light. How can you see that by which other things are seen? When you meditate you must keep in mind that the meditator is formless. When you go to sleep, keep the thought that you are not the body. One without the body has no caste, no sin, no virtue, no time. The sky cannot be stained and you are purer than the sky.

Ananda (bliss) is subjective, but the Self is not. Unless all things are forgotten, there is no bliss. As you get more faith in yourself, the individual mind will fade and you will be one-pointed.

Until a certain stage the deities are there. When that stage is transcended, the deities are not there. (Until a certain stage of meditation, the seeker has powers i.e. deities. When he goes beyond, there is only Brahman.) You do not understand your own personality, so how can others? The scriptures are for the ignorant, not for the one of knowledge. Whatever can be told through words has no permanence. It can be compared to a dream. Break off this deep-rooted habit of identifying with the body.

Dwell on this: 'What do you think of yourself?' Your body is food material. It is the food of consciousness, the life force within. Consciousness and the world are one and the same. They arise simultaneously. World is an illusion. However, you are the knower of the illusion that is caused by the play of the three gunas. This puzzle will be solved only through discrimination, and not by rituals. With that, offer yourself at the feet of the Guru. This, itself, is Guru's grace. You ask of what use is Paramatman to you? When Paramatman has no use for Himself, how can He have any use for you?

Why do we ask about That which has never come into existence? From the point of view of the jnani nothing has ever happened. How can one recollect what was never forgotten? Actually, what is remembered will surely be forgotten. After saying this, Guru Ramadas still made people sing the praise of the Lord and made idols of *Maruti* out of cow dung. Was he a fool?

Maya means illusion that has suddenly appeared. It is the illusion of having a shape and form. It has come over you because you have forgotten your true nature. Think of how and when you got your concept of beingness. One who knows the Self has no problem with anything good or bad. To have any want is beggarliness. Be still. Gradually, you will know what really happens and why. In fact, even when no harm is done, the jiva, feeling that a great calamity has happened, keeps on struggling, eventually to die in vain. In the stage of body-consciousness, all are beggars. Each one is asking for something or the other. Until ignorance disappears, the concept 'I want to go beyond' will remain.

There is only *maha-maya* (the grand illusion). She has to be dismissed after first worshipping her as God or Brahman. Then Godhood is also dismissed simultaneously. A rare one will tell you this most secret knowledge.

After worshipping the Self as God, ignorance will be revealed. Then no knowledge will be left. As spoken in the Vedas, one can go beyond *karma* after achieving knowledge of Brahman. It is rare to find one who knows correctly and yet does not claim that he has the knowledge. Who is the knower? The jnani? He only knows that all this is ignorance.

The union of you having the knowledge of your beingness and you not having the knowledge of your beingness is *maha-yoga* (the great union). One who knows this great yoga has transcended the knowing of beingness. Self is light. When the jiva emanates light, he sees the world. The reflection of the world appears in your knowingness. If there is an experience of happiness, there will be an experience of sorrow. Remember well what you have heard and put it directly into practice.

Nirupana 20
Sunday, April 2, 1978

Truly speaking, an individual has no form. The so-called form is made up of the five elements. Inside the body there are five senses. Which of these are you going to continue to live as?

Most people want to hear what is based on the body-sense. They do not recognize the body as unreal. All the knowledge in the world is based upon words. Find out if the one who has this wordy knowledge has any form. Contemplation on anything which is not the Self is untrue. Meditation can only be that of the Self. Knowingness that is in the body must be traced. It has no individuality. Sugar melts in the mouth but its sweetness remains. Does sweetness have any personality? There is only a trace of manifestation there. That is all.

No experience is lasting. The experiencer cannot be described through words, and we are the experiencers. That which depends upon life force and consciousness is not lasting. The everlasting is beyond these. We must expose the concept 'I am somebody or something'. Everything happens according to the nature of time. Desire to attain Self-realization also arises according to the dictates of time.

When consciousness arises, the world becomes visible. This is the ultimate principle. Childhood is put aside as you grow older. Similarly, after getting correct knowledge, the body-form is put aside.

As you have to say something through words, you call God the doer. Would the all-merciful God create such total chaos? Without us there is no God. God is nothing but the certitude you have of your beingness, the love you have of your beingness.

The sense 'I am' is Brahman. The One beyond it is called Parabrahman. First you will become Brahman and then you and Brahman will disappear. (Your subtle consciousness will expand, pervade the whole universe and then dissolve. This happens in deep meditation.) The jnani says ultimately there is nothing. Then why does he teach others? The answer is like this: when one has to go (urinate), one has to go urgently. While urinating, does not one temporarily love the act? Similarly, the body of a jnani is a temporary sensation that makes him preach.

The primary dream is the feeling that 'you are'. So long as you address God (out of duality), you have not reached your destination. Paramatman has neither birth nor death. Then why did Krishna say: 'I have had many births'? All these births were of the five elements. Such births are happening by the millions, every second, in the Paramatman.

The scriptures are concepts of poets. They offer bribes as well as they threaten. During sleep there is no experience of one's self. Sleep cannot be seen after waking up. In the same way, maya is unimaginable. Just as sleep cannot be known, so maya cannot be known, either by gods or by men.

Maya appears out of the manifestation of consciousness. Prior to that there is no maya. The thought of 'I am' is the disturbance. Even greater gods do not understand maya, as they are created by maya. They are not self-created. Their actions are illusory. The detached one has no touch of maya. Deep sleep means total ignorance. From that the feeling 'I am' arises. That is the beginning of maya. With the feeling that he is awake, one goes about dealing proudly in the world that does not exist. The feeling 'I am awake' creates the world. It is born out of maya. When you realize this, the feeling that 'I am the doer' will vanish.

When you see your Self, it will be seen as an empty void, emptier than even a dream. The image that 'I am like this, or like that' has seized you. What has been created will surely be destroyed. What is created? It is our consciousness. When the feeling of 'I' arises, it becomes the ego.

You would not be listening to this unless you are worthy. After hearing it, it has to be remembered again and again. That is the beginning of the process.

This form has come to you spontaneously. No one created it. You would not be here unless you were inspired from within to get the true meaning of life. This is not the type of devotion whose purpose is to acquire something. The purpose of this devotion is to get liberation through listening. The idea that you are a man or a woman with characteristic behavior patterns is false. It is an appearance. To know this, some worthiness is required. The knowledge 'I am' is your Godhood. Understand that. Various names are given to it.

The fact that a liking to hear about this knowledge has arisen in you is a good spiritual sign. When the knowledge of your beingness becomes clear, you will transcend maya. Consciousness will reveal its own worthiness. Manifestation is all one, but the names are many. All the names pertain to maya. After knowing the fact that 'I am everywhere', the knower will not be different from the knowledge. No experience is lasting. Whichever way you look at yourself will surely go. The sense that you are awake is also a concept. Sleep and wakefulness are indicators of your transient nature. When you enter into deep sleep, you let go of yourself every day. If that sleep does not end, what are you going to do?

Whether death arrives today or a thousand years from now, it should be the end of it all; there should be no problem. Detachment is the feeling that all this is an appearance. When Truth is attained, false things drop off.

No special effort is required to let them go. That is called an offering to Brahman.

The scriptures say that, 'At the proper time Bhagavan takes an incarnation and nourishes *dharma*'. It is the dharma of one's own true nature. When ordinary people preach dharma, it is the dharma of the body. The Guru is an incarnation of God. Due to devotion to the Guru, maya, which appears demonic and vast, is reduced to the size of an atom.

Do not neglect the consciousness that is now listening. It is pure and clean. Keep this in mind and worship the same. Do not forget that Self-knowledge is the knowledge of our own beingness. Due to impurities of the mind one goes to the forest and bears hardships. If your impurities are removed here and now, as you listen, you will not have to go to the mountains and forests (in search).

Nirupana 21
Sunday, April 9, 1978

Consciousness is boundless. It cannot be foretold when realization will shine upon you. Someone gets it spontaneously, the other does not get it even with much effort. When a particular stage is reached, there comes about an appropriate change and a proper ground is prepared accordingly.

Dattatreya, a great sage, was perfect Brahman. Where was the necessity of a Guru for him? Yet it is said that he approached 24 Gurus. In order to eradicate egoistic consciousness and to pacify a particular quality, an appropriate Guru was approached. Dattatreya was the knower of them.

You feel that 'you are' and that self-feeling behaves according to the nature of time. The modification that flows from it is the mind. Fear is created through the effects of the mind. The totality has no fear.

Earth is the quality of steady vital energy. The seed that sprouts from the earth does not die even when it is tortured, beaten, cooked or roasted. Because of this, your growth is sustained and accelerated. The earth bears everything. That is why she is peaceful. The consciousness in the body is the pure consciousness 'I am'. It has infinite names. Unknowingly, you have come to know 'you are' and that is God. The names of the deities pertain to that only. Before the knowingness was known, there was no experience of absence of peace. That is the stage of real peace. Until you know 'you are', your life is infinite. If you strive to know it, you will not be able to know it. In order to overcome 'absence of peace', consciousness has to be worshipped with non-dual devotion. The meaning of these words is not familiar to you.

Can one take support of what is transient to know the Truth? Your consciousness has a beginning and, therefore, it will have an end. First put aside your intellect and then take the Guru-word and meditate on your subtle consciousness. Know that it is prior to the pondering. Make friends with it and it will blossom within you. (You will realize that it is your true nature.) Believe that you are what you know, before you know anything else. That is the Guru-word. Consciousness has various names like God, Brahman, etc. It is known and experienced without making any effort. For Its sake, ignore your mind and body. 'Word' (mantra) means Brahman plus the guarantee that precedes it. The meaning of it all is 'I am'. Maintain that assurance with the initiation given by the Guru as proof. (The word comes out of the sound, which comes out of space. Consciousness is prior to space. It is called Brahman or God – the manifest reality.)

Mind knows nothing else except for the impressions gathered from childhood. That is the reason why good impressions are sought. That is the reason why the importance of good company is extolled. In the company of sages our mind emulates them. Happiness and misery are there because they are believed to be so. Due to the nature of time they are true for that time only. As time passes, they become meaningless.

Do not ever forget that we are exactly what our Guru has described. As you progress in watching your consciousness, without the body, by the same measure you will experience your worthiness. After listening to this, compare it with your present state of being. As consciousness arises, it becomes the individual's world. To realize this consciousness is to attain peace.

Can you stop sleep from turning into wakefulness and vice versa? Keep faith in the Guru's words as you live your daily life. Realize that when you act, you are not the doer. You only witness what happens. The sense of doership is because of body-consciousness. Unless you realize yourself, your ego-sense will not end. Even with proper initiation, if you do not follow it, it is of no use. Without uttering a single word of the Supreme or the mundane, that which is naturally there is your consciousness. Who knows the knowledge that is in the world? It is your own consciousness, also called the Self. It has no color, no form, and no design. It is pure knowingness.

You behave according to what you have heard. But do you pay attention to That which is hearing now? That listener is your consciousness. One deals with the world from knowledge gained by the five senses. Does that knowledge have any color or form? Yet you superimpose wrong ideas on that and become unhappy. Your consciousness is of the nature of love and devotion. The proof of God's existence is your own consciousness. As you meditate on that knowledge, the five elements will come to serve you. You unnecessarily believe that you are weak and sinful. Drive out the negative by contemplating on your consciousness and recognize your true nature.

The knowledge of the Self will dawn on you at the appropriate time and your worthiness will be boundless. Then the mind, which wants something or wants to get rid of something, will disappear. The five elements will be at your service. Peace cannot be achieved unless pride of knowledge is given up. The sage is very peaceful.

Nirupana 22
Thursday, April 13, 1978

You have read and heard a lot. Now get to know the reader and the listener. The fact that you know 'you are' is misery as well as joy. God is the source of joy whereas the root of misery is maya. But at the root, it is only consciousness.

Find out what you have with you that is your own. Meditate on and know that one who contemplates on God, is himself God. Only the Sadguru can tell you that it is so. Other teachers tell you to live as a servant of God.

In the beginning, your mother teaches you to understand sound. Had she not done that, what would be your language? I am talking to you in that language, which was yours before sound was first introduced to you. Yet you have to understand the meaning in the language you have learned.

All the religions of the world are mere concepts. Have you any other knowledge except what you have read or heard? The way of the Self implies the way of the life force or consciousness, because we are consciousness. The manifested consciousness is not steady, whereas the unmanifested is the everlasting Truth.

When they prepare the horoscope of a child, the first consideration is the time of its birth. Then who is born? Is it the child or is it time? Worldly dealings are done according to the dictates of time. Time is duration. The sense of doership can be called the mind. In all these dealings, there is the One who has no birth. With the

Sadguru's grace, the illusion of birth will vanish forever. Beingness comes with the combination of body and prana. This experience has no form of its own. As a result, the mind identifies with the (tangible) body. Birth brings on time, yet for practicality it is said that the child is born. The witness, who believes he is the body, is the victim of time. Does time have any form? This cannot be understood by performing rituals. Discrimination is necessary.

All that is heard from childhood is taken for granted. Discriminate about all this thoroughly. Take hold of your true nature. Whatever is believed or retained will not remain with you. This will be understood when you know the Self. Worldly dealings take place on the belief that what appears is true. Actually, it is a fraud. From deep sleep sprouts the feeling 'I am', then that of the body and the world, followed by happiness and sorrow. If you do not realize this you have to suffer.

Your consciousness is luminous, formless and spotless. The body is dirty, that is why you are on the ground. If it were purified, you could fly in the air. *Hatha yogis* do that. Keep in mind the consciousness (that is listening) and meditate on it. It has no attachment. There is no such thing as sin or virtue. You limit yourself by thinking you are the body and, hence, experience them. The one who is listening is the same as Brahman, and the same is the Guru. Contemplate on this. Respect pure consciousness as the Guru and it will become your friend. Stop looking outward and behave as if you were the Self. Worship the higher knowledge while saying, 'I am That'. Do you stay with your consciousness even for a moment?

One who wants to know this will not die without understanding it. There is nothing like 'I will die with the body'. Can the light die? How long is your consciousness going to live with you? It is seasonal. Contemplation of the Guru is contemplation of consciousness. Contemplation of consciousness by consciousness, is the same as non-dual devotion.

Nirupana 23
Sunday, April 16, 1978
Occasion: Birth anniversary of Bhausaheb Maharaj
(Maharaj's Guru's Guru)

Such is the glory of devotion to Bhausaheb Maharaj, that so many of you have gathered here. If you cannot appreciate the greatness of the Guru's teaching, all else is in vain. It is conveyed to you because of its total worthiness. Such a conviction will remove your ignorance. The firm belief in the Guru's word gives the knowledge of the Self. You are Parabrahman in whom the word (mind) dissolves and nothing remains. He is alone. He is neither the Guru, nor the disciple, nor God.

The devotion of most people is for fulfilling their needs in the world. Such devotees cannot realize the Self. At least before sleeping say, 'I am Paramatman'. You are the Paramatman. He has been called by many names. He has had many incarnations and will have many more in the future. You are the Atman of all these incarnations.

The word Atman means 'I'. 'Whatever happens in the world is because of Me. I must be present prior to everything.' Therefore you are the universal Self. You are the Paramatman. He is neither bound nor liberated. But you have embraced body-consciousness instead. You are attached to yourself.

What you are hearing is familiar and simple. Have complete faith in the Guru-word. With that you will become Brahman. Paramatman does not even know that He is. That does not mean that He is asleep. When you say that you had a good sleep, who was the witness? Who knows 'I am'? Then what is the meaning of the words 'He awoke'? How is it possible? This is the result of maya. Each one of us knows the answer to these questions, but we do not believe it to be so. Body-consciousness is cuddling you.

This is a journey within consciousness. You are the knower of it. (You are prior to consciousness as a passive witness.) The fact that you know 'you are' is the main impediment. To remove the impediment, first believe it to be so. Your beingness or your sense of 'I am' is the obstruction. It is God Himself. This is the way you should worship. When He is pleased, He gives true knowledge. Know that you are the Paramatman. Do not think that you are separate from Him. That is only the concept of body-consciousness. If my light is spotless, then how can I be stained?

The moment of death is the time of great happiness. For the body-conscious individual, it is death. If you die saying that you are pure light, you will be free.

The moment of death, that is so terrifying, becomes a happy time with devotion to the Guru. Such is the greatness of the Guru's word. As an example, how happy one feels as he slips into sleep. The experience of happiness or misery comes because of our consciousness. It becomes happy by the grace of the Guru. The joy of the moment when the vital force leaves the body cannot be expressed in words.

Worldly dealings are not true. So what is there to renounce? Carry on your worldly activities as it suits you. Remember the Guru-word, not by the mind but by beingness. Once you are convinced of your true nature, you will not be concerned about slander. With your light, you observe all other lights in the world. How can that light be stained? Without words, realize that there is no other God, no other Brahman besides you. Remember this without any words. That is the Guru-word. One who belittles the light of the Self will suffer great misery. Everything you recognize is based upon its colors and designs. The Self cannot be recognized because it has no color or design.

Nirupana 24
Thursday, April 20, 1978

Is it a small thing that you know 'you are'? Is it not that you alone know that? Then unite yourself with your consciousness. See what a miracle happens! Spirituality is simple. The rest is all entertainment. The word (thought) that rises in your mind will certainly have some effect on you. It is obvious that everything is untrue, so what is there to be negated? Even if there is nothing in the world, there still is delusion!

It is very difficult to get an opportunity to hear this kind of knowledge. Liking it is even more important. One who is having his last birth only comes to me.

What is not steady is called a phase. Samadhi is also a phase. That which is worshipped by all people and That which is worthy of worship, is the same as yourself. It would be unfortunate if you did not accept this. Devotion means union. Be one with your knowledge of beingness. Then the work is done. All methods, philosophies and rituals are of no use. Attainment of special powers through various yogic exercises is a hindrance. It creates false pride.

As long as there is fear in the mind, there cannot be devotion. Jnana means realization. It is also devotion. Does one know what has brought this knowingness to consciousness? When consciousness goes, everything comes to an end. Krishna says: 'My devotion cannot be practiced through japa or austerities, it can only be practiced by observing the Guru-word'. That is the highest devotion.

The Guru's word is: 'You are not the body; you are the consciousness in the body'.

Who is caring for whom? Is it not consciousness caring for itself? Consciousness dissolves in the state of Paramatman. It is not affected by time. After Self-realization, not a trace of ego will remain with you e.g. 'I am like this, I am like that'. Hold onto the Guru's word: 'I am self-luminous, pure consciousness'. Then you can involve yourself in all worldly activities.

While sleeping, remember the Guru-word. In deep sleep there is no body-consciousness; hence the identification will be broken. Start again when you wake up. God is there where you are. Without the devotee, where is God? Remain with your own Self. Do not get involved with others. Practice non-dual devotion. It is not time-bound. It is without ego. You will know how the five elements are created through consciousness, through you.

Silently repeat your mantra. Meditation should be on one's own nature. Slowly the mind will become pure. The formless consciousness will be uncovered and your true nature will be understood. Till then, rituals may be practiced. You will come to know that you are spontaneously there. God is not greater than the Sadguru. When you realize your consciousness, you will realize the stage of Brahman.

The mind always keeps comparing. Leave the greatness to others. Become so small that no one can see you. The conviction that ensues from the ever-growing devotion to Paramatman is 'I am formless, pure Brahman'. What you are listening to is the description of pure knowledge.

With devotion to the Guru, you will come to know that you are That. Be firm in your determination that you are formless, pure consciousness.

Nirupana 25
Sunday, April 23, 1978

Throw out concepts like 'I have become very virtuous' or 'I am a great sinner'. What is the entity that senses this? Body-consciousness will not lose its grasp on you with the thought that your well-being is the result of some spiritual activity. All you need to do is keep observing your Self.

Do not befriend anything that is visible to you. (Do not be attracted towards worldly things.) If you have to act at all, do only this: please your consciousness. It is very merciful. It will show you all that IS, directly. You will realize that the immense manifestation never existed. You are so microscopic that you will not be able to see yourself through your knowledge. Take the Guru's word as authority. You have no body. That which is prior to consciousness is fathomless peace. Surrender to it. Do not make everlasting bliss an object (a goal). You are beyond objects. The moment of death is the most blissful of all. There is nothing else to gain in this world except death. The irony is that where there is fear of death, at that very point is the ocean of bliss.

Nirupana 26
Thursday, April 27, 1978

The entire universe is sporting in a single cell of your subtle body (seed consciousness). That which is seen with your eyes closed is the dark blue Absolute. It is the shadow of the subtle body. A person with body-consciousness cannot understand this. First of all you must acquire God-consciousness through meditation. You must have the conviction that 'I am not an individual, but I am God'. With transformation of the intellect, the ego disappears. Whatever is sought is always there at the Source. Due to a misunderstanding, That is meditating. What is most worthy of worship? Is it not the knowledge 'you are', your consciousness? Only Paramatman exists, nothing else.

What is called birth is really the birth of the three gunas. The center of the gunas has no duality. A lamp requires oil. Similarly, consciousness presupposes the existence of the Paramatman. As long as the jiva has the experience of having done good or bad, there is no gaining the state of Paramatman. Your consciousness is the essence of sweetness. It is proof of the existence of Paramatman.

What can you do on your own? Can you sleep? Can you wake up? Can you excrete or urinate? Then why is there pride of doership? The life force with its three gunas is itself the indicator of Paramatman. Because of maya, each jiva thinks that it is responsible for its actions in the world. That is false. Childhood and youth have come and gone. What out of this remained with you as yourself?

Will your own company last forever? The reason for this situation is the play of maya. When the concept that you are your body is proved false through your own experience, you will know the nature of Paramatman.

I do not talk to your body. You should not talk as the body either. Let the body be. Keep it well. Get to know in the present who will leave the body. Know that you are not the body, but the knower of the body. Give full attention. Keep in mind that you are the light in the body and then act. Consciousness is a lamp, the source of light. Do you see the sky because of this light or are you seen because of the sky? Discriminate on this. Go into the Source that is beyond space. Does your sight have any stain? Does space have any holes in it? Is not the sight of your eye itself the light of the Self? And is this light male or female? As you use it with the concept of the body, it causes the fear of death. You hope for and expect so many things. But why not go for the Source? Has anyone seen the light of the Self dying?

You must hear all this from the Sadguru. Liberation comes through listening. It cannot be known through austerities or japa. When the words of the Sadguru are understood and remembered, perfection follows without effort. Through the mantra given to you, you have been asked to open up the Godhood within you. You are the Self; there is no question of attaining it.

The light of your Self is spotless. There is only the light. How can there be death? Who is listening now? The listener is your own Self. When consciousness forgets itself, there is peace.

The dark blue Absolute as seen with the eyes closed is similar to space. There is no break in it. It is all-pervading. Follow devoutly what the Guru says and you will realize that you are consciousness. When the blue shade disappears, the void remains. It is an all-witnessing state of being. It is the fourth stage: 'I am all that I see'. Your consciousness is the flavor of the Absolute. The Absolute contains an infinite number of universes. Many may have conceived Brahman intellectually. However, out of millions a rare one follows the Sadguru. There is no greater fortune than having Self-knowledge.

You have committed a great sin by calling yourself the body. Then the same Absolute becomes the great death for you in your last moment. Who else is there except for Him at the time of death? Make your own decision, choose for yourself. Do not depend upon other people. You must worship this knowledge, which is listening to the word of the Guru. You will see countless universes playing within your consciousness. There is no other deity besides Self-knowledge. There is no greater misfortune if it is not realized. Self-knowledge itself is the Paramatman stage – the home of liberation.

If someone writes down my words and keeps ruminating on them, he will get the state of Paramatman effortlessly.

Nirupana 27
Sunday, April 30, 1978

Sin can turn into virtue and a virtuous act can become sinful. One may feed a thousand brahmins to acquire merit. The food may get poisoned accidentally, hurting these people. This is the way of destiny.

All names have a duration. What is fancied, will be effaced. Then what remains?

The experience of God (consciousness) is there so long as there is life. However, I am timeless. Yet my true state has to be described in relation to something. The unmanifest got manifested with the feeling 'I am'. In the prison of this concept, 81 years have gone by. There is no such thing as my realizing God, or God knowing me. It is only hearsay. God is only a concept. All concepts are bound by time. My everlasting state is desireless and beyond thought. The concept 'I am' came unexpectedly and along came the world. A king dreams for five minutes, wherein he goes about as a beggar for a hundred years! When he wakes up, he is the king as usual. The dream 'I am' is momentary. In this dream many worship me, many kick me also. That does not affect me. I am perfect, always.

It is an accident that you suddenly came to know that 'you are'. I tell people to do something so that they have some purpose to live for. When a man dies, it means his body has fallen. Prana has left. The one who died, was he other than prana? When prana merges into the universal prana, it forgets itself. Without prana there is no beingness.

People have all kinds of suggestions regarding what to do. They are like a hollow bamboo.

Who decides what honest behavior is? It is all a great fraud. It is the primordial illusion – maya. Yet one would say, 'Speak the truth, do this, do not do that, etc.' It is because of this great fraud that you feel 'you are' and identify as men and women.

Your consciousness is of the nature of space. The knowingness that has come over you unknowingly is your consciousness. What do you witness first? It is the consciousness that 'you are', and after that you witness the world. The form of a human being is the form of Brahman incarnate. Catch hold of That which is known prior to any other thing. That is the one that listens. What is the difference between you and the world? Is your light any different from the light of the sun or the light in the sky?

It is the space of consciousness (*chidakash*) in which 'I am' arises. Consciousness is the certitude of one's own nature. Take good care of your body. However, be certain about your true nature. Love and devotion are names of the knowledge 'I am'. It is pure knowledge, not imparted by someone else. It has come over unasked for. Get a firm hold of that knowledge. It is the one that is listening. It is your own true nature. The teaching offered to one who dwells in body-consciousness goes to waste. Meanwhile, pride in the body increases.

In the universal life force, a child who is not yet born is joyfully playing. There is no difference in the life force of an unborn child and the one that is born. You cannot say that the one that is not born does not exist. It is joyfully playing in the whole of consciousness. Meditate on consciousness. It is *in* the body. It is *not* the body. All is seen by virtue of that. All names pertain to consciousness. The world is for the entertainment of that concept. You will worship the faith in yourself, if you have faith in the Guru. When faith is created, proper understanding will take place. There is no difference between us. If one is without form, how can there be any pride in the action that is performed?

From a jnani's point of view, the world was never created. Whatever is seen is false. The cover, that is the body, is not your form. You are the luminous consciousness within. You may identify with this or that as experienced in consciousness. The knower of consciousness is perfect. He is without any desire. This true situation is not such as can be consciously noted, because it has no form or color. With faith in the Guru's word, one's realization never wavers.

Nirupana 28
Saturday, May 13, 1978

The words of a jnani are imbued with the essence of the Vedas. Nothing is in your hands. Whatever is to happen will happen, when it has to happen. Identification as a man or a woman is a stain on consciousness. It has to be wiped out. Nothing else is to be done. You are already perfect. Worldly dealings depend upon names and forms. When there is no identification with the body, either as male or female, the cause and effect relationships have no power over you. Then what do you have to lose?

What is the enjoyment of sages of the Himalayas who have lived for thousands of years? Are they not enjoying their consciousness, or perhaps just a sweet sleep?

My period of samadhi is endless. I was in samadhi for ages and ages. At this moment there is some knowingness. When there are no words, what can you call yourself? Everything depends upon what you take yourself to be. That is the reason why the word is all-powerful. When you bathe at home it is customary to say, *Jai Ganga, Jai Ganga*. Does that tap water really come from the Ganges? Your word itself is the Ganges. The One on whom the water is poured, is the One who makes the Ganges holy. He can never be an object to Himself. He does not have the sensation that 'He is'. When one is certain that he is neither a man nor a woman, that one is the Self, will there be a thought of personal gain or loss? The past incarnations that you worship are not aware of your devotion. Krishna and Arjuna do not know each other in the present.

Patience, faith and determination are necessary. Association with a sage is the same as association with peace. It is prior to consciousness. *Chidananda* (consciousness-bliss) has a sense of duality. It is enjoyment. It is movement. It is there when one knows 'I am'. In non-duality, there is no guna at all. Therefore there is no bliss in it. There is no knowingness in the supreme state. When one does not know that 'he is', there is everlasting peace. What has been created will vanish. Get Self-realization before that happens. There is no peace in knowingness. Mind itself is the absence of peace. He (as Absolute) will be there even when billions of suns come and go. How omnipotent He must be! That power is yours when you do not know yourself (prior to the manifestation of consciousness). The appearance of the word means the appearance of the sky (space). The fact that 'you are' is the appearance of time.

Do not get stuck to what you have been taught, or what you have learned. Eventually, you will have to throw it away.

Nirupana 29
Sunday, May 14, 1978

Time comes into existence with our sense of 'I am' (beingness) and then everything happens. When it disappears, nothing remains. It is not possible to be totally without worry, because that is inherent in the nature of time. We are just helpless onlookers. Things happen as they will. All dealings in the world go on spontaneously. A rare one will deliberate on this point and discriminate. We carry on with our practical life only on the basis of what we have read and heard. (Maharaj says each one of us is pure consciousness, a passive witness. The impressions recorded in the memory are performing all the activities. This goes on automatically.) We have forgotten our true nature. Our behavior is like that of a king behaving as a beggar in a dream. We have knowingness in the waking state, but it has the entanglement of the gunas.

Carry out your worldly dealings but remember that they will not last. It is said that God created the world. It is our own consciousness. It is formless. When it is realized, the work is over. Think of yourselves as free without bodies. Contemplate on the contemplator.

All things are said by the word, to the word, through the word. However, your true identity is different. Your pure word – will it purify you or will it itself be purified? Is there any part of you that has to be purified? You have not realized as long as there is the desire: 'My well-being should be achieved or I should get some benefit'. Truth cannot be an object of knowledge. Whatever is transient can only be an object for knowing. Unless there is silence in meditation, one has not reached the correct level. (In meditation, one forgets oneself.) The mind flows only if there are impressions. Can it think of things that it does not know?

Paramatman is speaking of the experience of how He has made Himself conscious. So long as you go about in body-consciousness, in body-form, your identification is of a jiva. Jiva and Shiva are two names given to the state where there is action. The functions of the jiva are limited to the body. Shiva (pure consciousness) is formless and unattached. The understanding that you have got after listening is Parabrahman. The belief that you are like the body is the delusion. No action can change the fact that you are pure consciousness. The root of maya is consciousness by which you know yourself.

Our true nature is unknown to us. How can we talk about That which is unknown to us? Hence, the scriptures keep quiet. 'Clean, without dirt' does not mean white. Even whiteness is dirt. The lotus that comes out of the navel (the Source) symbolizes our consciousness. From consciousness, the five elements (including space) have been created. When you did not have knowledge of your consciousness, was there any fear? Consciousness through which the whole world has been created; can you catch it with your senses?

If you remember what you have heard now, there is nothing in the world that can harm you. Why? It is because you have understood the meaning of the Self. The birthless one is never born. Still, consciousness is created.

The impression of the body goes very deep; it is difficult to make it lighter. That is why it is difficult to remember this. (Since childhood we have intimately identified with the body. Now, we cannot even imagine that our true nature is formless.) The remedy for this is the mantra given by the Guru and faith in the Guru. Can the dream world be created by one's own efforts? Yet it creates itself and moves about. The meaning of the wordless silence is 'I am awake'. This is followed by the mundane activity with names and forms. After waking up, when we feel 'we are', the word is created.

Your great discomfort is your own consciousness. It is like a child of a barren woman (non-existent). Whatever is not fancied does not materialize. If you do not understand, at least respect consciousness that is listening. Treat it as the holy feet of the Guru. Have you understood the meaning of the birth of Brahman at the navel lotus?

All the cleverness of the world comes from imitation. For example, those who are fond of movies behave like what they see in the movies. Like that, see the film of consciousness properly, attentively. Then you will go beyond it. All this information is of the knowledge that is listening. Everything is a result of the play of consciousness. The flavor of our beingness at the navel is He, *Sri Hari*, who cannot be seen as someone or something. You are in the body but you are invisible by nature. Your true nature does exist but your eyes cannot see it. If you are like this, then there is no bondage for you.

What is a liberated soul? The answer is: he is the one who is listening now. When you hear, you must feel —

'Oh, is that so?' So long as you consider your body as your form, everything is true. When you realize that you are not the body, you will know that everything is just 'word' only. (There are only words and nothing else.) The meaning of the word will prove true as you want – or as you insist on it. Insist on the word, only then the word will manifest accordingly. Whatever you say will happen.

Worship by the mind is the worship of space, by space. Mental worship is higher than bodily worship. Before all this happened, I was there. If I am the cause of everything that happens, then what is the use of all that? The fact is that manifestation is all-pervading and individuality does not remain. (Maharaj means to say that realization is of no use to the seeker. When he attains it, he is no longer an individual to enjoy it.) When space and I are not different, wherever I go that will be the place where I am already present. If you go as a body, this is not true. If you apperceive this, will you ever die? The form of your consciousness is space. The knower is you. Whatever way the 'I am' behaves is called sport – maya. It is not real. Sport means fun, where there is no gain or loss.

Nirupana 30
Sunday, May 21, 1978

Sugarcane is a plant. When its form changes, it becomes sugar. What is there in the heart of pure sugar? Is it not sweetness? Like that, there is sweetness in the body. It has no form but has a flavor; it is our beingness. In the process of search, the pure consciousness is uncovered. Consciousness means pure Sattva guna.

What is born are the gunas. It is not my birth. Even if That has many qualities, many forms e.g. that of a man or a woman, still, That is beyond birth or death. How can One who pervades the whole universe have death? All have one and the same guna – the quality of being a jiva, the quality of knowing, the information 'I am'. The quality which is like space is the Sattva guna. Whatever misery is experienced, is by the gunas only.

Just keep silent while saying, 'I am not the body'. All will disappear spontaneously and your true nature will be uncovered. I am not the Sattva guna (consciousness) because I am the knower of it (I am prior to it). I was there already before the body came over me, but I had no information.

All this knowledge is not honest. The reason is that it undergoes change. The manifestation is called birth. But whose birth is it? The manifestation is atomic but it has pervaded the whole universe! The original ignorance has become a hundred years old and one says, 'I have become a *mahatma* (great soul)'. But if that ignorance (or consciousness) goes away, then what?

How is it that you experience good or bad odors?

Or does it happen spontaneously? Who is doing this? Who is holding up the picture that you see? Do you purposefully keep a thing in memory, or does it stay there by itself? All kinds of needs come with the body and make us beggars. Where there is no consciousness, there is perfection. Where there is awareness of the body, God (consciousness) is there, and where there is God there is also a body. (The Absolute – Parabrahman is beyond both.) We have sorrow, but the root of it is our own consciousness. Where there is no knowingness, there is no form, no gunas, no actions. Just concentrate on your consciousness and nothing else. Whatever you do will be an obstruction.

Everyone has got a taste of it (the feeling 'I am'). It is transient. Neither the Krishna-taste has remained, nor the Shiva-taste. There have been great sages, but they no longer have their 'I am-ness'.

The same vital force is there in all bodies. Yet one body does not know the other, though millions of bodies are born every moment. That is the wonder of the vital force (maya).

When Krishna talked about the nature of his Self, it was not the description of a person. Krishna said: 'Arjuna, kill all the Kauravas, but I say not a single one will die'. Krishna gave this knowledge to Arjuna at that fearful occasion, but does anyone think about how He did that? Though Krishna was a truly great teacher, yet that bodily idol of Krishna was ignorance only. (The consciousness of Krishna is the same knowingness, which by nature is ignorance because it is transient and does not last. Krishna had recognized that Truth so He became a jnani.)

There is nothing in the world except for this ignorance, which is the greatest fraud. This consciousness itself is dishonest. The world-tree has come into existence through the growth of the root ignorance (the seed consciousness).

I have understood the reason why I have a body. It is enough to know that 'I am not that'. I have understood why the accusation of birth has come over me. Contemplate on this: 'You are pure Brahman, you have no death. There is nothing – no one except you'. Therefore do not talk against anyone, do not blame anyone. You are the subtle manifested consciousness. It is the seed of the universe, seed of Brahman, seed of Atman.

There is no importance to how one behaves. Knowing he is neither 'this' nor 'that', one sits quiet. I am not even the one who knows 'I am'. There is bliss after 'this is like this, this is not like that' goes away. After the body is forgotten, one becomes free from the pride of body-consciousness. When bliss becomes compact, impenetrable, then it is not consciously felt. This bliss is not such as can be remembered or forgotten. Mind, intellect and consciousness cannot speak of the supreme Self. They dictate behavior, but is He affected? One who is listening does so due to the conglomeration of the mind, intellect and consciousness. But the One who is Bliss Impenetrable is the knower of the mind, intellect and consciousness. He is not affected by them.

One should be ashamed of saying that the body is his form. How much is being done in order to keep honor and to avoid shame? All gunas belong to the mind, intellect and consciousness. There can be no action without them.

One's nature means one's conduct based upon previous impressions. You arc inside the collective of mind, intellect and consciousness. Bliss is beyond that. The One with Bliss Impenetrable is under no rule of conduct.

Direct knowledge means your own Self. There is no teaching there, nor a teacher. What has been manifested has no use, either for good or bad. Until you transcend consciousness, the sense of doership will be there. The body is introduced only in the beingness. Beingness and dreams are the same, and all is felt and fancied in that. So long as this 'I am-ness' was not known, there was no interruption in the Compact Bliss. The dream looks very real, but it is dishonest and not true. 'I am-ness' has no limit or standard. You have to understand this only once, and then there is no concern for the body at all. The 'I am-ness' is a passing phase. It is borrowed. Beingness means the feeling 'you are'. It will not last. A rare one knows this beingness with the help of the Guru. He becomes timeless. Without the grace of the Guru this consciousness will not be stabilized. After knowing this, a rare one gets rid of his body-identification such as 'I am a man or a woman'. The rest die with such identification.

In this vast consciousness there is no religious system, no karma, no time. It is prior to the sense 'I am'. Do not try to know it, but hold onto what you have heard. It is the natural state where there is no memory that 'I am the body'. One remains in his natural state of being. The one, who holds the Guru-word as ultimate, will get forbearance and will get the state of Brahman. Even if there is knowledge of Brahman, it is not everlasting or true.

As it is an experience, it cannot last. All is Brahman; all is blissful and peaceful. The sense of individuality, however, is a misery. Remember that.

Nirupana 31
Thursday, May 25, 1978

Here we only talk about why we need our beingness and what its actual use is for us. Here, nothing is said about past or future.

Whatever is known will come to an end. Everyone feels he should 'be', but this beingness will not last forever. 'We are as we appear' – this deep-rooted concept should go away. We should realize the fact that we are not as we *appear*, but we are as we *see*. The belief that we will die is false. The known will become unknown. We are 'unknown' by nature. Just as water evaporates, or the sun sets, or the lamp is extinguished, it does not mean that it dies. Understand death to be something like that.

One should treat oneself as pure consciousness and not as a body. Anything that depends upon memory will not last. Whatever is known will be forgotten. The one to whom knowingness happens is always at peace. We are not going to die, but whatever is known will become unknown, it will not be seen. The unknown is called God, Brahman, etc. It is all a bazaar of names. All actions are performed by virtue of the name. Take your consciousness to be God who is formless, and worship it as taught by the Guru.

All the action is mere entertainment. The nature of the entertainment varies with time. Life force is one. Due to difference in form, everything looks different from the other. Every sage has a different pattern of behavior. There are thousands of men but each one is different. *Avatars* (incarnations) are the same. Yet Rama is different from Krishna. Days have different names, but the sun is the same. This puzzle will get solved slowly and finally there will be no trace of ego left.

The one who has doubts regarding devotion to the Guru will have trouble. The Guru is your own Self. This Self (consciousness) has come over us naturally, it gets realized naturally and remains in its natural state (state of a *siddha*). It manages the activity of the body but the body does not control it. You have no other heir. You are your own heir. You are Brahman, you are maya, and you are 'you'. Through words we are Brahman, but by nature it is our own Self. Remember the Guru and keep your devotion to him. If someone listens to me and remembers five or six sentences, he does not need to do spiritual activity anymore.

Krishna says: 'Because of devotional singing I become manifest. Without the devotee I cannot be manifest. I gave My all to those who were devoted to Me. Whatever are My names, they are My devotees' names. They do not die. Their fame spreads. Their names uplift the world'. So long as the world and the devotee exist as true, till then the miracles are also true. All temples are dedicated to the ones who gave devotion. Krishna says that a realized consciousness is necessary for My becoming manifest.

The same is called 'Guru'. Krishna has spoken the ultimate spiritual Truth. He always said: 'I am the perfect Atman'.

One who uses the five elements is the Atman. He illuminates space. He is without any stain, without attachment, always and ever alive. He gives all His worthiness to a true devotee. Devotion has to be without expectation. One must be devoted because one wants God. Be aware. When the last moment arrives, have full faith in whatever the Guru has said. Offer your body by saying, 'I am not the body. The activity of the five elements is due to me'. This you will know only through devotion to the Guru.

Do not speak ill of anyone. This is very important. Such an attitude must stop.

Each being has got the certitude that it is alive. It is self-luminous. This luminosity has come spontaneously. One who offers this faith (beingness) to the Guru receives the same in return. The Guru says, 'Accept your consciousness as a gift from me and use it without words, just as you know you are male or female without saying it'. Treat your consciousness as God or Guru. Take it away from the body and direct it to the Self. The supreme state of being is called the Sadguru. The manifested consciousness that is moving about in the world (through human bodies) is called as Sri Guru. Our consciousness is the holy sight (*darshan*) of the Guru. He is formless. He is motivating all the bodies. He has manifested as my own consciousness.

If the devotee has full faith, God takes an incarnation and helps him. That form has been taken by your own

Self. There is no other deity besides Him. If you hold onto the Guru-word, you will understand that true happiness is the quality of your own nature. Your consciousness is the Sadguru. It is the non-dualistic devotion that says with conviction, 'I am God'. That is the true situation. This is very difficult but when understood, it is easy. All the gods and deities have used my life force, my consciousness. I am All-Perfect. This should be the conviction. A jnani does not need any certification.

After listening to the Guru-word one must be thought-free. Stick to the simple conviction in your heart that your nature is in accordance with the Guru-word. 'All living beings are motivated by me, not verbally but actually, because all visible forms are the reflection of the Self. My atomic consciousness pervades the whole world. When it manifests, only then the world comes into existence.' In deep sleep there was a stirring and it manifested as the universe. The 'I am' has created the cosmic panorama. It is the source of all the sages and saints. When that wakefulness goes back to sleep, all deities melt into it.

Devotion should be accompanied by faith. The original faith 'I am' should be properly understood. Then the whole puzzle will be solved. Devotion states 'I am the life force – consciousness. All this is due to my own light'. This should be enjoyed within in silence.

Nirupana 32
Sunday, May 28, 1978

The form of consciousness ('I am') is space. As you are formless, will you have any needs? Take space as your identity. Holding onto this identity permanently is called spiritual austerity. Do not bring humanness into this. Once you realize this, would there be any need for a house or a family?

What instrument do you have for this search? Is it not the knowledge that 'you are'? This is the main capital that is spread throughout the world in the form of the five elements. Krishna also taught this knowledge in various ways. What was His capital? Was it not His consciousness? With most people the same capital is smeared with sin and virtue. Whether you see a deity or a ghost, it is seen in the light of your light. Most teachers recommend rites and rituals. No one talks of such self-evident facts. If there is conviction that space is one's form, is there ever any gain or loss?

The knower of consciousness comes prior to it. That which is prior to consciousness cannot be described in words. Existence-consciousness-bliss (sat-chit-ananda) is the quality of knowingness. It is still objective. The knower is not an object. My talk is like this because I have seen existence-consciousness-bliss in its bare form.

The knowledge 'I am' is bliss. So long as you have not experienced this, you will not be able to understand your Self. As soon as you become stabilized in your Self, the continuous commentary of the mind will stop.

You still have fear; it means a little sin is lurking inside. Identification with the body is the sin. Your consciousness works through five channels i.e. touch, hearing, seeing, taste and smell. Consciousness is you; hold onto it. Have you understood this? Remembering this is meditation. Gradually, its worthiness will be inspired. Pay attention to the greatness of this knowledge. It is so atomic, yet how colossal is the creation out of it. That which is already there need not be searched for. Do not mix it with the mire of body-consciousness. So long as you do not treat your beingness as God, you will not understand anything. Had it not been there, who could have said, 'I am Krishna, Vishnu, etc.'? Instead of believing in facts, you believe in illusory things. That is because of maya. If you want to drive out this illusion, pay attention to your subtle consciousness. It is as great as the entire universe.

When you get up from deep sleep, it is the Self (consciousness) that wakes up, but you take yourself as a man or a woman. Then you face death. Do not repeat the knowledge that you have heard here, till the experience comes. The flood of light of this atomic consciousness is so vast that it has become the whole world. It is the same through which you feel yourself to be sinful or virtuous. If the truth and untruth are known only once, it is enough. There is no use then of sitting down and going into samadhi all over again.

You have fragmented yourself. That is why thoughts harass you. Pay attention to the fact that you are all this in its entirety. The 'I am-ness' can be understood in the waking state only. Your pure consciousness is prior to any concepts. The Truth suddenly is felt as 'I am' and immediately thereafter the universe comes into existence. If the knowledge of your consciousness dissolves into the Truth, people will throng wherever you go.

Maya is that which is seen, felt, fancied and known, but it does not last. The Self is the base for all that happens in consciousness. That which is known becomes unknown and this is called death. It is evident that the five elements are all that is. They are sporting within me. To wake up from deep sleep is also the moving power of the five elements. It is the power of Sattva guna that nourishes *Rajas* and *Tamas*. The most important power is to understand that not I, but the world I see, is born. Through this everything is seen. The sense of waking up is the birth of the world.

Birth means knowing the 'I am-ness'. With it the world is created. Once this consciousness is born, the world comes into view with individual bodies and their joys and sorrows. Unless you meditate on this, the puzzle will not be solved. The world is born spontaneously. Dissolve your consciousness at that point. It is of the nature of God.

Consciousness – just the simple knowledge of our beingness – is the Guru, the Lord of lords. One who believes that consciousness is the body and the mind is lost. Through the mind, 'I-am' is sensed. Good and bad are known through the meaning that comes out of the mind. And you are not the mind.

How true can the experience be that comes through breathing? Had you seen the world before you were born? The world is born along with you. The 'I am-ness' in the human body is the birthplace of the world. When consciousness arises, only then the world is born! There is no birth or death for you. Consciousness has not created an individual, but the whole world. Body-consciousness is the obstruction. Otherwise, it is easy to understand this. Body-consciousness has delivered the perfect One into the hands of time (death). It has measured it by counting its days! You as Sadguru-Self have never been born (it's only the body or maya that is born). You are the proof of the Sadguru's word. 'I am really the One that my Guru told me I was. Whether the body falls or not, I am the proof of what I heard from my Guru, and the proof of my conviction is my faith in the Sadguru.'

When the jiva and Shiva both are proved to be unreal, the Paramatman still remains as the Witness. By virtue of my sacred offering, pure consciousness is realized. The concept 'I am' gets dissolved. The one who is before such a concept cannot be destroyed. So long as consciousness has desires, be watchful. The illusory consciousness has given birth to the world, not to you. To move that illusory world, do you require any power? If my words pierce someone, he will become a siddha!

Nirupana 33
Tuesday, June 6, 1978

What is needed in order to recognize one's Self? Is it the mind? The knower of the mind is consciousness. The Self can only be known through consciousness. Here, the intellect is of no use. Intellect is the essence of the collective mind. Consciousness has to be realized through consciousness, which is prior to the mind.

You say you know the flow of the mind and yet you flow with the mind. That is false. That means there is no conviction of how you are and till such time, fear is there. The greatness of the whole world is in the heart of a human being. However, he fails to understand that. He considers himself as the body and suffers misery. All great sages of the world became so by meditating on their own consciousness. It uncovers itself and acquires greatness.

That which was already there came to know 'It is'. This is called birth. The name maya is given to birth. Maya is the behavior of gunas. Its source is consciousness. It is the knowingness created at birth. Birth implies beingness. You are prior to that knowledge. All this is the sport of your own consciousness. Whatever is felt, fancied or known is actually not you. One who knows this is the Self. The creation, sustenance and dissolution of consciousness happens on the base of the supreme Self. All deities are a projection of consciousness. It is the result of the action of *guna-maya*. You are the support of all these. Maya means the experience of consciousness. Dying does not mean annihilation; it is like the setting of the sun.

No one has death as such. The matchstick is the food for the flame. When it gets extinguished, it does not mean that it has died.

The apparent conviction that one's body is the Self is what is called maya. It has an infinite number of names. Maya, herself, has been given the status of a deity. There is no truth at all in this world, hence it is not necessary to observe its rules and regulations. It is fictitious. Consciousness is moving about as beingness. Consciousness that is experienced is in fact not real. The meaning that floats through the feeling 'I am' is unreal. For example, to say I am like this, I have done this, etc., is unreal. When consciousness goes, the world also disappears. Consciousness and the world are not separate.

The work is done for the one who clearly knows his own Self. Consciousness has to know only this: the form, which is fancied and known through consciousness, is not one's true nature. Consciousness means the Guru, and the Guru means consciousness. They are not apart. The 'I am' was not known, and is now known. This is the primordial maya. The Lord or a blade of grass is the same for the one who has surrendered to the Sadguru. Maya means self-love. Whatever consciousness achieves is never full; it is incomplete, as it is not true. This attitude is born in one in whom the Paramatman wants to manifest. Therefore, constantly remember the word of the Sadguru. Become one with your consciousness. The oil disappears after giving light. Similarly, your consciousness will spread throughout the world and then disappear. Then what will remain? It is the pure nature of Paramatman. Continue with your silent repetition of the mantra. Then the Guru-ness in your heart will suddenly burn intensely and show you how it rises and sets. Your true nature will be revealed.

Nirupana 34
Thursday, June 8, 1978

The meaning of the mantra is your consciousness. You should make it known to you. While reciting the mantra, whatever you feel, let it be felt. It will go away. The import of the mantra is your beingness. In order to realize it, become more and more quiet. You are not dependent on the five elements, or sleep, or wakefulness. Until such time that this becomes clear, go on contemplating. In the end you will realize that you were never born, neither have you carried out any worldly action. When you are enlightened you will say, 'It was not necessary for me to gain the world or worldly knowledge'. Renunciation means to detach from the five elements and consciousness.

Without air, fire has no soul. Without the light of Brahman (consciousness) there is no space and without space there is no air. In the five elements there is no static form as such. To know this thoroughly is called renunciation. We know that 'we are' because of the five elements and consciousness. They will not last. One who has recognized this cannot be seasonal. If there is no consciousness, what can be known? One who has not thought of his own nature, has to believe in things he hears in the world. A rare one, by the grace of the Guru, will pay attention to That through which the worldly phenomenon is sensed. He will not be attracted to the world. He will only pay attention to his consciousness.

This knowledge is about Him through whom the world is visible. The sense 'I am' is known through Him. This is the work of consciousness. As a result of the Guru-word, this knowledge will be created spontaneously. When the atomic consciousness in the body awakens, it pervades the universe. When asleep, it pervades the dream world. The universe is filled with consciousness and it continues its existence. The one who knows this is called a jnani. A person may get to be the king of the world but as long as he has not realized his consciousness, his achievements are like a mirage.

All religions are the religions of tradition. The true religion is to know the nature of the Self. Be in That.

One who is dead – does he get the experience that he is dead? Someone else says that he is dead. Such is tradition. The sight of the knower is consciousness. In view of that sight, all this performance is going on. After realization, there is no place for individuality. But there remains a memory, in some form or the other, of being an individual. Consciousness that has pervaded the universe does not pertain to someone in particular. It belongs to all. However, it is seasonal, temporary, time-bound. When its duration is over; it is gone.

People take to saffron robes just to take advantage of a tradition. Other people fold their hands and bow before them. Catch hold of consciousness so that your renunciation has a true meaning. Meditate on consciousness. It will show you its Source. The world is seen within consciousness, which itself has been created through ignorance.

What you have heard from other people is the source of fear, bondage, and liberation for you. Can the one who has understood time see death? Consciousness has no support. It does not depend on the five elements or the three gunas. One's own nature is the true knowledge. It is not dependent on anyone or anything.

First you must see your own Self. Renunciation happens through Self-knowledge. One who has understood the ultimate meaning knows his Self. The rest are all selfish (who look after the well-being of their own individual self – ego). Call your consciousness as the Guru. Then it will show you the right way. It is consciousness that takes renunciation. A rare one out of millions can give initiation by saying, 'you will not die'.

Nirupana 35
Sunday, June 11, 1978

The more you understand about spirituality, the less will be your needs. When a jiva dies, it means the sense 'I am' ends. To understand this one should get stabilized within. Whatever you take yourself to be will come to an end. The 'I am-ness' that you have taken for granted will not last.

Wakefulness came from deep sleep. Along with that came the feeling 'I am'. When the mind is busy with daily activities, we bind ourselves to what we say or how we act. Otherwise, the beingness by itself is detached. Unless we give ourselves a name, there will be no activity. Actually, no one acts and no action is really true; nothing is done.

Brahman is true as it has no sense of 'I am-ness'. So long as consciousness is not understood, one has to act through the mind. The vast universe arises from the *Brahma-randhra* (aperture in the crown of the head). All knowledge comes out of the *Brahma*-atom and it merges back in the end.

One who considers his consciousness as the Guru has no ritual to follow. By taking the Guru-word as authority, one is not bound by the cycle of karma. This happens spontaneously. All worldly dealings are the movement of God. The devotee does not differentiate between himself and the Guru. Take yourself to be pure consciousness and behave accordingly. A simple devotee becomes limitless by holding onto the Guru-word. By reciting the mantra given by the Guru, he becomes one with the Guru. When the inner God is pleased, He gives the gift of the Guru.

On dissolution of individuality, the fear of death goes away. Any identity you take will be temporary. The identity given by the Guru will remain forever. To realize consciousness while in the human body is priceless. There is no one as generous as the one who offers Self-knowledge. If you realize that, there will be no difference between you and the Guru. You will become immortal.

Even without dying you have fear of death. There will never be an experience of death as such. Still the fear of death does exist. You know that you have awakened. Does it not mean that you were there before awakening? This memory could come only when one existed prior to that. The five elements are the characteristics of the memory 'I am'. It will never be able to see the One who is prior to the memory. You may believe in God, etc., but it has no steady existence. You consider your memory 'I am' as yourself. There are thousands of memories; are we those memories? All action is the result of memory, but we are not the memory. The nature of memory is to forget. Even the memory that 'I am God' comes to an end. Discriminate, deliberate on this point and be free. Get rid of the memory 'I am'. Identification as a man or woman is through that only. What does it mean? How did it get created? If by the grace of the Guru someone understands this, he will become the eternal Brahman. Do your words belong to a mortal human or to immortal God? If you make just one sentence out of this discourse as your own, you will become immortal.

Nirupana 36
Thursday, June 15, 1978

Bliss that comes by the grace of the Sadguru cannot come from anything else. Bliss that you enjoy at the time of death is infinitely more than the greatest happiness you may have experienced in your life. The time of death is the time of perfect life, the time of immortality. Unless you embrace this knowledge, there will be no peace. You may talk about this to others but you will not be blissful. Contemplate on the Self with whatever name you call it: Brahman, Guru or God.

All over the world people love themselves. Out of millions, a rare one will understand the meaning of this. The love of the Self looks after the body, whether it is ugly or beautiful, without getting tired. How does one meditate on consciousness? It should be done without holding anything in mind. Make it easy by calling it the Guru. You want every entertainment to while away the time. The Source of all is the love of the Self. All your relations and possessions will ultimately disperse. Get to understand the Self before this happens. Searching through the mind will not be enough. Discrimination will bring it to you.

Do not hurt anyone. Just go on tolerating. You will get the limitless power of tolerance. Endure with patience the censure and harassment from one and all. Do not, as a reaction, censure that person. All foolishness is due to selfishness. Quarrels are due to selfishness. With realization, your selfishness will come to an end.

He (God) who may not be found in the world is

found in the heart of the devotee. The world seems to be outside, but it is seen from within. The idol in the heart, the idol of knowledge, has no form. It is similar to the sweetness of sugar. Krishna says: 'I am present in your heart as Bhagavan, the Luminous One. It is consciousness. It is the same as you'. The sun of knowledge in your body is that through which you know 'you are'. It is the supreme devotion. It is non-dualistic. It is called love. All living beings have this devotion in their heart, but only a human being can understand it. A busy person acts through this devotion but does not know it. Devotion means the love 'you are'. It has been created unknowingly. It protects the body. Have you realized that you are love yourself? Be aware of this supreme devotion and meditate on it. In the first stage it is difficult. Therefore this devotion is called God or Guru.

Who is listening now? Is it not the love in the body? One who knows this love directly achieves the state of Paramatman. Because you take yourself as the body, you have to face miseries day after day. The body may be of any quality; yet the love, the supreme devotion, is never displeased. The love of Self in the body performs devotion. For understanding Self-love you will have to meditate on it. Treat it as the Guru. All the incarnations, as well as maya and Brahman, are not different from Self-love. These are names to understand the fact. What is nobler than Self-knowledge?

Out of millions a rare one will meditate on the love of Self. You will come to know your totality through Self-love or through devotion. For whom do you suffer hardships and do this laborious work? Is it not for this love? To meditate on Self-love, recognize it as God. It has thousands of names. That which is worshipped and praised is the self-luminous love in the body. A rare one realizes that he is that Self-love and that is where the Paramatman manifests Himself. Self-love is Self-knowledge, which is of the nature of Brahman. How long will it last? So long as there is consciousness in the body.

One realizes the Self-love by following the Guru-word. It will bring you eternity. To him the universe that is infinite looks like a sesame seed. It may be true that you do not know this Self-love, but without it you do not exist. Krishna says: 'I am in the heart, but am not found without devotion'. People worship outer covers and get devoted to them. A rare one devotes himself to consciousness directly. This devotion works in each being; the love of one's own nature. The love that wakes you up in the morning is Self-love. One who realizes this achieves perfection. This love is naturally in the body, it is self-sensing. Once you realize it, your work is done. It can neither be held, nor can it be given up, no matter how much one tries. So, it is the same as the Guru.

What makes people adorn themselves? Is it not Self-love? However, it is transient. There is going to be a separation from those whom you call your own. Self-love is not concerned with anything else. It is without attachment. What you have known will surely go away. You are the love that is formless, nameless and indestructible. Keep it in mind. Once you know it, the five elements are sure to surrender to you.

People are unable to grasp the deep secret of spiritual truth. One gets enjoyment from various things. What enjoyment have you derived from your consciousness? To love another is adultery. Do not love others with your Self-love. Love the love itself. By adulterous devotion, you may get a temporary benefit but you will not be happy. The whole world is really brimming with your love and is created out of your love. The crowd on the street is the love in body-forms. It is the primordial illusion or *mul-maya*. Her action is moving the whole world. Love is working through all bodies. However, it is wrongly identified as the bodies.

You may meditate on a deity, but the meditator is the Self-love. The experience of this love has come over you unasked for, and everything depends on it. If you please this love, you will realize that you are everlasting and perfect. Presently you can only see it in the form of the five elements; the sixth being God. To achieve Love, through love, names are given to that love. Many rituals are performed to recognize this love for our consciousness – 'I am'. If this love determinedly worships itself, it will be the same as the worship of all gods and deities. The names of gods and deities are the names of love. They are the embodiment of the love.

Nirupana 37
Sunday, June 18, 1978

In the old days, whatever the Guru had to tell the disciple he would say it only once. When they met again after twelve years, the disciple would be ready. The meaning of this is, it is not necessary to go to the Guru constantly.

First of all there is the Self, our true nature. Then consciousness appears. Through that all the dealings take place. They depend upon the memory. But nothing stays forever. The entire behavior is traditional. A rare one looks within. Consciousness and all that is known through it is by nature universal. That which knows this is atomic and impenetrable. Whatever is known through consciousness goes on changing and in the end consciousness also disappears. Then who was born and who died? You have held everything within consciousness. But consciousness has a beginning and an end. It is your delusion that you treat yourself as so-and-so within that consciousness. What you know through consciousness will be gone. Then what, ultimately, is the use of what you have done?

What is created is the lotus of the heart and the world is its petals. From there various pollens are created. But its source is the stalk. (The subtle consciousness is called the lotus of the heart.) Whatever you know is part of consciousness. One who knows that consciousness rises and sets, is liberated. One is bound when he considers what is known through consciousness as true. It has been given the status of God. If you have no consciousness, where is God?

The Guru plants the seed in your consciousness that 'I am God'. It germinates and grows. Then the seeker realizes that the form (body, world) has no use. The learned man of pure intellect or even a simple believer gets liberated. Only those who are somewhere in between, fumble.

Do not just meditate; live in meditation. The Guru's words are the only Truth. Hold onto that. The Guru gave the advice 'You are pure Brahman'; hold onto that. That is the seed consciousness. Do not forget that you are consciousness. With conviction, firmly insist that 'I am Brahman'. What is your share in the world? Then what are you proud of?

Hope and desire are the oils that keep the flame of life going. When hopes and desires are finished, one is extinguished right out. He is not dead but is extinguished like a lamp. According to the Vedas, the thinking during the last moment of life decides the destination. For example, a Hindu and a Muslim kill each other while their attention is fixed on each other. The Hindu is born as a Muslim and vice-versa, so the battle never ends.

Remembering the Guru means remembering consciousness. When you see yourself as consciousness, you will come to know how free and open everything is. You and your world are void. The efforts you make will be an interruption in this. Your consciousness is like a visitor (transient). The world is seen through consciousness, but consciousness will not last. It is a passing phase. Then why be concerned with the world? When consciousness goes, does it mean that you die? Consciousness has been given the status of God. When you become of the nature of God, you will understand that everything is unreal. Then you will be free from bondage. If the effort is given up, there will be no interruption. (Efforts create the mind, which is an interruption.)

The consciousness that talks of God and the consciousness that listens are not different. Listening to the teachings creates detachment. The company of the body does not remain forever. Besides, it changes through various stages of life. Consciousness has no form, hence it is neither a man nor a woman. The sense 'I am' depends upon the five elements. You wish to get rid of your body-consciousness, hence you have to pay attention to the consciousness that listens. It is not important whether you carry on worldly dealings or not. But the concept 'I am the doer and I am responsible for the dealings' should vanish. Your temporary consciousness is subtler than space. You are all. Any identity you have taken up will not last. The one who knows this is immortal.

What you know is only through this consciousness. It experiences happiness and sorrow. The one who knows consciousness is beyond experience. Consciousness is the birth of God. Remember that. (When you come to know 'you are', God is born.)

The seed of Brahman is sown in you through the word 'I am'. The more it takes root, the less will be the identification as a human being. God means consciousness, the same as your beingness, the sense 'I am'. Your actions are the actions of God-consciousness. Without Self-realization, you cannot be a jnani.

Recitation of the mantra is the remembrance of one's own true nature. It is the meditation on 'I am'. Practice that. It requires no other proof. The mundane concepts of an individual determine his behavior. However, your consciousness is natural and spontaneous. It is not a result of your concepts or ideas. When there is no longer any necessity of 'I am' or 'I should be', it is liberation.

Death is only a projected fear. It is not a matter of experience. Death of the body is not your death.

Concept precedes action. But consciousness is without a prior concept. What was not noticed before this, is noticed as 'I am'. It is still time-bound. It has an end. To listen to the story of God is to listen to our own story. When you are just aware of your beingness, is there any need for God or the world? Words cannot describe Self-realization.

One in whom God incarnates, can discriminate. This knowledge will not come through the recitation of the mantra or austerities. (These are not direct means for Self-realization, they are a means to keep the mind quiet.) Who sent you here? Is it not your own Self? Where you are not, there is no God, no religion, and no world. Wherever you are, there is everything. God is characterized by knowingness. You are That in which all characteristics are dissolved.

Nirupana 38
Thursday, June 22, 1978

The nature of Paramatman is such that He has no coming or going. At this time you have two bodies before you. One is your own, the other is the world. Worldly dealings are managed by concepts. So long as you have not realized the supreme state of being, you have to follow traditions. All actions happen through concepts. You have taken for granted that you are created; this is based upon someone else's concept. Concepts decide your state, whether happy or unhappy, as also your ideas about birth and death. All this is the sport of concepts. It is the concepts that act, while you think you are the doer.

According to the Guru-word, you are formless. You were never born. Worship consciousness and not the body. Whatever you understand as yourself will not last. You conduct yourself as directed by your mind and intellect. You do not have the courage to teach your mind and intellect. That courage will come when you act according to the Guru-word. By constant remembering and worshipping, consciousness is pleased and it uncovers itself. Then you will know what non-duality is. There is no sense of separateness in the Self at all. The dilemma whether to act or not goes away. When two opinions are united, there is no conflict. When consciousness is pleased, duality ends and there is totality. When there is no duality, there is bliss. For this, hold onto the Guru-word.

There is no God other than consciousness. Meditate on the sense 'I am'. It is the meditator itself. It is so simple yet people do incredible austerities for its sake. Like Krishna, you should also say, 'All this is I'. One that is listening is the consciousness. Are you not aware that 'you are'? Previously, you did not exist and were not aware of your beingness. Presently, you know that 'you are' and this knowingness is consciousness. Meditate on your Self, but not as a body-form.

Does the memory that you are a man or a woman belong to you or to the body? Is that memory 'you'? As soon as one feels 'he is', the five elements are perceived in consciousness. To further qualify 'I am' as 'like this' or 'like that' is ignorance. The remedy for that is the search for the Self. As it is difficult to meditate on your own consciousness, worship it as the Guru. You can think of the Guru as standing on your back, with light spreading all over. But you cannot imagine that you, yourself, are standing behind you. The early stages of meditation require support of dualism.

Your identity has no body-form. Everything will become clear when you realize that there exists nothing other than you. Where there is God, you are there; where you are, God is. You are not dependent on the body or upon the knowingness in the body. You will understand clearly without any support that 'I was eternal and am so forever'. Just worship that through which you know everything. The nature of Paramatman is ours as our personal right, as our own existence.

There is no Self-knowledge for the one who considers himself as a physical body. The Self has to be realized with full determination. That is the reason for your longing to come here.

Fate and destiny are traditional words. What is the destiny of one in whose opinion the subtle body is not born at all? If you mention this to others, you will disturb them.

One without duality has no occupation. The non-dual has no intention or desire. There is no other proof for non-duality except for 'I am That'. Your sense of doership will not remain with you. The jnani has no desire to live. He has no such concept.

Nirupana 39
Sunday, June 25, 1978

There should be a firm understanding of one's own nature. What you talk must be supported by a firm conviction about it. There is a verse: 'God inspires what I am saying. It is not I, but it is God talking through me'.

What is being talked about is the manifest consciousness. The unmanifest is beyond word, devotion and love. What the Guru teaches should be remembered continuously in all the waking hours, no matter what activity is being performed. When there is samadhi during waking hours, it implies that there is no worry and no thinking.

Do not hurt anybody. If there is dissension, just ignore it. The body is going to fall someday. Then why should we undermine the Guru-word? He has given us absolute assurance. What is the use of living if you do not believe it? Erratic behavior is not allowed in spiritual effort.

One has to be steady. All practical dealings are based upon opinions. The Truth is one, but people express it in their own way, according to their own opinion. They get experiences accordingly. With the strength of austerities, whatever is said comes true. The Principle is one but on the basis of that, thousands of opinions have come about. This is the power of maya. Krishna says: 'Without maya I cannot even be mentioned'. Maya performs all activities, but the Purusha (Self – Paramatman) is always silent. He is the non-doer.

Those who know that they are Brahman are the true brahmins. People claim to know Brahman and yet hold onto their egos. They start preaching their opinions. This again is the play of maya. There have been many sages and saints, but not one behaved like the other.

Only after 'I am' has occurred comes the concept 'I am Vishnu' or 'I am Brahma'. But before this happened, who was I? No one thinks of that. Maya does what she wants by taking suitable forms. To create appearances and dissolution is the characteristic of maya. Purusha is only the onlooker. If maya were not there, there would not even be a mention of Purusha (Absolute). When there was no experience of maya, what knowledge would you have about yourself? All your knowledge-information is illusory. It is not steady. It is visible, it is felt, but it is not the Truth. Purusha is actionless. Whatever is seen and felt is due to the color of maya. Purusha is the knower of maya.

Sometimes, sages developed pride of their realization. This pride became a hindrance to them and made them live for thousands of years. Whatever is known will never be steady. Why? Because maya is illusory. You cannot ward off maya even with penance performed for thousands of years. Even with different religious traditions, the states of sleep and wakefulness are the same for all. Due to the superimposition of maya, some accumulate merit or some accumulate more sins. After the body falls, there will not be a vestige of memory left of what you did today. Then how are you going to utilize that merit?

Rebirth is the opinion of those sages. The knowledge based upon opinions is intellectual knowledge. It is illusory. It is not Self-knowledge. It is temporary. It lasts as long as the body lasts. Can there be consciousness without the body?

What do you have as your own? You have the consciousness that is in the body. It depends upon the essence of food. So long as the body is healthy, you feel that your thoughts are true. After the body falls, there is no 'I' and there is no 'you'. But recognize it today itself. That duality was not there and even now it is not there. It is illusory. All this is not created, yet it is moving about. There is no such thing as a realized sage. No one lives and no one dies. All this is maya. Even the sages get dazed with the power of maya. Otherwise, there would not be so many opinions.

The most important thing is our consciousness. It has come as a guest for a few days. Eventually it will go. What was originally not there, will return to that state. How and in which bundle are you going to preserve consciousness? Are you your consciousness? Can one say, 'I was there before consciousness'? It is only consciousness that is created.

Sin and virtue are all a matter of words. When one starts discriminating, the words run away. Only the supreme Self knows how the word got the experience of the word. The rest are slaves of the word. Each one is a slave of the mind and intellect. Your true nature is prior to consciousness. Can you preserve this consciousness? Discriminate on this right now.

Nirupana 40
Thursday, June 29, 1978

Only the Paramatman knows the nature of time. The rest who identify with the body become a victim of time. All names belong to time. When you come to know 'you are', it is the birth of time. It is time that is born, not the child. For the one who has Self-realization, the movement of the clock and time are one and the same. For the ignorant one, the experience of time is a mountain of sorrow. For the jnani, time has ended. The ignorant one lives thinking he is the body. He is trapped in time.

Just listen to this. There is no need of rituals. Whatever you hear here, be aware of it and then your meditation will work. Your beingness precedes meditation.

The body depends upon time. Consciousness in the embryo is latent. It emerges in the form of beingness. The latent consciousness slowly starts expanding. Does the embryo experience time? It does not know its body. After birth, it starts identifying with the body. There is an experience of time. It starts knowing the mother. It recognizes her voice.

A body's growth is the result of time. One cannot will it. Strength and weakness come according to the nature of time. Therefore, understand the passage of time. Whatever you say is the result of time. One who knows time has neither birth nor death. Without consciousness, one does not know. One does not know 'I am' or 'I am not'. Time is movement which is also consciousness. The measurement of how long time is experienced is the duration of your life. You are the support of time. The knower of time is not in time. The Source of the creation of time is nameless. You may call it Paramatman or Parabrahman.

Time shows you its own movie; your birth is part of it. The dormant consciousness comes out of the womb. It is sustained by time. There were people who knew the three times – the past, present and future. There still are. But who is the knower of time? When they are told that the knower of time is Paramatman, people say, 'Yes, we understand'. Do you know that you yourself are the knower of time? The one who is beyond time has no birth at all. He is not born out of the essence of the five elements. He knows that he is not the essence in the embryo.

You were born without your knowledge. The knowingness arose after the birth of the body. This is the result of the nature of time. In deep sleep, the next day's activities are programmed. This program is recorded and behavior happens accordingly. To make this your own understanding, be one with your beingness. You have to do this on your own.

Time has all these names: the sun of the world, the sun of the Self, the sun of the universe, etc. This sun is your own consciousness. When you are with your Self, it is the sun of knowledge. The sun means time. All these names are given to your own consciousness. It is the sun of Self. Various names such as consciousness, life force, knowledge of Self, love, etc., are given to the beingness. Be devoted to that consciousness. Give it the status of the Guru. Contemplate on it, make obeisance to it. Whatever else you do will be eaten up by time. Recognize the sun that knows time and then time will serve you.

Take a vow to practice devotion. One who practices devotion definitely gets an extension of life. You cannot fool the supreme Self. If this extension is misused, it will result in disaster.

Because of the delusion of maya, the jiva does not understand this knowledge till death comes. You do not require a vow or determination to realize the Paramatman. He is the Witness of this determination. Be aware. Always remember to whom you have to be devoted to and why. Remember that the knowledge 'you are' is the Guru-God.

Nirupana 41
Thursday, July 6, 1978

The difference between 'He' (God) and 'I' (Self) is gone; neither really exists. The sense of individuality has been extinguished. The sense of universality is pervading. Neither the duality of 'He' and 'I', nor their unity is there. If there is one, relatively the other must be there. But if one is not there, how can the other be there?

Pleasure and pain, both should go. When a thing is useful, it brings joy. As long as individuality is there, there is joy and sorrow. You are tortured by miseries and elated by happiness. From where do such experiences come? They come from your consciousness. What is the evidence that one is realized? The individuality is completely uprooted. There is absence of sorrow and happiness. Your consciousness realizes that it is universal. When this knowledge *really* comes to you, there will not be any individual identity.

The source of happiness and sorrow is your sense of 'I am'. What causes the greatest sorrow is also the means of eternal happiness. Once you know your consciousness, individuality will not be there. But who is watching this? It is the Sadguru, the changeless One. Have this conviction. He is the same in deep sleep, in wakefulness and in samadhi. There is none other than That. The total experience that comes to you, is it different from your consciousness? Your money order has come but you have not taken the cash. Your knowledge has come to you, but you have not taken its delivery yet.

However great a thing is in the world, it is still a piece of information. If there is no consciousness, of what use is it? Who would have the conviction like this except for God? When you did not have consciousness, was God true or false for you? This knowledge is your own. Never lose sight of the holy consciousness that is listening to this knowledge. There are millions of seekers; how many have realized the Self?

Miseries abound because we identify ourselves with the body. It is the nature of the body-mind to experience joys and sorrows. If you know that you are not the body, there is no suffering. In deep sleep, there is no identification with the body, male or female. Hence, there is no experience of happiness or sorrow. Yet the mind goes on working, taking itself to be the body. It is false. If there is no mind then nothing can be witnessed. You have to accept the holy feet of the Guru to stop the mind. You have no knowledge of your birth, you have only heard about it. The past and the future, as projected by the mind, are not yours. Mind determines the past, present and future, and makes you behave accordingly. Mind says you have had millions of births, but you do not have the knowledge of a single one. Do you at least have the knowledge of your present birth? All your experiences are untrue. With the conviction that you are neither the body nor the mind, you will understand this fraud.

Religions have come down through traditions. Is there a religion without dogma? Even a jnani has to follow traditions until a certain stage has been crossed.

Discriminate. There is no understanding without

discrimination. Until then, there is no peace. You are the knower of the mind. The knower is beyond the body-mind. When you realize that you are not what your mind tells you, you will understand why Atman is unborn. A rare one turns inwardly on his own, without hearing about it from others. Gradually learn to discriminate. The awareness of the Guru-word will enable you to do this.

When the mind-connection is severed, you will see the void. To purify the mind one must remember the mantra all through the waking hours. Then your mind will come under your control. When you pay attention to your true nature the mind will disappear, bringing in the whole.

In the perfect state, there is no experience of bliss. It cannot be witnessed. Did you witness anything prior to your birth? There are great learned men, but can anyone of them step outside the mind? Wherever there is mind, there is prana (vital force). Where there is prana, there is consciousness. After realizing the nature of the mind, the life force is dissolved. The delight and bliss of that moment are unique. It comes to the one who knows the Self. Just as it is a concept that one is born, the dread of death is also a concept. The mind surrenders to you if your incantation of the mantra is continuous. It tells you what you need to know.

When prana leaves the body, does it have any pain? Prana carries out all worldly action, but you say you are the doer. When there is no prana, is there a mind? When there is no mind, there is no pain. This means that the mind has taken the form of the body. When prana leaves and the body falls, where does Atman go? This can be answered when one is clear about the Self. For this, according to the sages, the mantra must be recited.

Without prana, what is your identity? Without it, who is a man and who is a woman? Body-consciousness brings joys, miseries, and ultimately the dreaded death. It is all a play of concepts. When you discard the concepts, there will be a celebration of liberation, right in this body. Those who give up the addiction of the mind and recognize the Self will surely be provided with sustenance. Remember the Guru always and you will drop the mind and be free. Keep on the continuous incantation of the mantra. Make the mind i.e. prana say, 'My true nature is indestructible and eternal'. The mind will disappear; there will be the manifest Brahman Itself (thoughts disappear and pure consciousness shines).

Nirupana 42
Sunday, July 9, 1978

Do not compete with anyone in the world. Put such things aside. Your devotion to the Guru-word must be infallible. Such devotion is not dualistic. In such devotion, there is no fear and there is no begging. You will never attain peace in association with worldly matters. Once Self-realization is achieved, it is never lost. Let go of your body-consciousness: the feeling 'I am a man' or 'I am a woman'. That which has no color, no design, has no expectations. If you fully understand your weak points, they will become your strong points. Until the age of forty go on learning something. That way one gets some encouragement, some zeal to live by. Eventually you will be proud to say, 'I know nothing'.

To mention the word *nirguna* (unmanifest) requires relativity. Nirguna can be recognized only if there is guna. What happens when there is no guna? Guna means the knowingness that has come in unasked as the feeling 'I am'. It is consciousness that is listening. When there is no feeling of 'I am', it is called nirguna. When a person becomes one with his consciousness and forgets himself, he gets Self-realization. The same consciousness is in the form of the five elements. It is in the form of our beingness. The knower of consciousness is without any characteristics (gunas). When consciousness becomes illumined, you feel 'you are'. However, it is identified with the body. The only way to remove body-consciousness is to hold onto the Guru-word.

One who has imbibed my words will not have any complaints. To imbibe my words, one has to meditate on the consciousness in solitude. When consciousness is purified, it recedes to the unmanifest state and there is everlasting peace. You have been enchanted with consciousness and you have identified with your body. It is very difficult to break this habit. After listening to this, you may live your life as you please. There is no need for rituals. There is no separation between us. I see you as formless, whereas you take yourself as a body.

Out of the nirguna, many characteristics (manifest forms) are created. This must be understood while the consciousness (Sattva guna) in the body is still there. Otherwise, it will take birth time and again. Worship it with love-devotion. It will be purified. It will clearly understand the functioning of the three gunas. You will come to see that you are a non-doer and there will be eternal peace. The manifestation of your consciousness is called birth. It is also called the subtle body.

Despite intense effort, the habit of body-consciousness does not break. It is possible for the one who holds onto the Guru-word without fail. By reciting the mantra, 'I am pure Brahman', you will become limitless. There must be unshakable faith in the Guru. His words will become one with your breath. It will become the joy of your feeling 'I am'. It will correct the subtle body.

One who has no body, has neither remembrance nor forgetting. Hold within: 'The Guru-word is my true nature', with every breath. The fact that our nature is nirguna has never been forgotten, therefore it does not have to be remembered. The devotee of the Guru-word is the devotee of his own true nature. The Self exists and It is changeless. Do not attempt to change It with your intellect. With devotion of the Guru in your heart, you will never have any sense of duality. The supreme state as described by the Guru is naturally there. No remedy is required.

For bringing worthiness into your consciousness, your faith in the Guru must be absolute. It is the treasure house of the life force. Brahman is the Lord of words and It contains the universe. A great miracle is hidden in the seed. What a big tree comes out of it! The guna was latent in the nirguna. Whatever was hidden in the golden womb came out and with that the world became visible.

You will never get Self-knowledge if you impose your body-consciousness on the Guru. When you live with the faith that your consciousness and the Guru are the same, you will get Self-realization.

Such a vast world is contained in the microscopic consciousness! Such conviction comes with the Guru-word. Reading countless books is of no use. It will bring pride and with that the desire to undermine others. All troubles will be over if you yourself become the Guru-word. Do not ever forget the Guru-word: 'Brahman is eternal'.

Consciousness will expand and in the end it will become extinguished. 'I am beyond the body' will become manifest without words. It would not have to be looked after. It is easy, straight and natural. The habit of body-consciousness is the only hindrance.

In order to be convinced that you were never born, it should be known what is born and from what it is born. Just as there is a tree in a seed, the (universal) consciousness is latent within you. The Guru brings it out and it becomes all-pervading. Has anyone seen the end of space? Why is it so? It is because space is formed with the expanse of your own light. Make spiritual effort out of real and sincere necessity. His Majesty, the Guru, kills your individuality. The tree along with its fruits, flowers and branches enters the seed again.

The Guru has said that you are present everywhere. You must believe this in its totality. Self-realization is liberation. Then there is no need to go to heaven.

You are what the Guru has described. Do not bother with anything else. Spiritual truth has no concern with the body. It does not matter whether you are a man or a woman. Remember this.

Nirupana 43
Thursday, July 13, 1978

Mind is a kind of fever that has come upon you unknowingly. Whatever you do brings on suffering. You carry out all your actions to put up with the mind. When the body-form comes into existence, 'I am-ness' is sensed. Mind is created out of that feeling of beingness. There is rest in deep sleep. After waking up, you run around doing things that you expect will do you good. Why so? It is an attempt to put up with the fever called mind.

There are several names given to the mind: Brahman, prana (life force), etc. So long as there was no mind, how were you? Before mind came into existence, what was one like? One was perfect Brahman – beyond concept, beyond existence, beyond the three gunas. Parabrahman is always known to all living beings. Until such time that the mind was not sensed, there was no need for anything. There was no knowledge of 'I am' or 'I am not'. When you understand that the worship of Brahman, etc., is a joke, fever in the form of the mind will vanish.

Really speaking, you struggle for your good because you are confused by the basic delusion. Whatever is seen is not your true nature. That which was motionless stirred a little and created the dream world. It really means that you are the creator. The vision that has created the world is itself untrue. It seems many things were done in that dream but, really speaking, was anything done? Can anyone take credit whatsoever for the doership of this body-form?

You are living as a body, therefore you behave as one commanded by time. You do not know that time has been created out of you. The feeling 'I am awake' is time. Who upholds this universe with its sun, moon and stars? It is the same One who sees it. This is how Krishna says: 'I uphold the universe'.

Time is a season. The feeling 'I am awake' is time. Then comes mind as the knowingness 'I am'. It has occupied everything. But this is a temporary phase. Krishna says: 'I have observed this phase and that is how I am the creator of the universe'.

Time is associated by its very nature with the three gunas: Sattva, Rajas and Tamas. Time rules over people through their desires. Who carries out the action? That which is One is doing everything. It becomes many and moves about through desire as long as there is an experience of time. What is mind? Mind is the feeling 'I am awake'. When the mind dissolves, it knows nothing. The names of deities are after all names of the mind.

This is the story of Paramatman, which you are. You are not letting go of your habit of body-consciousness. Wakefulness is time. However, in time there is duality. Therefore, you have to become your own proof (of non-dual Absolute). There you will meet no other. You know the mind; you are not the mind. Hopes, desires, passions are of the nature of time. Yet the person says, 'I act' or 'I do'. Is there any difference between an expectation and a passion? With rites and rituals, you trade an iron cage for a golden cage.

Only after the arrival of the mind you require food, a home, a wife, etc. You call it desire. Yet it is of the nature of time. Recognize the fever of the mind. The mind is also called Brahman (manifest reality) that takes millions of births every day. All activities in the world are a result of the nature of time. To say one is a great person, etc., is of the nature of time. Time is the foundation of the whole universe. However, you are beyond time (unmanifest). Yet, body-consciousness does not go. You do not have to let anything go. You have to understand it. There is tremendous light-luster in the body. The light that comes out of your eyes pervades the sun and the moon. This dazzling, fierce light is absorbed by the Absolute. It swallows millions of suns. The dense, dark blue Absolute (seen when your eyes are closed) is so vast that innumerable worlds play in it like pebbles.

When one hears this he should say, 'Oh, is it really so?' Are you going to know this after you die? This world is so vast and yet the seer is smaller than an atom! For understanding this, worship That with which you are listening to all this. What did you know before consciousness came over you? The more you reduce your hopes and desires, the happier you will be.

The guna means the consciousness that has suddenly come over you. An infinite number of universes are sporting in consciousness. Who is the knower of this? Who is prior to consciousness? Is it the seer or that which is seen? If there is no seer, can there be the seen? By the grace of the Guru, the idea that 'time is my great death' goes away. When prana leaves the body do not say, 'I am dying'. Otherwise, you will have to take a new form again. Bhausaheb Maharaj (Maharaj's Guru's Guru) clapped when his prana left the body. Did he not mean to say that, 'I am Atman, I am indestructible'?

Liberation is attainable while the body is there. Can animals achieve it? When does another birth take place? After one dream, a second dream may immediately follow if it has to come. Remember that the one who is not afraid of death lives for many years.

Nirupana 44
Sunday, July 16, 1978

The true essence of spirituality is to understand life properly. At first, we felt a need for ourselves. Because of that, many needs have arisen. The goal is to find out where exactly we stand in all this, whether there is any everlasting Truth in it.

The stages of life are subject to change. They were not there before birth. Even the state of being a woman or a man does not last. Religion, God, etc., are medicinal doses for these stages. You know that no state of being is permanent. Yet due to delusion, you take them to be true. A rare one knows these stages. The fundamental state is that you know 'you are'. This is the root stage and it is miserable.

One must know for oneself what is changeless in this. It is not found in wakefulness, in sleep, or in samadhi. Our consciousness itself is not permanent. When it ends, we say one is dead. One no longer knows that 'he is'. Realize that no memory lasts forever, and be free. The feeling 'I am' will not last forever in any form or by any name. What was created will surely end.

The life force has no consciousness by itself. When it gets a form, beingness is created. The form is beingness. For the one who knows his true nature, this puzzle will be solved. The rest of them talk by inference. The main attachment is your beingness.

Have you not got the knowledge of your beingness now? And is it not a fact that you did not have that knowledge before? It is said that the world is an illusion. Why is it so? The reason is that your beingness does not last.

Consciousness is the seed of the world. When it sprouts and expands it becomes space. Seed means, 'What was not seen before, is now being seen'. The light of consciousness means the light of the sun and the moon. It is like a dream of daylight in the middle of the night. Wakefulness is like that dream. The seed means duality. The seed quality of God's consciousness is present in all beings.

One who knows himself perfectly is called Sadguru. He also knows how and why this imperfect consciousness is created. Krishna said: 'Whatever is, is Myself only. Yet I am different from all this'. Krishna's discourse in the Gita is truly unique. It is a great fortune to be able to hear it.

It is a greater fortune to be able to contemplate on it.

The greatest secret is consciousness. Put your faith in only that. One who understands this will not have rebirth. People worship deities for their personal satisfaction. However, the lasting satisfaction is one's own true nature. You alone can achieve that. One who takes himself as the body is never satisfied.

Always contemplate on what you have heard. That is the most important worship. If there is no listener, what will be the need for God? Worship consciousness in your heart. When you are successful in your contemplation, your worthiness will show. In the waking state, to remain without thought is the greatest worship. You should not feel 'I am so-and-so' while carrying out your activities. Put aside your knowingness and worship your true nature.

The Ganges flowing from the head of Lord Shiva symbolizes spiritual knowledge. As long as you believe that you are not everlasting, the eternal will elude you. You cannot ever forget the eternal. Endless rituals are not able to uncover the Truth. They may wrap you up even more. Whatever you see and sense will not last. When you have the awareness that you are neither a man nor a woman, you will be beyond consciousness. Once the Self is realized, everything becomes sacred. Bathing in holy rivers will not remove your ignorance, nor will mantra, nor spiritual penance. Association with one who abides by the Guru-word is enough. That is the knowledge through which sleep and wakefulness are known. It is the light that illuminates the sun and the moon. This light is yours only, but not as a human being. It belongs to consciousness.

It exists in the heart of every being. It is the self-sensing consciousness in the body. There is nothing more glorious than this knowledge. To be exactly like the meaning of these words, full faith in the Guru is needed. His word has to be taken as the authority. One who abides by that, acquires the bodiless knowledge. Krishna says: 'This is my true nature'. It is behind your memory. Neither the body nor the ears have the power to hear. It is the true nature that listens through the ears. It knows samadhi, yet samadhi does not know it. To achieve that with conviction is all that is needed.

No ritual can ever reveal one's true nature. All methods are of bodily nature. Without the existence of this atomic consciousness, there is no support at all for any being, the world, or Brahman. The essence of all knowledge is the Self. When falling asleep say, 'I am only the pure consciousness'. By following various methods, you will not find that which is already and naturally there.

Who recognizes consciousness? Is it not the one who knows time? Krishna says that consciousness, which knows all this, is My true nature. When there is the conviction that this birth is not true, the various concepts will not arise. One who knows the transient is eternal – perfect Brahman. A true devotee is not bound by anyone. He may perform rituals, but he is beyond them. To worship God means to be convinced that God is none other than ourselves. If there is no saguna (manifest), how could a mention be made of nirguna (unmanifest)? Hence, both are not there.

Nirupana 45
Thursday, July 20, 1978

When you take refuge in the Guru-word, birth and death will come to an end. Your consciousness is the Guru. If you identify yourself with the Guru it will be seen that there is no maya, but the manifest Brahman pervades everywhere. The Guru-word is, 'You are without body-form, without karma, without birth and death'. You will realize that maya does not give miseries, instead she serves spiritual effort. When you get identified with the word of the Guru, you will spontaneously realize what maya and the Self are. It is the idol of the Guru. This identification will create knowledge of the Self and understanding of maya. Remain with that, always. Deep sleep will be the only break. Love of the Self in the body is self-luminous. All the names belong to Self-love. You should meditate. However, consciousness itself is the meditator and also the listener. Meditate with love and devotion. Then you will understand all this through your consciousness. It is the essence of the body with its sweet flavor and is the most important. Who does not love his beingness – the sense 'I am'? Without consciousness, who will practice devotion? By nature, we are consciousness, love and joy. Surrender to consciousness without duality. The ever-luminous consciousness shines as the sun of your own true nature. When properly understood, the mire of body-consciousness will be removed.

Non-dual devotion is devotion to our own Self. Pay attention to That which is continuously with you.

You must feel its necessity. Your consciousness has gone through millions of incarnations. It knows its greatness as given by the Guru. It is the knower of time. It is your true nature. The great sages became like that by worshipping their consciousness.

The Guru-word is that 'you are the subtle consciousness that has become the world'. The world can be known only if consciousness is there. It is also called Brahman. The Self is immortal. It is the Peace Eternal, an ocean of bliss. Without this knowledge there is no day or night. This knowledge does not forget you even if you go about in body-consciousness. One who realizes himself becomes Brahman. His word uplifts humanity.

Your consciousness is the idol of the Guru. It is the Love of your love (as 'I am'). You have loved many things. Have you loved the one who motivates you to love? Become worthy of the faith of consciousness. It will provide you with everything.

One who knows prana cannot be seen. Prana is ever awake, even in deep sleep. One who knows that all worldly dealings are untrue is indestructible. Remember that.

Nirupana 46
Sunday, July 23, 1978

As long as prana and the body are together, there is consciousness. When prana leaves the body, consciousness disappears. What does one have to lose (by dying)? First there is consciousness, and then the body is sensed. One who knows consciousness is called a jnani. Your consciousness is the seed of the universe.

To be without words is to be in samadhi. You will not meet Parabrahman through intellect. What did you have before you were taught anything? Only wakefulness and sleep. The rest (all concepts) is based upon what you have heard. Even the pride, 'I am the seeker of Truth, I shall renounce', etc., has to go. One who manages worldly activities is of universal nature.

The only purpose of the human body is to realize Brahman. That is the reason why all the idols we worship have a human form. The word and the existence of the word can be sensed only through the human body. Word means Brahman (the manifest principle), existence means consciousness and, therefore, Brahman is sensed through the human body. But due to body-consciousness a man remains a man. If 'I' is taken aside from the body, it contains pure Brahman only. Brahman is consciousness and vice versa. The irony is that the ego that takes the body as itself is trying to know IT. Body-consciousness has to be dismissed. Nothing else has to be done.

Does your body know your consciousness? The body is a material object. Without prana, it is a corpse.

Consciousness in the Brahma-randhra knows pleasure and pain. Who is aware of consciousness? When this is clearly understood, the pleasure and the pain will go and there will be peace. In the body there is nothing else but pure Brahman. The one who knows consciousness, the feeling 'I am', is the knower. The knower cannot be described. Consciousness in the body is itself God. It naturally knows Brahman. It has the form of space, water, fire-luster, air, and earth; yet it is consciousness only. It is our consciousness that is acting through the five elements. It has no identification as a man or a woman.

The purpose of the body is to know Brahman. The mistake is that the same Brahman identifies itself with the body. It cannot know itself without the human body. However, it has accepted itself as body-consciousness. The five characteristics of the body are based upon word (hearing), form (seeing), touch, taste and smell. The vibration of Brahman in your body senses them. Therefore the human body has great importance. Do not waste a single moment without paying attention to your true nature.

The awakened consciousness is the image of Param-atman. It is easy for the one who recognizes it as God and becomes one with it. Catch hold of that Truth. Continuously remember that consciousness is your true nature (the manifest Brahman). It has been praised with a million names.

When consciousness sprouted, it took the form of a child. What do you possess except for consciousness? It *is* the light. Always remember that this is your true nature.

One who has this knowledge is Paramatman. It is the evidence that He is. If you understand this there is no need for austerities.

Identification with the body is the cause of turmoil. When there is no experience of a single word, while awake, it is your true nature. Your consciousness is the golden womb through which the world has been created. Through conception the unmanifest becomes manifest. Your everyday life, wife, children are nothing but entertainment. The various spiritual methods are also entertainment.

Can anyone feel that his body is sacred? If you do not feel sacred about yourself, then how can others feel it? When you are convinced that you are pure 'I am-ness', people will come to have your holy sight. When you become convinced by the Guru-word that you are pure Brahman, pure consciousness, you will feel that your body has become sacred. When you get realization, people will naturally want to have your darshan. One who is the 'soul of death' itself, how can he die?

The greatest negation of religion, the greatest sin, is to believe that the body is your true nature. Your religion is to remain as the Self. You must have the conviction of your true identity. You must recognize your relationship with your own Self. The mind gets modified and behavior changes with repetition of the mantra. The body serves as the food for this consciousness. The mind flows from prana, the vital force. When you realize all this, at the last moment you will clearly witness that you do not die but prana leaves the body. The enlightened person has no hopes, no desires and no passions. Therefore he has no death. It is the most indescribable event when the manifest becomes unmanifest (at the time of so-called death). But the ignorant one says, 'I am dying', even before prana leaves the body. This is because he has not known his true nature.

The time of death of a sage is very sacred. It is more sacred than sunrise. This is the reason why their death anniversary is celebrated. Decide now who you are going to die as. The thought at the time of dying will decide the future. There should be no other thought except 'I am perfect bliss'. Your state will be in accordance with what you take yourself to be. This is true now and it will be true then.

Nirupana 47
Sunday, July 30, 1978

From birth to death, all actions are performed in order to pass the time. The greatest good in life is to know who we are. It is impossible to establish order in the world. Meanwhile, those who teach and those who learn, all pass away. Religion is formed by the concepts of its followers, nothing else.

Our consciousness is the base for all worldly dealings. However, there is no base for consciousness. It has come uninvited. It rises and then passes away. There was no memory of 'I am' before, and now it is there. Except for this, what do you possess as your own? One who has realized himself has no concern about his well-being.

Wakefulness, sleep and hunger have no substitute. No law applies to them. Without these, nobody would do anything. Realized men are silent in spite of the knowledge they have. They know the secret of birth and why it has arrived. How was this consciousness imposed on you and since when? This must be understood. To get into samadhi means to let go of the mind with its memory.

Your breathing is proof of the existence of the breathless One. The word comes upon waking up, therefore you are prior to the word. The wordless meaning of our consciousness is the sense 'I am'. If you remain completely silent, you experience the Self. There is only one Self for all. Prana works also in sleep. It has no meaning then, as it has no knowledge of its vibration. Waking up is to feel 'I am' without pronouncing the words.

The three gunas are the names given to three types of behavior. They function in all living beings. We should not judge anyone's behavior. One who understands gunas will understand this. People with Rajo guna and Tamo guna will meddle with others' affairs instead of working on themselves. The bodies may be different, but consciousness is the same in all. It is formless. You might say that it has a flavor, a quality, which is love. The knowledge 'I am' loves itself and, hence, we can distinguish between good and bad. One who understands its greatness finds it all-pervading. Such a person does not criticize others. All things are being done for the sake of the love of Self. One who has devotion to all beings, as if they are God, cannot hate anyone. He sees clearly that he is not the doer.

Hold onto the fact that you are Brahman. First you know that 'you are' and then the words follow. Whose information is it? It is the information of the one who feels 'he is'. Consciousness is knowingness; a sense of being. All the activity of Purusha (supreme Self) and prakriti (creation) is based upon this. One who reaches this stage keeps quiet. He knows that in its absence there is no happiness or sorrow. Can you recede back to this stage?

So as to know who you are, understand consciousness with determination. What is more important than consciousness in the whole world? When you reach that point, you will not utter a single word about others. Without consciousness, there is no word. Pay attention to consciousness and nothing else. The one who does not recognize this has to suffer many miseries.

The world is a fun-game created out of one's own existence. No one can stop the process of creation, maintenance and dissolution of the world. This is because there is no creator. With a slight illumination of consciousness, the universe with its infinite space is created. It is the wonder of the subtle consciousness.

What came first, the body of the world or our body? Your true nature is formless, yet it identifies with the body. In the same way, the world looks real through the senses! Who is prior: the world or the one who sees the world? Your wakefulness is the same as the world.

First comes consciousness, and then the world is seen in it. Consciousness is unstable. It likes to be. However, when 'I am-ness' goes so does the world. You have to see this with a very subtle inner discrimination. This vast panoramic world is the reflection of your consciousness. As such it is nameless; yet name gives it support and transactions are made possible. All names are concepts. When Parabrahman remains in the unmanifest state, can He have a name?

Krishna says He is all-pervading. Because of the sense of duality people differentiate. They either praise or censure. The concept 'I am like this' is the basic reason of misery or happiness. If you stay with the feeling 'I am', the basic vibration of 'I am', you will digest miseries as easily as happiness. Whatever is visible, whatever appears, has not happened at all!

Do not indulge in flattery or censure, even if it costs you your life, as there is no other. Unless the sense 'I am like this' goes, the duality will not go. You must understand the ultimate meaning of your Self, by yourself. Then nothing can harm you. One in a million tries to know it. One who realizes it, his consciousness merges peacefully within his own Self. Consciousness disappears into the knower. That is called Parabrahman.

You know what you are before you know anything else. Convince yourself that you are pure consciousness. All worldly dealings will be carried out spontaneously. It is the only way. The notion that you do something is utterly false.

Nirupana 48
Thursday, August 3, 1978

The unmanifest is motionless. Where can it be? Deliberate on this point. With a slight stirring of the unmanifest a little maya is created. If there was no sense of selfhood, one would be beyond maya. You are eternally unmanifest by nature. Consciousness implies an individual and the knower of consciousness is the unmanifest. When suddenly you know that 'you are', it fascinates you. It is the same as love. Your consciousness has been created through ignorance. This is the primordial maya.

The vital force permeates every cell of the body. The center of knowingness in the body is the cerebral cortex. Without consciousness, it has no knowing faculty. Do not ever say you are the body. You are only the knowingness. You are consciousness. It is like light. It is the sense 'I am'. It paints all the pictures. Worship it as the Guru, infinite and boundless. You expect the fruits of the actions of the three gunas, because you think you are the body. Doership depends upon the presence of God, so He is called the doer. The consciousness in us is God. Every living being wishes to be immortal. That is the greatest desire. The flame which is lit up inside, with the body as oil, is called the universal flame. The sense 'I am' caught fire and became visible as the world. At the base of consciousness is the unmanifest, the supreme Self.

People think that the world is old. Actually, the world rises with your consciousness. This is called maya. There is nothing there and yet it plays so much havoc! As the memory of 'I am' changes, everything changes. If the memory of 'I am' vanishes, then what? Does anyone have a memory of his death? So what happens? The memory of 'I am' forgets itself, that is all!

What is your state when you do not know that 'you are'? There is no delusion such as 'I am' or 'I am not'. Such a state is called Parabrahman. Memory or ego-sense is time-bound. It is of the nature of time. When this is understood, an ordinary person becomes a jnani. One says, 'I did this, I behaved that way'. When memory goes, what happens to action and behavior? All the names are given to the word, by the word. The Source of the word has no form. While awake, when there is no self-memory, one is in a state of the Absolute. All titles are acquired. They are not natural. If you take a single sentence from this and put it to use, it is enough.

Nirupana 49
Sunday, August 6, 1978

Be free of the need for consciousness while it is still in the body. It is because of the grace of the inner Self that one is inspired with devotion and pursues a spiritual path. One becomes silent and holy. With this awareness, you do nothing that ought not to be done.

Desire to find Self-realization leads to the Guru. It becomes easy in the company of his word and with constant attention to the meaning of the word. The supreme Self, which is unattainable, is naturally there. It is perfect, whole and unchanging. The Truth, thus achieved, cannot be analyzed by the mind. The nature of the sage cannot be seen with the intellect. The knowledge achieved with this association is constantly being trampled on by people. Hence, how can there be any pride in the company of a sage? The world appears all right, as it is. There remains no differentiation of good and bad. For me, life has no gain or loss. Life and death are individual concepts. An individual becomes what he takes himself to be.

The world moves on the strength of the word, but the word cannot point out the Truth. Within the unmanifest principle arises the feeling of beingness. Within that the word is created. There is chaos in the world. Who is prior to that? Is He not always there, the One who knows it? The knower of the word is prior to the word. That which is prior to the word is the blessing of the Sadguru. The disciple surrenders his beingness to the Sadguru and He returns the same as blessings. He gives the eternal peaceful nature that is inherently yours. After investigating the Self one becomes silent, while the rest are busy fulfilling their needs.

The scriptures say that abuse of the everlasting Paramatman leads to death, leading to another birth. The jiva lives in order to die. What is death? You know that the vital force leaves the body. Does that mean that 'you' die? What you experience now will not last as it depends upon the breath. When faith in the Guru is established, you will know what death is. Do not use devotion to God, chanting or austerities for returns. Know that you are prior to the first day you witnessed. Wakefulness comes in the morning from the east, so to speak. One who wakes up is prior to that. Truth is not achieved without the grace of the Guru.

Your sense 'I am' is prior to words. Speech means mind, which means prana. The sense 'I am a man' or 'I am a woman' comes only after the word appears. We are prior to speech, wakefulness and sleep. That which is prior to sleep, prior to wakefulness, and prior to speech is your true nature. You learn this Truth in the company of a sage. After God forgets His Godhead, what remains is the nature of the sage (your true nature). The real rest comes when the memory 'I am so-and-so' comes to an end. The true nature prevails, which is prior to memory. Recognize what is different (from true nature) based upon this.

Nirupana 50
Thursday, August 10, 1978

You have problems because you see yourself as a body. All worldly species are of the nature of the body, not the Self. If there was no body, what would you look like? You want to enter into heaven, taking yourself as the body. This is not possible.

Consciousness witnesses everything. Who witnesses consciousness? Is it not true that you are the witness of consciousness? Does mind or prana have any form? Is there a form for consciousness? So long as the oil is there, the wick burns. Consciousness is there as long as the body is there.

Wakefulness that comes in the morning is the pure sense 'I am'. It stays with you until you sleep. It is of the nature of space. It is called Brahman or God. Immediately thereafter the thought process starts; body-consciousness takes over and all actions take place. Unless you get appropriate worthiness you will not understand what I am saying.

Where are mind, intellect or consciousness? When are they present? Are they not there only when prana is there? Can you eat when there is no prana? Do not forget that you are the Witness of all this. If the body and prana separate, what will be your position? If you recognize prana, how can you be prana? So long as there is unity of prana and the body, you feel 'you are'. In fact, when you talk it is prana that does the talking.

At the time of death, prana goes into space, the body mingles with the five elements, but nothing happens to the knower. He was never born, therefore he has no death.

One cannot listen to this and like it unless one is worthy. The rest will leave. Basically, without the grace of the inner Self one would not like to listen to this. For some the worthiness is created at birth, for others it comes with time.

When you get up in the morning, before the thought process starts, you are pure Brahman. Once the mind comes into action, you see yourself as male or female. It sees itself as the body and acts according to its impressions. Otherwise, you cannot do anything. The knowledge

'I am' that wakes up in the morning is formless consciousness and is your true nature. Do take care of your body, but do not say you are the body. Even your memory does not have a form. Then how can your self-luminous consciousness have a form?

The memory of a thing is not the thing itself. Similarly, the memory of your form is not your true nature. The various deities are adornments of your sense 'I am'. If one ponders over the same, it becomes all-pervading. Meditate on the meditator. It is not possible without consciousness. It is the feet of the Guru. The flame of consciousness is lit because the essence of the body is burning.

First there is food, then the living beings come into existence. (First there is a body-form, and then consciousness arises in it.) In the body of any living being, the vital force and consciousness arise simultaneously. No activity is possible without consciousness.

Catch hold of the feet of your own consciousness, treating it as God. Recite its name. It is your true nature. Have your own holy sight rather than going to a temple. Can God have any importance without your knowledge 'I am'? So far you have only heard about this. Now you have to reach it.

If you are unable to do anything else, at least salute the wakefulness that comes in the morning. Similarly, at bedtime, salute the sleep and surrender to it. Keep in mind that your consciousness is God. At least remember what you have heard. By practicing this, your circumstances will change; you will avoid difficulties.

By worshipping God, one becomes God and is free

of sorrow. Day by day, difficulties are reduced. No joy is lasting, but the happiness of Self-realization is everlasting. The consciousness within you knows everything. Your intellect is of no use.

Your consciousness is spontaneously taking photographs of everything you do and see. The minutest details are recorded. Until this is realized, their effects have to be faced. By practicing devotion to God, bad things are avoided. In association with a sage all miseries end and one day you realize that you are of the nature of God. Meditate in solitude on 'I am formless, luminous, pure knowingness'.

The vital force acts through the body. Consciousness witnesses. It is Bhagavan, the Luminous One. It does not act. Do not identify it with the body. That would be a sin. Wakefulness spontaneously rises in the morning. You are miserable because you treat your wakefulness as the body. The lump of dirt (the body) looks beautiful because of the light of God within. The light has no color. It is your Self-love. It is of the form of God.

God helps one who says he is not the body. As there is no reason for your experience of beingness, can there be any reason for death? The body will not last. Hence, understand this now: my Guru is always with me as my consciousness. There is no speech, no movement without him. Though he has a thousand names, he is my true nature.

Your consciousness is the source of devotion. Who worships whom? You worship your consciousness while taking yourself as the body. It has caused duality and with that there is death. Without pronouncing words, say, 'I am formless, desireless and pure as space. My sense 'I am' is of the nature of God'. The smallest presence of God is the size of the whole universe. Worship your sense 'I am' as the Guru.

Nirupana 51
Tuesday, August 15, 1978

Names are mere letters, whether it is your name or God's name. As God has been given names, similarly, you have been given names for practical use. It is like a village having a name. God is of the nature of the word, He is of the nature of space because the word has the quality of space. You may call your concept God. The basic concept is your consciousness, 'you are', but you have taken it to be of the nature of the body.

You say you do spiritual activity but have you ever thought of what it is? What is the evidence that 'you are'? The love for your beingness is the only evidence. It comes up spontaneously just as grass shoots up from the earth. It is prior to the heart, mind and intellect. The Source lies prior to the sensation 'I am'. It has no form. It is like space. Nothing can be said about the Self. One who knows consciousness is only a witness. He is a non-doer. One who has realized the Truth is not required to do anything special for the benefit of the world.

Mind is the language of prana. It speaks according

to the impressions that it has collected. Mind means the impressions recorded in prana. Your behavior is the result. Mind is created if you accept the meaning of words. Your silence must be led to the extreme. After becoming a jnani, you will know that the thoughts that are in your mind are not worth two paise (cents). 'You are possessed' means the mind itself is possessed by the mind. Who, or what, is ever going to possess 'you'? Are you in any way concerned with that? Who is it that is concerned about your children and the household? Is it you or your mind? Does the mind recognize you, or is it you who recognizes the mind? Why do you accept what your mind tells you as your past or your future? What is your true identity within the body?

You are void just like space. Just as space is unbroken, so are you. You are neither small, nor big. You have filled each and every void, and still you are. (You are all-pervading.) Space that is prior to the word is called consciousness. It is of the nature of Self-love. It is prior to the word and, therefore, it has no meaning. Can it be experienced?

Who is the source of this fraud? Is it not consciousness by which we feel 'we are'? Why is this consciousness untrue? Because it is an experience that has come upon you accidentally. It came in unasked for.

Each one of you is a master of doubts. Is your behavior ever bereft of doubt? The universally acclaimed 'intellect' has possessed you. It is your front. Is the intellect prior to you or are you prior to the intellect? Without intellect, would you be happy or unhappy? You are suffering from the fever of your consciousness. You may feel good for a while, the rest is all unhappiness. Is there any suffering during deep sleep? It is a state of ignorance. What would make you completely blissful?

A teacher can impart all the practical knowledge in the world. However, only the Sadguru gives the knowledge of beingness. Every living being has consciousness. One who introduces this is the Sadguru. You have been told that there is someone who sustains the world. Who is this someone? Is it not the consciousness in the body? The Sadguru introduces you to consciousness. He is the Witness of consciousness. He is prior to consciousness. This consciousness has no information regarding how and from where it was created. If you want to realize this, keep on chanting 'Guru, Guru' without pronouncing the words. If you have faith in the Guru, his word should be taken as authority. You have a strong desire to live. It will last until you know your true nature. (This desire goes after realization.)

When consciousness is pleased, God is pleased. Meditate on consciousness. This is as easy as it is difficult. If your faith in the Guru is unshakable, it is easy. Consciousness, through which you get the experience of good and bad things, is complete in itself. In deep sleep you take rest in your own being, you require no outside help. The sense of duality is the cause of sorrow. If you take the Guru-word as authority, you will not experience sorrow. You will know that you are bliss yourself.

Your consciousness is more expansive than space. Though it is void, it is compact and impenetrable.

Keep faith in your own consciousness. Heart, mind and intellect are the operational channels of consciousness. So long as there is consciousness, there is no rest. You will realize that everything is created through consciousness. Hence, there is no need to ask for anything. Everything is moving through consciousness only. Yet its hunger is never satisfied. Surrender without duality to consciousness. Then it will also surrender to you. You will be like the river that becomes the sea, when it meets the sea.

To meditate on consciousness with consciousness is maha-yoga (the great union). Then there is bliss. On the ocean of bliss, the waves are also bliss. If one wants to worship God, one must worship the Guru. That means one must surrender to the consciousness that listens to the Guru-word. To follow what you have heard is the ultimate devotion.

Nirupana 52
Thursday, August 17, 1978

If you are convinced that there is no future, you will have no fear of any kind. It is true that you are the world, but the world will not provide an answer to your questions. You have to provide it yourself. Find out for yourself what it is that is changeless. Do not take anything for granted.

Witnessing is of two kinds. First, our consciousness witnesses, and the second is the Witness who witnesses our consciousness. He clearly knows that the word and its meaning have no value at all. He is found sitting silently without words. Words make it possible to listen to the knowledge.

One gets boundless peace in the company of a sage, which is prior to words. Wrong thinking drops off.

There are many kinds of learning in the world. Real learning is knowledge of the Self. Knowledge means recognition of God. Before knowing God, we have to recognize ourselves. 'We' means the consciousness in body-form. One must see what 'I am' is. Knowledge of the world also depends on our consciousness, 'I am'. What gives you existence? Is it not consciousness? To know it and to know our true nature is called realization.

To have direct, correct knowledge one must worship one's consciousness. Treat it as Brahman. The opposites of 'I' as transient and 'I' as everlasting eternal have to be recognized and understood. Devotion to the Guru gives you courage for achieving this. To make this happen, you should surrender to your consciousness as your Guru. One who has surrendered to the Guru in order to seek the Self will get the same status as that of the Guru.

If you follow these words of the Guru: 'The body is not your nature; the priceless consciousness in the body is your true nature', you will become a realized person. Chanting the mantra, meditation and bhajans (singing devotional songs) bring worthiness beyond imagination. If a great difficulty arises, worship the Guru with devotional songs and surely it will be warded off. Due to devotion to the Guru, one gets limitless power. The seed sown by the Sadguru has sprouted; it is the vital force, *chaitanya* incarnate. Remembering the mantra constantly is meditation. Due to temptation of relationships with the world, despite the fact that they are devoted to the Guru, people do not rise to the stage of the Guru.

Consciousness is the God of knowledge – the greatest God. Do not treat it as the body. You will understand that your consciousness moves all the bodies in the world. Atman means our consciousness. The Guru has given you the nature of Paramatman. Worship him in order to become Paramatman; not to get food, clothing or happiness. Only a rare one maintains the conviction that he wants to be God.

Your consciousness is God. The picture gallery of His light is the world. God is your inner Self. It is not necessary to recite it with beads in your hand. You have to pay attention to the Source. With the expansion of the seed consciousness, you will spontaneously know what is everlasting and what is transient. Pray to your consciousness as 'Guru, Guru', then you will be worthy of Him. The body is the means for devotion. Understand that it is not your true nature.

While remembering the Guru's words, run your household happily. Contemplate constantly on your consciousness. Nothing else sustains the world except for your consciousness. You do not exist without God, and God does not exist without you. Do not get confused by attachments to the household. Do not deviate from your own nature. God has no form other than consciousness. Always remember this. Such matters cannot be casually talked about with common people. If you take only one sentence out of this as your own, you will be easily redeemed.

Nirupana 53
Saturday, August 19, 1978

Just meditate on the fact that you know 'you are'. Your consciousness has to be realized. It is worth all the effort and penance. You have to practice this meditation for a long time in order to get stabilized in this consciousness. Remember that you have no form. Your form is all-manifest and all-pervading. It is called Brahman. Once this understanding is stabilized, then nothing else has to be done. Then That which never dies, has no qualities and is without illusion, will be free. It is called Parabrahman.

One must have devotion for the Guru. Bhajan and *aarti* (singing devotional songs) are a symbol of your love towards the Guru. In order to be stabilized, practice meditation; you will naturally get the knowledge of your Self. Lots of hard work went in enabling us to flick a switch and light up the room. In the same way, those who achieved the Truth performed a lot of penance in the old days. Now it is open for us. If you have imbibed what you have heard from me will there be any question left unanswered? The only instrument for liberation is your own consciousness. Realize it and offer it to Brahman.

So long as you are entangled in any other kind of memory, you cannot progress. Continuously think of what 'you are' and not in what you know. Do not delve into money, wealth, glory, loved ones, etc. Hold onto your own Self. The center of all things in the world is your consciousness. In spite of the fact that It (the supreme Self) has millions of names, It is not tainted by a single name. Yet, without giving it a name, you cannot trace It.

You identify with the name given to you and that is why you have to bear abuses. If you let go of pride in that name, you will not suffer from them. Liberation means there is no longer the feeling of beingness. The ultimate Truth is that I am neither the name nor the form. Consciousness is the same, whether it is an insect or the highest deity. When consciousness is pleased with you, Brahman is pleased with you. The rest of the wordy knowledge is of no use whatsoever. Up till now, you have used your consciousness to remember other things. Now use it to remember consciousness itself.

Having heard all this, what kinds of sadhana are you going to do and how? When consciousness is understood, you will see that it is the support of all there is. It will also be known what is good and what is bad. Consciousness is the source of all there is. Without it, there is nothing. It is infinite and limitless. When you are pleased with someone, you will give everything to him or her. If you are pleased with your Self, what will be the result? You are no longer an individual with mind and intellect. You are the totality. Maya has manifested as existence and energy. She is intimidating you and threatening you.

As such, she does not have an iota of truth. In order to acquired such knowledge, you have to practice devotion. The infinite universe exists because of consciousness.

Nirupana 54
Wednesday, August 23, 1978

All emotional states eventually come to pass. They are transient. Childhood automatically goes away. Does anyone feel bad about it? In the same way, you will also pass away and God will pass away. Nothing will remain.

When you ripen with the mantra that has been given to you, spiritual knowledge will start expressing itself. Such is its power. You will do nothing. The realization will talk through you. The power of the mantra will increase and it will be understood that the Guru-state is within you. People have devotion, they love the Guru, but they have no inclination for Self-realization. Devotion to God is there, but a strong desire for knowing the Truth is not there.

An individual thinks he is a small entity in the world. The fact is that the experience of the world is dependent on us. However, we cannot be an object of senses, as by nature we cannot be known by the senses. Our true nature is unmanifest. The first experience one gets is that of God ('I am'). In the manifest world, when we search for ourselves, we find God; because God is using our body and our name. After discovering God, the eternal is discovered. You are eternal. Do not say you are the body. Consciousness lasts for a duration. It is called the tenure of life. Go back to the state when you had no experience of anything.

People are devoted to God, but to find one in search of true Self-knowledge is rare. God (seed-consciousness) is the center point. He spontaneously takes the form of the universe. With body-consciousness, we will not be able to discover that we are eternal. What is the use of making the mind blank? In deep sleep or while intoxicated, the mind is blank. Who is the knower of this?

Samadhi brings in various miracles. The experience of the awakening of *Kundalini* is like that also. That will not give you the experience of Truth. Love, joy, gain, loss – are all one and that is consciousness. As you go further, you will understand how the concept of beingness arises and where it goes. This gives rise to *Nirvikalpa* samadhi – one without any concepts. The sense whether 'we are' or 'we are not' is not there. Rest of the samadhis are *Savikalpa* (with concept). In Nirvikalpa samadhi there is no witnessing.

From now on do not consider yourself a human being. You are immortal, eternal and perfect Parabrahman. This understanding does not come from outside. It is known because it IS. It is our true nature. It cannot be made new, it cannot be invited, and you need not go to meet it. Remain as you are in the natural state of being. Do not imitate the Guru; catch hold of his true nature. You should not act through intellect, but act through natural instinct.

Nirupana 55
Thursday, August 24, 1978

Religions are created by and followed by human beings. How is one prior to the accusation that he is a Hindu or a Muslim? We are all bound by traditions in the world. They do not last, just as flowers do not last. In a village where Muslims live, is the land Muslim? The elements e.g. fire, air, space and water have no false pride of belonging to a creed.

Consciousness is the essence of the five elements. We call it the sun. The sun means the light of our own beingness. In that light there are an infinite number of images in time, and of infinite worlds.

I hope you do not have any pride of the body. Why not look at the Source? One did not have the memory of his consciousness. It has come now. How long has it been since you got this memory? As many years as your present age is. This memory is maya; it is a delusion, the mother of ignorance.

It is said that we are eternal and infinite. It is said through the consciousness. How can this be true if consciousness itself is unreal? Would this question arise if there were no consciousness?

Life-tenure means that there is consciousness and memory for that period. Whatever is said and whoever says it is quite right, but only at that time. Your sense 'I am' is a precious jewel. If you hold onto something in your meditation, it will manifest through your consciousness. If you meditate on Krishna, it will manifest in the form of

Krishna. However, all that is transient.

When someone says that he has become a perfect jnani, how could it be when the knowledge itself is imperfect?

Will Vishnu come here and ask me what I am prattling about? He will not. He may have been here at one time, but He is not here now.

When Brahman is dismissed through right discrimination, it is called Parabrahman. Space is everywhere, it does not go from place to place. Space, prana and luster are everywhere. Only human beings identify themselves as bodies and behave in various ways. The knower must be identified no matter what it takes. This may happen in a moment or not even in a lifetime.

You are the consciousness in which all kinds of knowledge are consolidated. It is not necessary to go all over the world in order to recognize the Self. Your consciousness has no form. It is neither small nor big. It is as good as nothing. What is the reason? It is because, so long as you know that 'you are', it exists. You have the need for the Self, but It is prior to the need. If you recognize it, you will understand that all needs have their source in consciousness and they all merge into the same. It has no beginning. It is atomic. If you go to look for it in the world, it will not be found because it is the One through whom you know 'you are'. It is the Lord through whom you see the world. It is the knowledge that 'you are', without saying it. As consciousness, It is also the Lord of the qualities. All names, male and female, belong to It. The Atman and the Paramatman are names given through words for the sake of understanding.

Till such time that this knowledge is consciously known, we need ourselves. Consciousness is there as long as one exists. He is the Witness of consciousness without the act of witnessing. Your awareness itself is the eight-handed goddess *Mahakali* (the great divine mother). If you are convinced that you are immortal, imperishable and indestructible, she is pleased. If she is pleased she will fulfill your needs. If you call her mortal, she will be displeased. She provides when the devotee becomes one with the consciousness 'I am'.

There is not a single living being that does not worship Atman. The insects also worship Him, as they look after themselves. All human bodies are temples of God. Unless there is duality, there cannot be identification e.g. Brahman and maya, God and devotee. At first it has to be divided like that, and then united. When you recognize yourself, you will know that there is no being on earth to whom you are not of any use. God is omnipresent. He has pervaded everything, everywhere. This is the view of your own consciousness. If you understand this, not even a trace of selfishness will remain in you. Whatever you do will be worship of the inner Self only.

In order to realize, you have to meditate on consciousness through which you know 'you are'. Call It the Guru. Hold Its feet tightly. From It you are getting the experience of the physical body and the world. It is your own nature. Remember It well. Worship It constantly by remembering it. It is the image of your true nature. Remember that and no concept will trouble you.

Nirupana 56
Sunday, August 27, 1978

Parabrahman conveys His own knowledge to Brahman – the manifestation as 'I am'. He is there from where the sound emanates. The 'word' is the assurance of Brahman (consciousness). It is the life force. Your sense 'I am' is the same as Brahman. The act of seeing is empty. Yet the very sight of the seer is the creation.

False identification with the body is the reason for all joys and sorrows. Remember that you are the offspring of your Guru. Therefore his word is your authority. What is his dictum? It is 'Whatever IS, that you are. There is nothing else'. There is no other method for the aspirant. Without faith in the Guru-word, people grope for other methods.

When prana leaves the body, what happens to the Self? It pervades everywhere. Its symbol is space. You are That. Space is purer than the four grosser elements. Your consciousness is purer than space. When a jnani leaves the body, he experiences bliss. When you realize the Self, you will know that there is bliss at the time of death. It will be the experience of one who knows that whatever is created is Brahman – the consciousness. There is no other except you. Even though a jnani may worship the qualitative Brahman, he has no delusion.

The impressions stamped in the body from childhood are flowing through prana. This is called mind-flow.

Can you put a stain on space? Then how would the light permeating space be? Your knowingness is the light of the Self. The purpose of your spiritual activity as a seeker is to know who you are. Your association with all other information will vanish. Wake up and be aware this very moment. Worship the Self, the king of knowledge. He resides in the body. To follow the word of the Sadguru is the most worthy effort. He is beyond the five elements.

Before you fall asleep, remind yourself that you are not the body. Slowly the Guru-word will bring joy. As it eradicates harmful things, it also removes the obstacles to your spiritual growth. The belief that you are the body is the obstacle. The Sadguru's message is 'I am all'. With implicit faith in the Sadguru, one becomes perfect Brahman.

Nirupana 57
Thursday, August 31, 1978

I know that 'I am' and, hence, I know that the world is. Both happen spontaneously. The world comes into existence along with my birth. Our true nature is the Self. It appears to me as 'I am', and the world follows. This will be understood when you know with certainty that the body is not your true nature. Out of a million, a rare one will say, 'The world is because 'I am''. All others will say that the world existed previously, I came into it. I am the world and the world is I. This information pertains to the manifested consciousness.

Where there is the word, there is a guarantee of beingness. When the word permeates all around, it becomes of the nature of space. Our talk is stored in space. The quality of knowingness which is within, is called chidakash. The light of the space of consciousness has blazed into such a dazzling conflagration, that it is called the great space (*maha-akash*). The space of consciousness is subtler than the subtlest. What happens in the chidakash is absorbed and its pictures are taken immediately. These are the impressions you store. Unless you know your eternal nature, it will go on the same way. The wish that one's consciousness should last forever is the root-maya. It is the source of devotion and love. That is called chidakash. The universe is created in that. The original nature of it is not to be, not to exist. If you know this well, will there be any loss if the visible comes to an end? Will there be any grieving if someone dies? Instead of saying, 'I am That' say, 'I am always and forever'.

Many people learn from the Guru and stop there. Nobody pays attention to the fact that 'I am' is different from the teacher and the taught. Even if you take to heart the fact that 'I am' is the cause of what has to be learned, and it is also the instrument for learning it, it is enough. Then you are already redeemed. Before learning something your natural state of being is in perfect condition. If you limit yourself to the one who has learned when instructed, how will you get out of it? (It will be an endless process.)

Krishna said: 'The ignorant jiva does not understand what is eternal and free; therefore I had to take this body'.

Witnessing the last moment of death is a festival of happiness. Time comes to an end but not I. I have no rising, nor setting. Carry on with your worldly duties.

However, keep to your true nature. In your spiritual endeavors, you claim 'I let go of this, I renounced this, etc.' How are you going to renounce that which was never there? Consciousness is the root-maya – the goddess of knowledge. The jnani is the Witness, he is not consciousness. The time of death is the end of time. You are the Witness of this. Then have you ended there? We feel the existence of body and prana, but the body and prana do not know us. You should reason until you come to this definite analysis. As the salt crystal melts, prana becomes fainter and fainter at the time of leaving the body. The bliss of the knower goes on increasing in the same proportion. This is the moment of great happiness.

The end of time means the end of prana. The fact that you are listening is the result of the 'chemical' consciousness. Teaching is imparted to this body-consciousness. When consciousness goes, the teaching fades away. You are beyond this. Who is learning? Is it not the body-consciousness? All dealings are done by time. Think of how you are different from what you were before this learning. Those who call themselves enlightened are wrapped up in concepts of their choice. They have not gone beyond concepts.

Why do you enjoy finding fault with others? Is there not a better way to feel good? Such is the characteristic of the jiva. Saint Tukaram used to call common people as saints. Do you see saintliness in every human being?

There is one in a thousand who really profits by what is heard here. What is recognized as a mold or a pattern is not the Self. The Self cannot be known. The body is an instrument. The One on whose strength the senses work is called God. He is not the supreme Self. (God, Brahman is the manifest principle; Paramatman, the supreme Self is the unmanifest.) Prana is also not the Self. Prana carries out all actions. Mind, intellect and consciousness are forms of prana. The one who has realized the Self, following the Guru's word, experiences total bliss at the time of physical death.

Keep to the state that you had before you were taught anything. Does anyone pay attention to how this occasion for learning and teaching has occurred? We are not what we recognize or are taught. You cannot contemplate on the Atman. What is known to us is not our true nature. The Self cannot be contemplated upon. That which is not known through the senses must be you. 'You' cannot be understood or recognized. One who understands is not the object of knowledge. The fear is due to ignorance in thinking of a rope being a snake. Nothing is to be done. Contemplate on what you have heard. Ruminate over it with determination.

Nirupana 58
Sunday, September 3, 1978

Why do they call a devotee, a devotee? It is because he cares for God, he contemplates on God. The rest are anxious about their households. All are concerned about what happens in their practical dealings. A rare one has a true desire about knowing God. For one who gets the supreme knowledge, there is no other thought except God. Then God has to bear the responsibility for the devotee's worldly needs.

Brahma, Vishnu and Shiva cannot stay eternally in their present forms. Therefore they are illusory. The experience that is known through the senses is illusory. The one who knows this is eternal.

The Guru illuminates one's true nature. One who considers the body as his true nature cannot do this. What is the instrument for devotion or worship? It is consciousness that is present in the body. It has to be called God or Guru and honored. Consciousness is Brahman. Meditating on it is all that needs to be done. (No other ritual is required.) Contemplate and meditate on the Guru. There is no other God. This is non-dualistic worship. In this kind of devotion, God who is qualitative or non-qualitative, with all His names, is of the nature of the devotee. Where there is God, there is devotee; where there is devotee, there is God. There is no duality. Unless you accept this and merge into it, you will not understand. Unless a man jumps into the water, he cannot swim. Devotion fills one with the nature of God. Actually, both natures are one and the same. When there is no consciousness, who is to say, 'it is' or 'it is not'?

How many serious seekers are there who will utilize this transient life to search for God? Meditate on the One who notices the transient and phenomenal world. When the devotee has become of the nature of God, he surrenders to Him. God takes care of him. His needs are provided. Who nourishes the fetus? Who generates milk in the mother's breast? When the teeth appear, will the food not be provided? This is the kind of faith needed in the true devotee. He lives with unshakable conviction. It is a pure position like that of a child. Will such a devotee ever beg for fulfilling wishes? He peacefully says, 'I am That'. He is blessed with the experience of a child. He has no fear. How can he ever worry?

When things become unbearable, repeat the word 'Guru, Guru'. He will show you both the form and the formless nature. By devotion to the Guru, God becomes eager to manifest Himself. Even after listening to all this, if one does not worship God, what can be done? Your consciousness is the image of God. With devotion it becomes the infinite Brahman.

Nirupana 59
Sunday, September 10, 1978

Various incense sticks give out different fragrances. Similarly, the body contains different ingredients. A person's behavior is the result of the three gunas. These are Sattva – knowingness, Rajas – motivity, and Tamas – consolidation and inertia. Behavior gives rise to good or bad results. That is called destiny.

You know that 'you are'. Contemplate on it. Do not meditate on any object. Penance is a sort of meditation. The jnani's destiny is the whole universe. You will know this through meditation. Once you know consciousness, you will never identify with the body again. I know that I have a body, but the body is not 'I'. One remembers his childhood, but will he become a child again? Only the memory is there. Similarly, after realization you will know that you are not the body, even while the body is still there. You will be beyond beingness. The concept 'I am' has been created due to God. I know that God will eventually leave the body. That implies that I existed prior to God. God means prana. This is opposite to what people who identify with the body think. They think God existed prior to them, they came later. Pure consciousness is called God. How can God kill me? He only departs from the body. (Maharaj says that the consciousness in the body is God – Iswara – the manifest Brahman. It is the same as prana – the life force. However, I as the Absolute – Parabrahman am beyond it.)

When one realizes that one is liberated, no worldly dealings are left for him. This is the true situation.

Those who got liberated but did not continue with devotion to the Guru were not useful to common people. They are not known to common people. Those who continued devotional practices after liberation, their presence is always there even if they no longer physically exist. After Self-realization when body-consciousness is gone, one does not require anything else for comfort; he becomes a 'nobody' and by being that he becomes extinct. There is no use of the Guru unless there is complete faith and devotion. Are seekers who go to the Himalayas and find salvation of any use to other people?

Many a great king has come and gone; people do not remember him any longer. Those who practiced devotion to the Guru benefited the people, and people are devoted to such sages even now. There is no greater charity than offering of Self-knowledge. One who receives it becomes like the one who gives it. This is not true for other worldly gifts. There should be devotion towards the one who gives knowledge.

Even if the Guru is worshipped in stone or clay, it bears fruit. Never let go of devotion to the Guru. His creed will manifest through us. Such is the greatness of devotion to the Guru. Those who were devoted to liberation became immortal in the minds of the people. One should never forget to worship the Guru (consciousness).

Obligations to the one who gives Self-knowledge can never be paid off. One can only offer continued worship and share his teaching with others. Where there are no instruments, do mental worship and sing devotional songs. Why is Guru-bhajan performed? It is for uplifting the world. By doing this one becomes as worthy as the

Guru. (After Self-realization, the teaching process should continue for the benefit of others.) God is the same as Self-knowledge, do not use other concepts. Never let go of devotion to the Guru.

Nirupana 60
Thursday, September 14, 1978

Your previous identity will go and you will speak with a new identity, but without taking yourself as 'so-and-so'. You will know nothing about the new identity as it will talk spontaneously.

Here is a beautiful flower; who is responsible for its growth? As it has life force, it has movement. That which exists beautifully and tenderly in the flower, also speaks through this body. In the case of the flower, It does not speak, but It shows 'It is'. It is both manifest and unmanifest, and It pervades everywhere. There is a minute sample of the infinite life force within you. You will merge into That. You will not be able to see It. Merging does not mean dying.

The mind is occupied by thoughts based upon its predominant concept. Each being identifies itself with its physical body. A rare human being, one in a million, identifies himself with God. Prana derives its support from food and all speak through the power of prana. Consciousness arises where prana and the essence of food are joined together. It is the source of the inspiration 'I am Brahman'. Atman or 'I' has no form. The tree grows tall because of the power of prana. Without the combination of food and prana, there is no consciousness. I am neither food, nor prana; I am there only when they are united.

People talk about God and Brahman (the manifest principle). I do not. I talk about my own realization. This knowledge comes from the meeting place of the world and That which is beyond the world. It is the meeting place of the manifest and the unmanifest. This must be thought through carefully. Those who feel they have understood have not understood anything. (It cannot be conceptualized.)

Thoughts come to your mind uncalled for. They come and go. Somewhere a person dies. People gather. What thoughts prevail in people's minds? The silence of the man who is dead has entered the minds of those present.

When performing any action through the body-form, the sense of doership is ignorance. You behave according to the image you have of yourself. It is not true. Consciousness lasts for a certain period. It is called the tenure of life, also known as time. Eventually all this will disappear.

Consciousness in the body is the experience of 'I am'. This experience does not belong to the body. It belongs only to the knowing faculty. The body does not experience anything. Consciousness in the body is your true nature. It has no form. A person identifies with his body and goes about. 'Nothing really happens' – this will be understood if you remain in the company of consciousness. In good company (satsang) bad thoughts are replaced by good thoughts. The jiva becomes pure by realizing its true nature. Till then, the dirt in the form of the body is its only domain. In good company, impure thoughts get destroyed just as the sun cleanses the world.

Bhagavan means the Luminous One. It is the consciousness that makes us feel 'we are'. Where there is devotion, there is consciousness. Where there is consciousness, there is devotion. Does the body have love for itself, or is it consciousness in the body that has love for itself? Love means devotion and devotion means consciousness, and the same is God. When ignorance is destroyed and consciousness is freed, the devotee becomes God. One must contemplate on what one has heard. One who loves the Guru, loves himself. Remember what you have heard. The Guru keeps repeating so many things, but do they stay with you?

Consciousness in the body is the image of God. If consciousness is not sensed in the morning, you will not be able to carry out any actions. The sense 'you are' that you get when you wake up is the holy sight of God. Consciousness was tiny when it woke up, but how far has its light spread? It takes account of all things, real and unreal. If you welcome this consciousness, you will know that you are infinite. It is the Guru. It is your true nature.

Worship consciousness that is prior to everything. Put your faith in it. Until then you will be dissatisfied and unhappy. Have the conviction that you are God. Do not prattle about it to others. It is not necessary to announce your awakening. People will know that you have attained Self-knowledge.

Nirupana 61
Sunday, September 17, 1978

Manifestation implies consciousness. It has no form. Mind has no form. When there is no body, there is no form. Presently, you are pure consciousness in the body. It is the sense of your own beingness. It is subtler than space.

Even in the case of great incarnations, there was no sensation of 'I am' prior to the incarnation. Parabrahman in His true state has no knowledge of His beingness. Sri Rama was Parabrahman, yet his Guru had to impart Self-knowledge to him. What does it mean when someone claims to have chosen his parents, claiming himself to be an incarnation? What evidence do they give? Such people are ignorant. When there is no body, there is no knowledge.

The word implies prana, the vital force. The food for prana is the body, and consciousness is the knowingness. It is the assurance of our existence. It is Brahman. It is the word. It is the vibration of manifestation.

One who punishes and the one who suffers from punishment have the same consciousness. One who punishes is the same as the one who undergoes punishment. To say this openly, it is necessary to be convinced of one's true nature. The root of sorrow is the very company of prana. It is difficult to bear your sense of 'I am'. Your existence, the presence of God Itself, is sorrow. All worldly activities are undertaken to bear this sorrow. If there is a disturbance in the body, have the courage to say, 'God (consciousness), now go away'.

It is only after birth that some become engineers, scientists or doctors and, similarly, some become *sadhus*, jnanis and yogis. However, what happens if there is no birth at all? What is called birth is filled with an infinite number of universes. You can meditate on anything and it will manifest before you. In whom is the dream world created? Is it not in you?

You are not yet free of the concept that you will get great good in the body-form. The vital force in the body is consciousness – the Atman. The pure nature of Sri Krishna is the same as your own nature. The One that makes the body move cannot be perceived.

You must listen without the body-sense. The real nature of the listener is of the nature of the Self. It is your true nature. Use your consciousness for worship. Rituals are for the satisfaction of the mind. There is no experience of the mind in the worship of the Self.

Much is seen with the eyes open. However, with closed eyes what is seen is the place where all the yogis have gone. Perfect sight is the one without 'seeing'. So long as you wish to get success in life for comfort of the body, nothing can be accomplished. All seekers have ultimately merged into the life force. The movement of the vital force is given names such as Brahman. One particle of consciousness is also the ocean of consciousness. The state of the Self has no duality. My speaking and your listening do not imply two Gods. It means I am speaking to myself. God does not have to enjoy the fruits of virtue or suffer from the results of sin. One who does not treat himself as God has to experience the same.

Till such time as your consciousness is properly satisfied, it must be worshipped with the mind and then with no-mind. (Worship with no-mind means to remain thoughtless as pure consciousness.) How does the Guru offer his grace? When he talks about his experience, know that it is your own. This should be understood with the fullest conviction. Repeated contemplation is like churning. It creates a poison along with the nectar of knowledge. The poison is the ego. It has to be swallowed up by right thinking.

One who is unsure about direct knowledge should practice devotion. It is the purpose of life. It is also the remembrance of the Guru-word. Keep repeating that you have neither birth nor death, neither sin nor virtue, you are not the body, you are eternal. Do mental worship. Wherever the mind goes, the Sadguru is there. Have faith in His word.

Nirupana 62
Thursday, September 21, 1978

People practice devotion with bodily identification and, therefore, they do not reach the Paramatman state. When you continue to listen, by virtue of your devotion, you will go beyond no-thing-ness. You cannot even carry out worldly dealings well by identifying with the body, let alone making spiritual efforts. The body moves because of prana, which depends upon food. You are not the body, you are in the body. With body-consciousness, your well-being, your hopes, desires and expectations are seldom fulfilled.

What you continuously meditate on, its vision must come to you. By pleasing that deity, you acquire the same status. However, you do not get the Truth. Anything you contemplate on can result in visions. This is the result of excessive love or fear. What is the source of these visions? Is it not consciousness? If you live with the conviction that you are the life force in the body, the universe will manifest itself to you through the tiny vital force, just as a big tree grows from a seed. A rare one worships the consciousness, with consciousness. Most worship with bodily identification. With that stance one does not go beyond the five elements. Due to consciousness in the body, the world is sensed. It is the result of the life force. Consciousness is the Guru. One must *live* with that conviction; mere listening will not create that in you.

All the impressions received from birth are flowing through prana. They constitute the mind. Prana, mind, intellect and intuition are formless. Does the Atman, who is the knower of all this, have a shape? Identification with the body is ignorance, illusion and delusion. Consciousness *knows* the body, outer and inner mind, sleep, wakefulness, etc. Can consciousness be identified with a person? It is naturally there in a human body. Animals do not have this understanding. It has no form. It is the self-luminous God. Carry out all your activities while keeping this in mind. If you have contact with pure consciousness even for a moment, you are liberated.

Actions through the four elements (earth, water, fire, wind) do not affect the fifth, i.e. space. How can it defile the light of space? I am pure consciousness, pure life force. I have no shape, no form. Therefore I have no birth, no death and no karma. The impurity of the karma cannot defile the formless, changeless Self that is the life force, the consciousness. If you try to put a stain in space, it will only stain your finger.

You should worship the word of sages. People go through life with the name given by their parents. Actually, is there a connection between you and that name? Can the knower of the name be identified with the name? Who is the one whom you call Brahman or the Guru, because of whom you wake up in the morning? Before waking up you were neither a man nor a woman. Had you not awakened, you would not have remembered. To say, 'I am a man' or 'I am a woman' is to identify oneself as a body-form. The knower of this body-form is silent. It is consciousness.

All your actions in the world will not fulfill your

expectations. Your consciousness is riding on your prana. It goes when prana goes. The Atman does not go, because He never came. Are you prana? What are you when prana leaves the body? To understand that, you have to make the Guru-word your own. You are the formless Atman, you have no form. It is a simple thing but if not observed, it becomes troublesome. Otherwise you will have to undergo birth and death according to your concept.

Get a clear idea of Atman beyond words and categories. Do not leave the feet of consciousness that is listening now. You cannot hold these feet with your hands. They are to be held with the conviction of your own nature (by saying, 'I am the Self'). One who drinks the holy water of the Sadguru's feet, his body and self are purified. He does not need to visit holy places. Wherever he goes, it becomes a holy place. Do not forget the Atman, repeat His name silently.

With devotion to the Guru, birth and death vanish. It is difficult to get this knowledge, but once you have it everything is possible. All happenings are transient. They do not bind Atman. Keep firmly in your mind that consciousness in the body is your true nature. When prana goes, does the body have any pain? It could be used as food.

Bliss is the fire of that knowledge. Fire does not burn itself. It burns the wood. Similarly, the Atman does not come and go. By sticking to the Guru's word, the perverse intellect will stop its mischief.

Nirupana 63
Sunday, September 24, 1978

'I am-ness' is a dream. When we sense 'we are', space gets created along with the world. You say the world is much older than we are. However, it is not older than our consciousness.

Meditate on your own consciousness. Be aware of that. Remember that the memory of your beingness has come to you suddenly, without asking. To meditate on That means to be one with That. To dwell on thoughts of your well-being is a misconception. To think that you are awakened is also a misconception. All these concepts are present only when you 'are'.

The experience of God comes in a state of sickness. The picturesque world has appeared in a state of sickness. It will not last. There is no Truth in it. Only 'you' are true when you recognize the state of sickness. One who is aware of this Truth is perfect. One who understands this naked Truth goes beyond the known. The last word of the scriptures is silent. Then there is no awareness of whether 'I am' or 'I am not'. (Maharaj says that the manifest principle 'I am' is a sickness. The unmanifest, without qualities, is beyond it.)

When water evaporates or when fire is extinguished, does it mean that it is dead? Whatever is visible has disappeared. Can it have any Truth? Drop all insane concepts and just be quiet.

When you are convinced that you have gone beyond the need of your consciousness, you need not come here.

There is neither creation nor dissolution without the Sadguru. One who knows this reaches the same state. The Guru-word is our true nature. This japa is to be repeated without words. The word of the Sadguru is your true identity. What remains after everything is extinguished, is your true nature.

Those who worship the Sadguru as a human being are doing so for worldly achievements. It is not devotion for knowledge. The five elements and the rest i.e. name, form, etc., will disappear. What remains has no sense of duality such as 'This is my Sadguru, and this is I'. There is no other support for the manifestation and dissolution of the world, except for the Sadguru.

That which is prior to the word has no identity. It neither 'Is' nor 'Is not'. Your consciousness is the light of the Guru, the holy feet of Sri Guru. It is your true nature. Even if you are a beggar, remember well that the Guru-word and you are the same. The eyes see, but the true seer is the Sadguru within. It is consciousness. It is the perfect Self.

The body is subject to death. The one who knows the body, is he known by the body and prana? Consciousness that illuminates is the knower. It is the perfect Brahman, the perfect bliss, the love-devotion, and your true nature. Do service to this consciousness, but do not take it to be the body. Do not neglect the body either. It contains pure consciousness – the Sadguru. It is Self-love. It is the nectar of the holy feet of the Sadguru. One's true nature, the uninterrupted bliss, has to be discovered. Obeisance to the Sadguru is the same as the obeisance to our consciousness. Is it not so? That by which you feel 'you are' is the same through which the world with its five elements and the living beings is created.

The holy feet of the Sadguru are the same as your consciousness. It is the same as the sensation you have that 'you are'. You must realize their pure movement. Then whatever appears to you will be pure and sanctified. To remove ignorance, catch hold of the holy feet of the Sadguru without duality. Remain in your natural state without doing anything. Worship that which is in the body and that which gives you the sensation of your beingness. Due to your devotion, the world gets uplifted.

Why do people suffer all kinds of miseries? Is it not for the sake of consciousness? Is it not the one that is dearest to us? Whatever you do is because of the love for consciousness. It comes to the Paramatman with great difficulty. It takes ages before He senses that 'He is'. Do not forego this opportunity as a human being. Do not leave the feet of the Sadguru. It is rare to find a jnani who is eager for the experience of the ending of time.

Nirupana 64
Sunday, October 8, 1978

To be aware of our beingness is meditation. We have understood what we are; keep that in mind. Unless the intellect understands it, the heart will not accept it. Always be aware that you are not the body, you have no form. Do you know how you were before acquiring the body? This knowledge is conveyed to you to remove body-consciousness. Your body is not the form of the Self. To think that the body is one's form is ego. One who understands this becomes Brahman.

The Guru-mantra should be continuously repeated at all times. With practice, even poison can be digested. Try to form the habit of sitting down in meditation. Increase it by a minute every day. There is nothing impossible in the world if you are determined. The world-phenomenon is made of our own vital force. Nothing is impossible for it. Rituals continue so long as you do not know who you are. It is easy to be someone different, but to be of the nature of Paramatman is very difficult.

It is ignorance to think that you are a human being subject to karmic laws. Consciousness is covered by the body. It is so because of ignorance. It is that by which we know 'we are'. Since you are not the form of the body, it is a delusion to think that you will die. Our true nature is of One who knows consciousness in the body. We are the knower of consciousness, without words.

Many actions take place after acquiring worldly knowledge. Yet that is not the knowledge of one's own nature. One should understand that our true nature is without activities, beyond birth and death. That which knows consciousness is changeless. What we know through our consciousness is not our true nature. It keeps changing. What is known without knowing never changes. That which is true is eternal. That which is eternal is the Truth.

Consciousness is God. Consciousness, world and God are time-bound and, hence, temporary. It can be said that God is of the nature of the universe. However, what is seen or felt will come to an end someday. Your true nature is neither seen nor felt. Hence, it is not time-bound. A rare one out of millions may know this.

Consciousness that has taken itself as the body is ignorance. The knower of this is eternal. It has no tenure of life. It is pure non-duality. After having heard this, see where you stand. Your true nature has no experience of wakefulness or sleep. In the beginning you have to realize that you are consciousness. In the end you are not that either. Our talk is material knowledge. The characteristic of the material (food essence) is consciousness. The effect of the food essence is beingness. The body is an object. You are not that.

One who is purified is God. The jiva is the essence of food. The realization 'I am not the body' is the end of objective knowledge i.e. 'I am like this', etc. What is important is the discrimination between eternal and transitory. Do not run after concepts. Do not try to be what you are not. Otherwise, you will again be wrapped up in concepts. Do not accept any worthiness. Do not qualify yourself. Your actions and their results are neither true nor everlasting. A rare one who is not deluded by the body-form will understand this. He knows that the world is born within his consciousness.

Do not be despondent. Take courage. Recognize all this and go about your daily living. You will understand that sorrow is like a child's plaything. The first thing each being feels is that 'it is'. It is time-bound. One who gets this knowingness is eternal. What rises, also sets. The knowingness quietly ends and all is peace. You are the knower of That which transcends time.

That which is timeless is surely known to you, but you do not have time to discriminate. That which is unknown to the mind exists prior to the feeling 'I am'. The birth of mind can be called the birth of God or Brahman – the manifest. The influence of Brahman – the creation, is very tortuous. Only the Sadguru can remove it. Therefore, keep the Guru's word. Then you will not be harmed by this influence. Insist that you are God. Through Him, go beyond Him. All this is material knowledge. Remember that you are not an object. One who is beyond any qualities, beyond the feeling 'I am', is timeless. Time comes and goes, but the eternal Truth is as it is. It has no color, no design. It is timeless. It is neither small nor big. One who understands this gives up all ideas of worthiness and becomes the smallest of the small. Body-consciousness is a misery. One who entertains doubts about the Guru will not get peace anywhere.

Nirupana 65
Thursday, October 12, 1978

You are accustomed to a body-form. If you experience formlessness during meditation, it causes fear.

The subtle body is spontaneously created. You experience your beingness through it. Five kinds of knowing (touch, hearing, sight, taste, and smell) are created through the same. The little child slowly grows and, if inspired, reaches Godhood. To acquire basic worthiness, a proper background has to be created within. The scriptures have prescribed rituals for that purpose.

By reciting the mantra you reach the subtle body. Space is created through the subtle body. The rest of the scene follows. There is no space before you are born. Space contains the world. The Absolute is beyond space. The characteristic of the subtle body is pure consciousness, your beingness. One must hold onto it.

Worshipping means pleasing your true nature. It takes out the impurities. Through that, God meets the devotee. As a result one realizes that he is not the body. As there is sweetness in sugar, as there is saltiness in the sea, likewise there is Self-love in the body. The panorama of the world is filled inside your subtle body.

The belief that God is greater than the Guru is a mistake. The holy sight of sages is of greater value than seeing idols in the temple. One who is soaked with devotion is holy. One who goes beyond body-consciousness and becomes one with the Self is a sage.

The word is the basic instrument we have. The name of God, the word itself, becomes of the nature of God. The name of a holy place itself becomes of the nature of the holy place. Your word is of the nature of God. Your speech will sprout with repetition of the mantra and your word will become God's word. The Guru's word is final. It does not change. This must be your conviction. It should be remembered constantly. As your behavior changes according to your word, it gives value to your word. Your word becomes the word of God. Never use it to hurt anyone. As your word becomes pure, knowledge will flow through it. The words flow out of your mind according to your worthiness. When you chant the mantra, the vital force takes shape according to the meaning of the mantra. Visions are created. The pure word flows like the Ganges, washing away the miseries of others.

To impart the understanding to a mortal jiva that he is immortal is like transmuting clay into gold. This is the purpose of spiritual efforts. One must be aware and vigilant. To live according to accepted advice is awareness. You will act, but do not behave in an unworthy manner. Do not identify yourself with the body. Identify with the formless and surrender to it.

Offer your food to God and eat it as His gift to you. You will become holy. Where there is no food, there is no vital force (prana), no mind, no intellect, and no consciousness. You can speak only if there is prana. Without prana, how is the Atman? Atman is the knower of the occasion when prana leaves the body.

One who lives according to the Guru-word does not experience death. Only prana comes and goes. One who practices devotion, becomes of the nature of the Atman. He never comes and goes. Atman has pervaded space. If there is no Atman, who will recognize space? A rare one thinks like this. If you take someone's advice, you should follow it properly. When Atman Himself has become all this, why expect the fruit of your actions? God is worshipping Himself. Once your word becomes pure, never use it to harm someone as it has a lot of power. Chant the mantra all the time without any desires. You will understand that everything is happening spontaneously. Hence, there is no reason for pride as everything is naturally there.

Nirupana 66
Sunday, October 15, 1978

Do not do anything to the one within us who is listening. Leave him as he is. The idea that 'I am the body' is ignorance. As a child, many expensive clothes were bought for you, but they were of no use when you grew up. The enjoyments of the body have no use when you transcend the body. Your true nature is consciousness. Treat consciousness as the Guru and worship it. Do what has to be done without expectation. Say, 'I am pure, luminous consciousness' and get absorbed into it. You are of the nature of God. All entertainment is supplied to you e.g. work, family, etc., for passing the time.

Be friends with your own consciousness. It will fulfill all your needs. Your existence is like a dream of daylight during sleep. In your dream, the mind creates a world. The world is false, yet it appears to be very true. It is seen within ignorance. Recede back to the point you arise from.

Religion implies a code of behavior in everyday life. The true religion explains the nature of that behavior. It is the religion of the Self. If you acquire wealth, utilize it for spiritual purposes. No one wants to know who he truly is. If you think you are the body, you suffer the consequences. After establishing yourself in your nature, you may carry on with worldly life. As long as the body lasts, there is time for spiritual activities. After the fall of the body, this cannot be done. The highest religion is searching for one's nature and stabilizing there. Whatever is done through body-consciousness is imperfect. What will be the form of your consciousness after the body falls? No one thinks of that. All collective phenomena are called maya. Truly speaking, no one has any form that he can call his own. If this is understood, one gains the eternal state of Paramatman.

Night implies ignorance and darkness. Yet in deep sleep, the sensation 'I am' is present. It is called God. It is created during ignorance. Wakefulness is the awakening of ignorance. Whatever transpires will pass away. One who senses this is motionless. There is no darkness, no light, and no direction in it. It just IS. Surrender to the consciousness through which you know 'you are'. Please the consciousness. Worship it. Keeping faith in it is meditation. Do not look here and there. Consciousness is formless and luminous. It is of the nature of love. Are you listening to this as a body? Or is it pure consciousness that is listening? God is pleased with the one who lives in that meditation. Then the devotee and God are not different. Stay with the feeling 'I am perfect, I want nothing'. With non-dual worship, one pleases the God-principle and achieves perfection.

Ignorance and knowledge both disappear into the Absolute. The Witness remains. That is called vijnana – direct knowledge. As long as there is consciousness, various sensations are there. All attachments pertain to it. When there is no consciousness, everything is all right. True nature is all-pervading and, therefore, has no movement. True nature cannot be known; everything is known through it. A rare one can see (realize) That through which everything is seen.

Nirupana 67
Thursday, October 19, 1978

The seed sown by the Guru will sprout. The tree that will grow is the same as the world. In the end it will disappear. It is of no use to you. Whatever you gain will ultimately be useless, as there will be no form to enjoy it. The memory 'I am' will not remain. When there is no consciousness, there is no need to be happy nor is there any experience of misery. As childhood did not last, our individuality will also not last. Whatever you are not will also end, whether you like it or not. The desire to 'be' leads to humiliating conditions e.g. the need to eat, sleep, and wake up, etc., over and over again. In truth, your true nature has no measure. It has no color. You will never know that you have died. How can death be experienced when there is no death? Consciousness will not last whether you like it or not. Whatever you feel about the body will not last. When you realize in meditation that there is nothing, who knows about it? When the knowingness ends, is it death?

Many names have been given to consciousness in the human body. It is not found in the objective world. It is not known to anyone. It is transcendental. One in a million realizes it. He realizes his own birth. He knows that where there is consciousness in the body, there is also the world. They go together. Pure consciousness by which we know we are is the Sadguru. It cannot be experienced objectively.

All beings have a need to continue their beingness. It is nourished through the five senses. In order to continue it, various activities are undertaken. Devotion to consciousness is its nourishment. That is our first love. It is the only thing that is worthy of love. It is of the nature of the Self. One must perceive it directly. Keep repeating 'Guru, Guru' silently. Finally, consciousness gets dissolved into itself. You may lose your prana or the body, but not this Self-knowledge.

Deep sleep is restful because the knowingness is not there. The memory of being a man or a woman belongs to the body. There is no need of anything, once the body is forgotten. Unless you understand your present state of being, you will not understand your true nature. When you let go the sense of being a body, your individuality will become the totality. Once the subtle body (seed consciousness) is realized, it becomes universal. All the names are given to the manifest. The world and Brahman are not separate. The light of consciousness is called the world. It is the manifest consciousness that knows the world through itself. It is called the feet of the Guru, and is to be worshipped.

In the first phase, one should sit in solitude and go inwards by paying attention to one's own consciousness – the Guru. It is self-sensing and luminous. It is knowingness and love. To assimilate this knowledge is very difficult. For that, be one with the Guru. While being awake, do not forget that you are pure consciousness. It must be firmly established that 'I am' is prior to whatever I have seen. What is there where we are not? With the grace of the Guru, you become of the nature of the Guru and see this. You will realize that you have not done anything at all, nor will you ever do anything.

When emotions become quiet, there is no need to go anywhere. The mischievous intellect will never give you any satisfaction. Right discrimination and faith are essential. The whole existence of the world is within you. As a spider forms a web from its saliva, the universe is formed from your own light. It is bondage to think that you live in the light of the world. It is the other way around.

All activities take place on the basis of the word (mind-concepts). One who is in the void of the subtle body becomes awake if invoked through words. What is the subtle body and when does it come into existence? It is That by which we feel 'we are'.

There is no God other than the devotee. As God, he is consciousness. You take him to be of the nature of the body and are convinced that there will be death. The universe is fabricated by your unique consciousness. Pay constant attention to your own true nature. If you feel uneasy, recite 'Guru, Guru'. One who has no fear has no death.

Nirupana 68
Sunday, October 22, 1978

Your beliefs will give you relevant experiences. Keep reciting your mantra. It will enable you to understand your true identity. You will come to know that you are not the body. For Self-realization it is necessary that consciousness and the vital force be united. This happens by reciting the mantra. It has to be done with love and a sense of urgency. In fact it is the vital force that recites the mantra. A persistent commitment is needed. There is no part-time spiritual effort.

The body is created out of food. The hum of consciousness comes through the essence of the body. That is the same as 'I am'. There is no true sense of individuality, right from an insect to God. There is manifestation for a duration of time. Maya means ignorance, which means fear. Under her influence, the jiva takes on an identity and accordingly gets experiences. The basis of your life is consciousness. It depends upon food.

What is said will not be understood until the 'sins' are eradicated. Concepts are the sins. Beingness has no meaning. It is just a movement (activity because of Gunas), but the resulting nuisance has to be suffered. The body is a form of food. In that food-object there is a taste of 'I am'. It is gone when the food material is exhausted.

Talk about this only if you understand it. Your thoughts and your words are bubbles in consciousness. When understood, the jnani is not bothered by thought. When the vital force is present in the body, there are an infinite variety of thoughts and actions. None of these is everlasting. Consciousness is of the essence of food. When it is finished, it disappears. Then who dies, a man or a woman? Root-consciousness is created out of the essence (Sattva) and it is felt as the sensation 'I am'.

The name of God is your own word. Your faith in your word will manifest as God. The devotional word (bhajan) has great importance. With time, this word has greater meaning. Your conviction also grows. Atman can take any form. Words reside in the heart and emerge as thoughts. The idea of the 'wishing tree' implies that your concepts will materialize. With fear in your heart, your actions will be fearful.

Krishna says: 'My devotees are the manifestation of My true nature'. It is love, the Self, the knowingness or the knowledge that 'you are'. This knowledge is formless. The nature of time is tied to the body. Your life span, place, activities, etc., are included in time. The realization of Self is bliss. It brings true happiness. The true devotee knows this. If we do not sense ourselves like this, then what is meditation? There is no other God except consciousness. It is the feet of the Guru. One deals with others knowing that there is no difference between him and other beings. They have the same consciousness. As God lives in all beings, he treats them all as God. When it is understood that God and I are the same, all actions become an offering to Him.

Consciousness that has come over you unknowingly has awakened as the 'I'. It carries out all the actions. One who knows that he is not the body, remains in constant self-attentiveness. The ego that says, 'I am so-and-so' is the doer of actions. Pay attention to the seed consciousness, the atomic wakefulness that arises at dawn. After listening to the Guru, what change has come over you? Has one sentence created a conviction in you? All creeds imply concepts that are agreeable to them. You should know that the one who knows is in the present. Then everything will be revealed.

All the incarnations have had different kinds of behavior. Each sage presents a different concept. Why is it so? If you want to know this, you must merge into your true nature. From the point of view of a true devotee there is nothing bad in the world. One who understands this has no value for his person. He does not have a single concept left with him. The state of being in which one does not know whether one 'is' or 'is not' is called the Absolute.

Your thinking creates your destiny. Your concept of yourself creates your circumstances accordingly. Therefore, see that you become nothing. When you see your true identity, it is called Self-realization. The knowledge 'I am' is the supreme God. Surrender to it without duality. You are not different from consciousness. It is your true nature.

Nirupana 69
Thursday, October 26, 1978

The experience of the world is through the body. The experience of God also comes through the body. He resides in your heart. He can be reached only through the human form. When the jiva reaches Godhood, there remain no karmic debts.

All actions happen on the strength of the word. That through which the world is created is in your body. One who realizes this becomes a sage. He is not disturbed by desires. One who is not troubled by his word (mind), will not get trouble from the world. One whose inner storms (thoughts) have become silent is a realized sage. By reciting the mantra, God is pleased. The sense 'I am' comes from food. It is God.

One should never think that he will die. Only the body dies. And you are not the body. It is inborn nature of consciousness to have self-love. It wants to continue. You live in the house, but the house is not you. There is recognition of 'I am' in the body; the body is not you. It is a natural instinct for the life force to safeguard itself. The body is food for prana (life force). One who gets this knowledge becomes deathless. To get that worthiness, follow the word of the Guru.

Good spiritual efforts can be carried out while running a household. As soon as you realize that you are not the body, you will not be affected by your concepts. Therefore, keep continuous awareness of the Self. Our vital force is called consciousness. The whole worldly phenomenon is made up of consciousness. Whatever you are now, is of the nature of time. One who understands this transcends time. As a result of the three gunas we feel 'we are'. The jnani is the Witness of consciousness.

Prana goes into space and the body merges into the five elements. Where does the Atman go? Know that you are not the body, you are consciousness. The sensation of knowingness is the quality of the essence of food. When the essence of food goes, so does consciousness. One who knows the consciousness is a sage. Orange robes do not make you a sage. Such a one is not free from fear. A sage is not bound by traditions.

If you take one sentence of what you have heard and make it your own, you will be liberated. At least, be quietly aware of the fact that you are not the body.

Nirupana 70
Thursday, November 2, 1978

One who has merged into his true nature is a yogi. Prosperity or poverty does not affect him. Do you take yourself to be different from your name? The name is only the letters. Are you those letters? The name has been given to the body. At present, the body has become your identity and the name has become yourself. It has become a habit. That is the influence of maya. Can you tell me about yourself when you are not the body nor the name given to the body?

How would you look if you say, 'I am not the name, nor am I the body'? Then what name can be given to you? And after all, what is consciousness? Is it not love, or taste, or flavor, that remains after leaving out the body and the name? What would one want when he is like this? Consciousness is love itself. That is the bliss unasked for in the feeling 'I am'. It transcends the body. It is not of the form of the body. Without consciousness is there God, or the world? How do we look at ourselves while in the body? It is pure luminosity. Its symbol is light. The light of consciousness means the light of Atman. It has no form. It has no divisions. It is without the body and the name. It is like space.

What comes first, space or your consciousness? When there is no consciousness, there is no world. How long does the world last? As long as one is awake. One who has realized the Self is a great yogi. God, Guru and consciousness are the same for him.

The sensation 'I am' is the beginning of time. First of all, consciousness arose and then the world was seen in it. Did anyone do anything to create it? When consciousness disappears, the world disappears at that very moment. What happened to the big mountains? Who swallowed them? No one, because the world was false, an illusion. With the birth of the knowledge 'I am', the world comes into existence. Both happen simultaneously.

Do not say you have understood. Be aware of what you have continuously heard. The use of the body is for consciousness through which we know 'we are'. It is the essence of food. One who sees the dream has to be the originator of the dream. Is it not so? To use consciousness means to convince us of this and behave accordingly.

Only a Guru can give true advice. The rest give consolation with false concepts. Consciousness is universal. God, Guru and 'I' are all its names. The common name is Brahman. It is there as long as there is the word (manifestation). Its characteristic is knowingness. This manifested, all-pervading Brahman merges into the Absolute. It has no identity of its own. It is timeless.

The foundation of our way of spirituality is self-attentiveness. The Sadguru is beyond time. He has no coming and going. Is it not so that one knows the Absolute and, also, is it not so that one does not know it? (It is our true nature, but it has no duality.) The body is the food for consciousness. Prana eats that food, not the Self. Prana carries out all actions. One who clearly knows that he is not the body does not suffer from worldly gain or loss, pleasure or pain. The knower of prana is consciousness. It only witnesses.

Can you take a fistful of Bombay to your village? The same is true of God. From the point of view of the Paramatman, you are prior to the world. From the point of view of the jiva, the world is first and then you. The jnani does not require any outside glory. Identification with the body and its name is ego. As long as the fear of death is there, you have not realized yourself. Dwell only on what you know before experiencing the world. Think on the metaphor of the dream I mentioned earlier.

For a man the company of a woman means desire. Where there is desire, there is expectation. Where there is expectation, there is hope. Where there is hope, there is bondage. The cause of bondage is desire. Where there is 'I' and 'you', there is pure delusion. Where there is no 'I' and 'you', there is pure Brahman.

Nirupana 71
Sunday, November 5, 1978

The true meaning of *ahimsa* (non-violence) is to not hurt anyone's feelings. One ought to develop such an attitude of mind in order to purify it. Our behavior gradually changes accordingly.

At the time of Sri Krishna there was no other method (for spiritual pursuit) than having a Guru. The Guru's word was the Truth. Hence, the Guru was treated as God. The knowledge of the Self cannot be achieved without the grace of the Sadguru. One is not really awake, but feels he is awake because of ignorance. The Sadguru gives the knowledge about how the wakeful dream has come about. A little light of the jiva has brought about the view of the universe! The Sadguru shows clearly how the wakefulness and dream world are of the same category. He introduces us to Self-knowledge. He is the knower of consciousness, the sense 'I am' and, hence, He is beyond it.

In ancient times it was difficult for people to avail of the teaching. Therefore they had to have the fullest faith in the Sadguru. Today, people do not have such faith. If anyone does keep such faith, he will be liberated. The Sadguru is of the nature of the Absolute. He is our perfect Self. He is our eternal true nature. A rare one follows this type of devotion (non-dual devotion). The Sadguru and your pure consciousness are one and the same. We know that 'we are'. It is the same as love (consciousness). Love itself is faith. Consciousness, through which all this is seen and felt, merges into universal consciousness at the end of life. What was already there but has now become manifest is Self-knowledge. What undergoes change is not eternal, hence it is not true.

Night and day are created by consciousness. Our true nature is not dependent on the five elements. One who wants it intensely will realize his own true nature instantly, provided he gets rid of body-consciousness. Observe yourself, keeping aside the name and the form. Now, how do you see yourself? Is this not enough in order to realize? Remember that you are not the body. No other effort is necessary. Consciousness is the pure essence of the body. Accept the Guru-word in order to understand your true nature. Identify with the Guru-word. When you remember a person, you remember his behavior pattern. The Guru is remembered by his word. The meaning of his word is: 'you are'.

Nirupana 72
Thursday, November 9, 1978

It is true that words can be deceptive. But who is the knower of the words? (Who is prior to the words?) What value can the words have if there is no knower? You say that in meditation the knower gets lost, but who knows this fact? When consciousness disappears, can anything further be known? Things are known only through consciousness. If there is no consciousness, what can be known?

Does the experience of the body or the world come about by any effort? Wakefulness comes and goes automatically. So long as there is consciousness, there is the individual. If there is no consciousness, can one be called an individual? Can this consciousness be driven away? In meditation you may see innumerable colors but what is the color of consciousness, the knowledge 'I am'? It is only love. It is non-dual. Your consciousness is the self-love. For the sake of this love, you have need of other things.

The puzzle of the five elements will be solved when you hold onto your consciousness. The five elements are within your consciousness. Truth is at the core. The root-maya, your consciousness, is sporting on the Truth. Those who have realized the Truth will not perform miracles. The knower of consciousness is beyond time and beyond beingness. He is without movement.

Your knowledge is limited to what you have learnt through your consciousness. Gradually you will know that the world is within your consciousness. The world is vast, but you will realize through meditation that it dwells inside your atomic consciousness. It is love. If you want to go back to the Source, stop wandering and go on meditating. Nothing is to be given up. Just realize that whatever you know is different from you. There is a place from where nothing is seen and there is also a place from where everything is seen. This should be properly understood. I am giving you this readymade knowledge. Just listen and absorb. You must reach the point that you (as consciousness) are the Self of the world. This gurgling stream of the world is flowing out of the love 'I am'.

To know and understand that the world is untrue is detachment. Giving up something is not true detachment. How can you hold onto consciousness, as that is what you are? The source, the seed of the world, is the knowledge that 'you are'. A rare one out of millions reaches this point. That which is eternal is the Truth. There is not a trace of beingness in it. There is neither light nor darkness in it. Your consciousness is called God or Brahman. It is not eternal; it is not the Truth. Whatever is seen in the world is God. That by which it is seen is also God. One who recognizes God is beyond everything.

Our prime worldly activity is feeding ourselves. Consciousness is nourished with food. The qualities of the five elements are sporting in the food. As they come together, you know that 'you are'. The birth of a body comes out of the sour food. The body is the food of consciousness. The life force is the same in all living beings. The vital force moves with greater and greater speed. It cannot remain steady. It acts through the five senses, namely: touch, hearing, seeing, taste and smell. They determine the behavior of the individual. One feels he has understood but does not feel contented, as it goes away.

God means light, which is the sight of our consciousness. It is created out of the essence of food. There is a connection between prana (vital breath) and knowingness. Without food, there is not even the strength to speak. The light is that of food. It is because of the juices of food that we have our consciousness.

Truth is eternal. There is no sense of 'I-ness' there. There is no 'I' and 'you' there. The eternal is beyond. The rest comes from the five elements. There is duality when one says, 'I know something'. There is no duality when I do not even know myself. All this together is One, and we are That. This is the goal to be accomplished. In order to achieve that, one must go on observing one's own Self as taught by the Guru. While doing that, one may see visions of various kinds. But we are not that. We are the knower of that.

The seer is one, but the things seen are many. Is it not true that the seer has only one sight? Is not the light of the seer only one? How can it be made steady? The seer should only observe himself. (He should stay with the 'do nothing' state of mind.) All that is seen and felt keeps on changing and ultimately goes away. No need to feel sorry for that. Whatever is seen, that we are not. We are That to whom seeing happens.

The shape of food is the body of the living being. Prana and consciousness arise simultaneously and disappear simultaneously. They are necessarily born out of the sour food. Consciousness is the same, right from that of an insect to that of a human being. It is the same as the vital force. Suppose a worm dries up in the hot sun, what does it mean? The food in the form of a body has dried up. The movement vanished along with that. Please discriminate as to what or how we are.

All books are true as long as there is ignorance of the Self. Once the Self is realized, they are all useless. The meaning of the great mantra is the certitude that 'I am'. The qualities of the deity you worship will descend on you. After that you have its vision. It arises from your own consciousness.

From where have you come and to where will you go? You never came from anywhere, then where could you go? Consciousness was created from food, and then it got extinguished. Atman means 'I', but from what point to what point? It is there as long as we consciously know ourselves.

With steadfast devotion to the Sadguru, one recognizes that the devotion is to his own Self. Knowledge is of no use until one becomes devoted to the Self. The great mantra is 'I am Brahman'. If you have no devotion to the feeling that 'you are', is there any world or God? With devotion to the Self, you will spontaneously recognize all deities. The meaning of the mantra will be revealed through you. It will be clear to you why it is that you 'are', and why you were 'not'. Without the devotion of 'I am', would we have any needs? Has anyone pondered over this devotion? Our sense of 'I am' is the Godhood of God. We love others because we love ourselves. If we do not get food or water, the love of 'I am' will get extinguished. When the food is exhausted, its characteristic (consciousness) comes to an end. The quality of food had appeared; now it has disappeared.

Your consciousness is itself the primordial maya. She behaves as she pleases. Surrender to that consciousness. She will reveal herself to you. Then you will be Brahman. That is the knowledge that makes us feel that 'we are'. Devote yourself to that knowledge. Perform your household duties to perfection. However, do not forget the Guru's word. It is your own true nature. Carry on a constant incantation without words. The extent of the incantation will bring corresponding change within you.

Nirupana 73
Sunday, November 12, 1978

Whatever is visible is within the purview of the senses. It is visible to the One who cannot be seen by the senses. (The unmanifest Absolute is prior to the manifest world; the unknown is prior to the known.) Sometimes it is said that it is all void, but one who understands the void, is he void? Meditate in such a way that you even forget that you are meditating. Truth will reveal itself when one forgets oneself. We are not what we know. We are prior to knowing. One who has understood this has no need to sit in meditation. Continue repeating the mantra. Even without repeating, one must know that it is going on within. Ever since the body was born, this incantation has been going on. This incantation stops only when a person dies.

We all have a strong desire to assure that our beingness is safe. When this is in doubt, there is fear. Hold onto the feet of the One whose presence removes fear. Hold onto the feet of consciousness. It is continuously with you. Guru means consciousness.

Do not consider yourself as an individual. It is the root cause of fear. Forget what you have read. All the hatha yogis and those who awaken the Kundalini have disappeared within consciousness. Bodies can be strong and weak, but the holder of the body is the same One. To achieve samadhi through sex is a foolish idea. Self-realization has nothing to do with it

All religions have their traditions full of concepts. They are ritualistic. There is silence when concepts are retired. Ignorance is failure to realize the Self. Conflict of opinions starts with the body sense. People believe what they hear. No one thinks about his inner Self. How trustworthy is the experience of the world that has come with the breath? What happens when the breath stops? You are proud of your religion, but how long are you going to stay in your own company?

The one who experiences day and night is within us. If he had been aware of his beingness before birth, he would not have wanted to be born. He would not take a shape anymore. He would not want to steam in the womb for nine months. One tolerates the dirt in the womb because consciousness has not become manifest.

One trusts what one hears or sees. With the resulting attachment, there is an urge to act according to the inclination of the mind. If one gets disgusted with that, it is called detachment – turning back. It brings perfection. There is no sense of beingness, hence happiness and sorrow become meaningless. Misery is what one does not like. Happiness is what one likes. They depend on the nature of time. You will understand the meaning of this when you will realize that things happen according to the nature of time and you are not affected by it.

The highest spiritual achievement is the art of right discrimination. That is the Sadguru. It makes everything easy. Without hurting anybody, look minutely at yourself. With this, joy wells up within you. It is very fortunate when this happens. It pleases the Atman. Hold onto the feet of That by which you know 'you are' and the 'world is'. Your consciousness has qualities. The sum total of worldly phenomena is God. Consciousness is prior to the world. The knower is prior to consciousness. This is the order. You behave as a body. When prana is ready to leave, you feel you will die. Therefore you experience fear.

God is knowingness. Surrender to Him. He is also the Atman; He is the world. No evidence is necessary for this. Do you require any proof that you have awakened in the morning? Do not treat consciousness as the body. It is an unholy act. Knowledge is power. It is the same as Purusha. So long as you have not awakened to the word of the Guru, the fear of death will not go. You never die; only the body is forgotten. Whose light makes the body so pure? Is it not the light of the Atman, your true nature? The knower of consciousness is infinite and eternal. One who is prior to the body is the knower.

There must be a conviction that one is consciousness, the knowledge 'I am' as taught by the Guru. After getting Self-knowledge, you will live as a timeless entity. Then time will have no measure. If you have faith in the Guru, then have faith in the knowledge of your beingness. With faith in Sri Krishna, Arjuna became liberated while listening to His words. Consciousness that is of the size of a sesame seed has pervaded the whole cosmos. Do not lose your divine faith in consciousness. That is the highest God. The jnani's advice is not an act of his pride. The meaning of the Guru-word is our true nature. Due to such meditation, the mind becomes silent. That results in detachment. Do not talk about this to others indiscriminately.

Nirupana 74
Thursday, November 16, 1978

At the core of all living things is the eternal. A fault has occurred in the eternal Truth. As a result, we have come to know that 'we are'. A pimple has appeared on the Truth. The pain caused by it is felt as 'I am'. The light that comes through a hole in the pimple is called the world. In spiritual language you may call this pimple an atom (manifest). The coming to awareness of the pimple is the same as the consciousness 'I am'. God who pervades the universe now dwells in a house of the size of a sesame seed!

Consciousness is hard to bear and that is why people get involved in worldly activities. A rare one out of millions remains in silence. Consciousness is not our true nature. Experience speaks a lot, but is there an experience of the experiencer? The sight of the world is the sight of your own consciousness. You take the scriptures as authority, but the one who knows them is you. You are the knower. The treasure of all the books in the world is in your consciousness.

The fact that you are alive and awake is the original delusion. Intellectual perception is superfluous; it is dry. Self-realization is like a cup of nectar (it will make you immortal). Why was your beingness not known previously and why is it known now? Real satisfaction will come when this is understood. God is contained in the knowledge 'I am'. When time ends, God also ends. You are primordial. The Atman is eternal. You say you were not there before a hundred years, but today you know 'you are'. One who was 'not', will he come to know that 'he is'? Only the one who has been in existence will come to know that 'he is'. The knowingness will go, but the knower will not. You think that you are consciousness. However, the knower is witnessing consciousness. Consciousness is not eternal, the knower is. The world is within consciousness. When consciousness goes, the world goes. Then what does the Witness have to lose?

During the dream of wakefulness you may see Rama and Krishna. However, the concept that 'I am awake' itself is false. Saint Tukaram said when there was no space, no water, I still existed as the Absolute. What is it that has pervaded everywhere? It is the love as 'you are'. If you keep witnessing your consciousness, there is no need for any ritual. We have no control over our dreams, similarly, during wakefulness everything happens automatically. You only do the witnessing. So long as you say, 'I am the doer', you cannot become a Witness. This dream of wakefulness itself is false. The seeing and the seen are both untrue.

The inner being of the aspirant is not yet mature. That is why he is wandering in the world with his verbal understanding. He has to understand clearly that his wakefulness itself is false. That should be the conviction. You like to consider yourself as a human form. How did it come about? You have the company of your consciousness and, therefore, the world. In my eternal nature, there is no company of any kind. You take support of God as you go about in the world. Otherwise, it is unbearable. It is no different from taking a stick while going through a forest to get some courage.

One who does not know that 'he is', will he ever take birth? He is prior to birth. All actions are useless when there is no Self-knowledge. After realization all actions are still useless. What is understood through words is false. That which moves is false. Either you follow what you have heard, or drop it altogether. Do not mention this to anyone. You will be laughed at.

The one who knows he was never born can only say, 'I am not the doer'. The feeling that you know (the Truth) is untrue. Have I done anything for the fact that you have come here? Only witnessing has happened. The Witness is subtler than space. Consciousness behaves as it will. It has come unknowingly. It is spontaneous. You are not consciousness. You are beyond that. The knower cannot be mentioned through words.

Truth cannot be seen. It does not know whether 'It is' or 'It is not'. One who knows, cannot be known. Your sense that 'you are' will also go away. With body-consciousness, the experience of being and the world has come to you. You have forgotten that you are consciousness that knows the body. You consider the body as 'I'. This causes attachment to material things. You are the Atman, the Witness.

You have not forgotten the Truth and, therefore, you cannot remember it either. How can you remember that which is not forgotten? It is like the lamp being the witness. In its light you do anything; fight or quarrel. The lamp is not concerned with that. Similarly, the Absolute is not concerned with consciousness and the resulting behavior. The one who knows this is a sage. Spirituality is to realize the absolute meaning of your beingness, not the meaning of what is seen or felt.

Wakefulness and sleep come and go automatically. You cannot change that. The knower has no connection with these stages. He is not awake and, therefore, he never sleeps. Wakefulness is a microscopic form of consciousness. Even that is difficult to bear. The one who has no experience of wakefulness and sleep is the all-witnessing principle. You may call it the knowledge of Brahman. It is your own knowledge. Happiness and sorrow are parts of your consciousness. The jnani has a silent sense of being. He does not know that he is a jnani.

As there is sweetness in sugar, so there is self-love in consciousness. This association with consciousness is transitory. To make it bearable, one has to treat it as God or Brahman. Consciousness is the seed that can create an infinite number of universes. Be friends with consciousness. When it is pleased, it will reveal itself to you.

Nirupana 75
Saturday, November 18, 1978

You are prior to any thought you get. Always be aware of this. You are prior to any experience you have. When you recede, what is then seen and felt will become empty. The experience of 'I am' is not that of an individual. It is the totality. It cannot be changed. There can be a remedy for an individual, but is it possible in case of the totality? The experience of 'I am' will go away in the same way it arrived.

I know that the experience of 'I am' was not with me. I also know that the experience will go away. I am not That which will go away. God (consciousness) cannot remain in my company forever.

Why do you wish for things to get better in your worldly affairs? That is foolishness. Is anything in this world going to remain with you? Do not find fault with any individual. Whatever happens, happens due to the nature of time. An individual is powerless. As time passes, the individual goes on changing. You cannot change the situation.

The experience that I have undergone is available to all. My identity is not based upon anyone's imagination, it exists naturally.

The nature of the mind is to think. It cannot stop. In fact it is due to prana. You say that mind is due to the result of impressions. However, in reality it is the flow of prana. Language (word) is created through prana. Prana is movement; it is the vital force (chaitanya). Mind is the flow of language; it must not be accepted. Awakening of Kundalini through the six centers is the action of prana. Amongst all these, who are you? Is there anything which can be claimed as your own right?

Is there a need to think when there is no longer any individuality? You are the same today as you were before your birth. The love that everyone has as 'I am' is the primordial maya – the root concept.

Birth is the worst bondage. I have swallowed this knot of birth itself. With divine understanding, it will all go.

Nirupana 76
Thursday, November 23, 1978

There have been many great sages. However, they could not make any changes in consciousness because they became one with the universal consciousness. This consciousness is not in anyone's control as it was not created by anyone. It was created spontaneously and all else followed. It is said that God incarnates and destroys evil, but it does not happen knowingly. It happens spontaneously, as summer follows winter. When evil abounds, good comes spontaneously into being. Self-knowledge is a matter of experience. What is the totality? Until it is understood that we are the same, we will not get ultimate satisfaction.

The feeling 'I am' is Shiva and Vishnu. Everything is created through consciousness. Without your consciousness, there are no deities. The sun is the same every day, yet there are names for different days. Really speaking, all days are Sundays; concepts have divided them.

Dwell on why and how this consciousness has come over you. The rest is meaningless. When there is consciousness in the body, there is the world. Consciousness is God. That through which everything is known is God-consciousness. It is the sensation 'you are'. Through its light everything is seen. The world is the result of the sensation 'you are'.

Parabrahman – the Absolute, is not pleased by worldly efforts. To reach that state, no method is of any use. Such means are nothing but multiplication of concepts. You revel in concepts until you understand yourself. What you believe or what you know is a type of entertainment. Even in this, there are waves of miseries and dislikes. You behave according to what you have heard as it suits you, but that is entirely false. Your image of yourself, whether in worldly matters or in spirituality, is not you at any time. This is true whether you perform mundane or spiritual activities. There is not a single experience in the world that is true and honest. Whatever image you have in your mind is not true. You cannot be like that forever. Your self-image and actions are dishonest. Neither childhood nor youth remain with us. The knowledge 'I am a man' or 'I am a woman' is untrue. Memory depends on a body, but is the body an honest fact? Is there anything everlasting in the world? Is there anything honest in this world that can be proven by evidence? Does honorability in this world have a proven standard?

The experience of our consciousness itself is untrue

211

and dishonest. How can the world that is vitalized by it be honest? All spiritual methods are untrue. And yet consciousness has been given a divine status. Does consciousness by which you know 'you are' last forever? No. Hence, the sages have asked the question 'Who am I?'

One remembers the charities and the rituals one performs. Does one remember how many times one urinated? With that difference, the Self would never come in sight.

Krishna says: 'You cannot come to Me unless you seek the company of a sage'. With that the concepts slowly melt away. When the seeker reaches his true nature, there is not the slightest idea such as 'I am Brahman'.

To meet a Sadguru is great fortune. (Three things are most important: the human body, desire for Self-realization, meeting the Sadguru.) Keep saying, 'Jai Guru, Jai Guru' within yourself. You will understand and the inner whisper will come out. You will see your true nature. There is no modification like 'I am' or 'I am not' within your true nature (the Absolute). Such is the condition of a sage. You must clearly understand what is in you that gives the experience of happiness and misery. You have your worries, but that through which the worries are experienced is not eternal. The eternal Truth cannot be forgotten and, hence, the jnani sits silently. He cares for no publicity.

Let all this cause no fear in you. Have faith in the Guru. Then That which cannot be described will be pleased. Do not call temporary disgust as detachment. You are fortunate as you have the opportunity to listen to this. God is like a stick made out of faith, like the stick you carry for safety while going through the forest. When you recognize God, He will serve you. Continue reciting the mantra. Do not be impatient. Consciousness is the feet of the Guru. It is a great friend. Be aware of this and keep quiet. Non-duality means whosoever is, is myself only. One who lives like this is protected from everything.

Nirupana 77
Thursday, November 30, 1978

Self-realization is a state of perfect contentment, both worldly as well as spiritual. After this the seeker does not require even his true nature. You have become a seeker because you are hungry for realizing your true nature. The goal (pure consciousness) has three stages i.e. wakefulness, sleep and dream. The one who knows the goal is beyond all the stages. The goal has three gunas – Sattva, Rajas and Tamas. When you have realization, you will know that you are prior to wakefulness and sleep. The alternating stages of wakefulness and sleep will not be there permanently. As you are beyond these stages, can you tell me what uniform you have?

Practice meditation. One should live with the conviction that one is not the body, but the pure consciousness within the body. The spring of Self-realization will flow from within. 'What God has created is given back to God. I do nothing.' This is the sign of a sincere devotee. That which is motivating the body is the true devotee. He has a pure heart. He himself is God. In the beginning, he offers his body and awareness to God and then he remains as pure consciousness.

Meditation means holding onto consciousness. The consciousness that appears in the morning is the holy sight of God. Everything is known through consciousness. When the heart is pure, one says, 'The Guru is the Self, He is everything'. The true devotee has no sense of doership. Consciousness is the vital energy of the whole world. If you are unable to do spiritual practices, at least maintain the pure feeling in your heart: 'There is no other God except my consciousness'. It will benefit you and others. Pay no attention to honor and recognition. There should be no pride such as 'I am a knowledgeable devotee'. Never publicize your charities or good deeds. Use the body happily, but never identify with it.

Keep this awareness: 'I am the seer, never the enjoyer'. Then the bad qualities will drop off. The pure feeling in the heart should never be lost sight of, even at the cost of your life. It is the inspiration of God that brings us here. Go on meditating. Then you will become convinced that whatever is, is not separate from yourself.

Nirupana 78
Thursday, December 7, 1978

God is pure consciousness that dwells in the body. When the body dies, prana leaves. However, the Atman does not go anywhere. Does space go from this room to the other room? No, because everything is contained in that. When consciousness and prana come together, pain and pleasure are felt. When prana separates from consciousness, there is no longer any experience of pain and pleasure. The body is made out of food. Are you of the nature of food?

When you remember that you are consciousness, the Guru is with you. The belief that you are a human being is a sin. You have no beginning. God comes later. God has His source in the primordial maya. This source has no cause. (God – the manifest, is created from Absolute – the unmanifest.) Your desire to continue with consciousness is the root-maya.

When there is no body, there is no word. When there is no word, there is no sense of whether 'I am' or 'I am not'. There is a verse: 'Prior to everything there is a seed, the feeling 'I am''. True religion is to live as the Self. You may do what you like, but do not ever identify your consciousness with the body. Consciousness is the Sadguru. Remember, wakefulness that comes in the morning is the holy sight of God. Keep that in mind as you do your daily work. The holy feet of the Guru are the movement of the Guru. It is your true nature.

In the essence of things, there is a quality e.g. sweetness

or bitterness. Your experience of the seed consciousness is your beingness. The essence of the body is the feeling 'I am'. Your body is the food for your consciousness. Your destiny is the result of impressions that are embossed in you. These are all concepts. Atman is pure, but He is bound by concepts. Consciousness is attached to its qualities. It is the result of maya. It is the love for beingness. The epithet guna-maya is given to the Self in the body; the consciousness in the body. It is the same as God. We know that the primordial illusion is that 'we are'. It is the quality of Sattva. Because of the root-maya, one wants his beingness to continue. It is self-love.

Paramatman, our true nature, has no such qualities. Maya is the name given to manifestation of consciousness. Paramatman is prior to these qualities; He is beyond time, beyond the feeling of existence or absence of existence. (Pure consciousness is called God. After Self-realization, the same is called maya.)

There is no difference between the speaker and the listener. (The same consciousness works in both.) When consciousness becomes pure, it reveals itself.

Incantation purifies prana. Prana purifies the mind. When consciousness becomes very pure, as the result of a pure mind, it reveals itself. Such a person is called a jnani. Consciousness, the sense 'I am', is the Guru. Do not identify it with the body. It can see space, but space cannot see consciousness, as it comes later.

The one who acts is prana. When prana is in the body, there is the quality of knowingness. Once out of the body, it becomes universal. As you hear this, you will understand that death is a false concept. The five-elemental body is produced out of the primordial maya. However, we are not the body. Sit silently for a while and meditate on the knower. The mantra is given to make the mind quiet.

Nirupana 79
Sunday, December 10, 1978

One's greatest need is one's own beingness. It is the consciousness created through the five elements. In itself it is false. Once you know that everything is untrue, then whatever you do will be untrue. This is because you have no existence in your own right. The fact that all is void is also dependent on 'you'. Without you who will say it is void? You may do whatever you want but it is false.

You can hear this kind of talk only here. The rest of them (spiritual teachers) will get you involved in some kind of a ritual.

Many great people were famous in their own time. Do they still exist? Can they be sought out today? All that has been created is false. All that was not becomes that which is not again. This knowledge is not useful to those who want to live and want to gain something for themselves. It is for those who want to realize their true nature. You know 'you are' and as a result you have needs and wants. It is the reason you want a wife, children and many other things. (Pure consciousness is void and it is not easy to come face to face with it. To escape from this void, people fill up their life with things to entertain themselves.) If you leave all desires, passions and fears you will clearly see yourself. Then you will lay prostrate.

Your love for yourself happens spontaneously. (Your consciousness is of the nature of love.) You want this consciousness, but at the same time you cannot bear it. To make it bearable you do so many things. If you realize your true nature, what can you do for yourself? It is Brahman that comes into existence of its own and disappears on its own. It is everything. Meanwhile, you feel you are the doer. The fact that you know 'you are' is the root cause of trouble. In order to realize consciousness, prana has to be purified with worship or incantation. After purification we realize ourselves. Then we do not have a need for ourselves. All actions happen spontaneously. The greatest of all things, visible or invisible, is consciousness.

For anything to happen in the world is it not necessary that 'I' should be there? The world will be there only if my presence is there. Your first act is to protect your consciousness. The whole universe is contained in consciousness. The source of consciousness is in the five elements. Your need for God is to protect the knowledge 'you are'. Death is the cessation of knowingness, nothing else. In fact, there is no death or birth. Only the knowingness becomes non-knowingness and that is all.

You search by asking 'Who am I?', but if there is no questioner to put this question, who is going to investigate whom? At the Absolute level such a question is meaningless. It is enough to remember daily that the evidence of Paramatman is your consciousness. It is the original love, the original devotion. Love it and you will be free from the experience of happiness and unhappiness. You have identified yourself with a form; however, your consciousness is formless.

There is no other attachment like self-love. It is the root-maya. Because of it the world comes into existence. When the 'I am-ness' is forgotten, the world disappears. Nobody dies. It is said that after death, a virtuous man goes to heaven. Then where does a donkey or a rat go? After the fall of the five-elemental body, all beings go to the same stage.

Nirupana 80
Thursday, December 14, 1978

The primary concept is the sense 'I am'. It is consciousness. Hold onto the basic concept 'I am alive'. Your sensation 'I am' is God. Do not forget this all your life. It is the same as maya. She signifies the power of God. One must be convinced that he is not the body; he is consciousness. All the names of God belong to consciousness.

A seeker has no form. One who still identifies with the body is an aspirant. The conviction that 'I am not the body' must be there. It must be firmly established that 'I am consciousness only'. This is the goal of every seeker: 'I have no shape. I am in the house but I am not the house'. You say, 'I am', but can you give me some information about yourself while keeping aside the word 'I'? The one who is before the words 'I am', is he a human being? Does he have a form? That knowledge does not have a body. There is no question of its being either a man or a woman. Yet it has a flavor. Consciousness is prior to everything. It is consciousness that remembers the Guru. A seeker has no form, just as thirst and hunger have no form. Have I not told you that you are not the body (even before the body dies)?

(In answer to someone's question regarding astrology, Maharaj said that its effects were true because we believed it to be true and as a result suffered from its consequences. If we take ourselves to be as pure, formless consciousness, how can the movement of planets affect us? The universe with its planetary system is within our consciousness.)

One who has no notion of devotion or God is truly bound. One who looks for Him desires liberation. One who follows a method is a seeker. He becomes the siddha, the liberated one.

When you see misery in the world, you feel pain because you consider yourself an individual. The individual is bothered by the sense of 'I' or 'mine'. The totality has no such botheration. If you meditate on 'I am the whole world along with its pleasure and pain', your personal sense of misery will go.

Consciousness with its three gunas is the same in all animals. It is the beingness. The subtle feeling of being awake is the manifest identity of maya. In her womb are the three gunas. Nobody wants death. That means the consciousness 'I am' wants to continue.

Such is the power of maya. To see the subtle consciousness is to see the world with its innumerable beings. There is no one who can be called a doer or a creator or a destroyer. The feeling 'I am' is the highest devotion.

So long as friction between prana and the essence of food is there, one feels 'he is'. When prana leaves, beingness comes to an end. In the body, the friction between pure Sattva (quality of knowingness) and prana is continuing. This creates the knowledge 'I am'. When prana gets separated, beingness disappears. No one can be rescued from the jaws of death unless all this is understood.

Tamas and Rajas are involved in everyday activity. Rajas is the worker and Tamas is the one that takes pride in the work. Sattva is the onlooker. Consciousness is the characteristic of the essence of the food-body. Once prana leaves the body, you will not remember that 'you were'. The world and the wakefulness are not different. Follow the words of the Guru to understand this. Your manifest consciousness has to become unmanifest again.

Hold onto consciousness at least before you go to sleep. When you wake up, hold onto knowingness in the same way. You are pure consciousness for a few seconds after awakening, and then the person becomes wakeful. The most sacred thing in the world is consciousness. Without doing anything else, meditate on consciousness. You feel you are the body, but you are only consciousness.

Nirupana 81
Sunday, December 17, 1978

What use are those seekers whose minds are not steady? One who has the most sincere desire in his heart finds his fulfillment sooner or later.

I feel I have been unknowingly caught in the trap of maya. Is it not due to my parents who have claimed birth of the one who has no birth? That I am born and I have parents is my defamation. Why should I take as true that which has happened without my knowing it?

The thought 'I am' is an ailment that has come spontaneously. The manifestation of consciousness means that all of a sudden we feel 'we are'. Because of this ailment one says, 'I am the body'. The Atman is the manifestation. However, there is identification with the body with its collection of desires and passions. Listen to all this. Liberation does not come as a result of any action. Whatever you know is not you. Discrimination with open eyes is necessary. Mere blind faith does not do it.

With our beingness comes the world, with the living and the non-living. Beingness is identified with the body. The root desire is to continue with the ego. It is the result of turbulence in the gunas. The rest follows. When beingness is gone, nothing remains. One who knows he is not the body is the enlightened one. There is no pain for him due to hopes, desires, passions, etc.

Did you notice becoming an adult from a child? Without knowing, your body grows. Your state before the turbulence of the gunas is not traceable by the senses. All is created due to the turbulence of the gunas. Understand this and keep quiet. It is not necessary to talk about this. As you know it, you will know that the universe is untrue – just an appearance. This understanding should be firmly established in the mind.

'I am-ness' means turbulence of the three gunas. Whatever is seen through it is a dream. It is called the world. It has come without any effort. What part do you play in all this? The easy remedy to know all this is to catch hold of what consciousness is. ('I am consciousness, I am God. The world is within me. I am prior to everything. I am the knower of it': this is Jnana yoga.) To believe that consciousness is the Guru and to catch hold of his feet is the yoga of devotion.

This 'I am-ness' has come spontaneously and uninvited. It was not there before. When it goes, the universe merges into the five elements. The 'I am-ness' has been given names like maya, the root principle, the golden womb, etc. One must know who and how he is and to whom everything is known.

Our mundane existence is to satisfy our hunger in the form of hopes, desires and passions. The turbulence of the gunas augments this transient life and the population increases.

Even with all your wealth, there will be no peace. Rest comes only after forgetting yourself in deep sleep. You forget that 'you are'. For whom do you sing devotional songs? Meditate on That by virtue of which you know the world. You will get peace in the form of samadhi. This peace does not come through the five senses. When you will understand your consciousness, you will come to know that you are the deep ocean of peace.

Nirupana 82
Thursday, December 21, 1978

You may say God is, or is not. The fact will not change. Who is saying this? Who says God is, or God is not? (It is our consciousness that is the real God.)

To be realized means to be perfectly silent. In deep sleep there is no pleasure or pain. One feels good when sleep comes. In the same way when you know who you are, death becomes an occasion of great joy. There really is no such thing as death. When one forgets that he is so-and-so, there is liberation. What is That whose characteristics are wakefulness and sleep? This will lead to the state of the Absolute. You will find that the knower of consciousness is a rare one amongst millions.

Have you understood your own true nature? The body is made of food material. Mind, intellect, ego and consciousness are the form of prana – the vital force. The knower of this does not do anything. As long as the incense burns, there is a pleasant smell. When the ingredients burn out, the smell goes. Similarly, as long as the essence in the body is burning, consciousness is there. It is a flavor, it is self-love. The knower of this cannot be pointed at. 'I am' is the direct knowledge. It is also the result of the three gunas. One who understands this is the knower of the gunas. The feeling 'I am' is the result of the gunas. When one praises God as someone different from himself, it is indirect knowledge. When he realizes that whatever is, is himself only, it is direct knowledge. The first phase has objective knowledge. Later, there is no object.

One who concentrates on his Self, having faith in the Guru, becomes free of all concerns. What is, is you. No other remedy is required. The need for a remedy implies that consciousness is not purified. One becomes happy when one forgets oneself. No outside object can make him happy. The meaning of these words is understood through the grace of the Guru.

In sleep one forgets oneself. The waking up follows automatically. Similarly, everything happens spontaneously. The only uplifting thing is faith in the Guru. It is in one's own nature. Do not look for greatness and its associated pain. Do not accept concepts like 'I am so-and-so'. After listening to this, if one still suffers the pain of body-identification, how can the Guru help? That sound with which you took cognizance of yourself is the first wordless state. The meanings brought later by the mind mostly cause pain. A jnani is even beyond all this as only the Witness.

One who is eternally peaceful while living is a jnani. He is pure Brahman. The world has been created from your 'I am-ness'. This fact is known through the absence of thought. It is perfect. Keep silent. When the mind recognizes itself, you will come to know that it is the operational power of God. Do not be tempted by honors when people might take you as the Guru. If a so-called jnani underrates others, you will know that he lacks knowledge.

Nirupana 83
Sunday, December 24, 1978

In my (approach to) spirituality there is nothing to gain and nothing to lose; there is only to know. Benefits have no use, as you have no form. Throw away whatever you have understood. For knowledge of the Self, just keep silent and discriminate. You are not the body; you are not the consciousness. One who says, 'I am not the consciousness' must be you only. All we need to know is that consciousness comes with the body and in the end it forgets that 'it is'. There is no such thing as death. How can you be the transient consciousness?

Krishna says: 'I am the knowingness in all manifestations. I am everywhere. All the manifestations are My manifestations'. It is a river of consciousness. The sages talk about how the One who speaks *is*.

When you wake up in the morning, the holy sight of God comes to you unexpectedly. When you realize your manifestation, you will understand that what happens is so by the virtue of That only. Hold onto consciousness. There is no God other than that. The knowledge is of your Self. It is best received by listening. It is of the greatest importance. The Lord in you is trapped by concepts. He becomes free through listening. This removes all obstructions. One is bound by body-consciousness. Listening cuts off identification with the body.

Be convinced that the consciousness in you is the movement of the Guru. The sense 'I am' comes when you wake up. Consciousness arises. God manifests as your sense 'I am'. You have put Him in trouble by believing that He is the body. Your consciousness is your true nature. Surrender yourself to consciousness. (This is non-dual devotion. It is true meditation. Sit comfortably with eyes closed and without movement. Observe your beingness with a passive mind until you forget your body-consciousness.)

The myriad existences are nothing but the manifestation of your consciousness. You take yourself to be of the nature of the body. Is it the power of consciousness that makes you believe so? Maya and God exist together. They are not separate.

In yoga, they take prana to the cerebral cortex (by breathing exercises). However, the greatest yoga is the knowledge of the Self. The word of the Guru is the perfect manifestation of God. Only the enlightened one can talk about Self-realization. It is only possible when the Guru's words are followed: 'you are shapeless, formless, pure consciousness'. The five elements are clean and pure. Atman is a result of the unity of the five elements. Get merged into the blue shade of the Absolute. You can call it an idol or an ocean; whatever you choose it would be that. In samadhi there is no sense of bliss. The joy is felt after the samadhi ends. You should reach the point where the Guru-word is never forgotten.

Different foods, because of different qualities, have different effects on the mind. The aspirant is advised to take simple food in the initial stage. Ultimately, you should realize that your true nature is untouched by the quality of food.

The steady state is without birth. One who is born has movement. Go on remembering the Self, then all conflicts will vanish and result in silence. That is the greatest worship. No experience will stain you. All I see and sense is myself only. It is the knowledge 'I am'. The Self is beyond thought. The first dawning of wakefulness in the morning is without word. We are prior to any word. The power of prana is the primordial maya.

When one is diligent in following the Guru's words, all difficulties are resolved. Keep hold of the words 'I am pure Brahman'. With persistent devotion that will become Parabrahman.

Nirupana 84
Thursday, December 28, 1978

The root-maya is love herself. It is the love to 'be'. One wants his beingness to continue. It has been spontaneously created. The process goes on. The love is being created through love. The reason we are meeting each other is this love for the self. This entire crowd has come out of that love. The primordial maya is the ocean of love. All actions are based upon self-love. If you realize this love, your attachments for worldly things will come to an end. There will be no difference between you and the world. The world has been created within the light of your consciousness. You will not come across many people who will say this so openly. I do not call myself a yogi or a sage.

Therefore I can talk like this.

When you do not have Self-knowledge, you may go to the temple and worship. It becomes unnecessary when you know your Self. There should be no desires except for Self-knowledge. It takes strong dedication to achieve this. All desire for worldly learning will fade away. Then you will reach your true nature. One can get happily involved in what one likes. But this does not lead to the discovery of your true nature. If your attitude is fixed on external things, you will not have this knowledge.

Krishna says: 'Forgetting everything, you should just worship Me'. Be steady within your own Self. Presently, you are only listening. When you get the experience, you will know. Where there is devotion, there is love. Where there is love, there is devotion. As long as we take ourselves as the body, the difference like 'me and mine' will remain. I cognize that 'I am'. That is consciousness. Worship consciousness with non-dual devotion. It is cognized in the body and its movement is due to prana.

The ears do not listen. The one who listens through the ears is not a human being. Really speaking, that which is listening is of the nature of God. It is self-luminous. You believe otherwise because of the body. One should continuously hold onto consciousness. The light of the Self precedes other lights. It has no form, hence it is neither big nor small. Therefore it is all-pervading. This love is formless. It has no body.

So long as there is prana, the Self resides as the seer. It neither comes nor goes. You are in the body but you are not the body. You are pure consciousness, pure vital force. The world is only the light of consciousness. The original state is 'Oneness'. That only has to be properly understood. 'I am consciousness': this should be the conviction. All names are my names. The best devotee is unwavering in the conviction that he is not the body. All your needs will come to an end with Self-realization. Otherwise, you will not be satisfied even if you were the emperor of the whole universe.

Nirupana 85
Thursday, January 4, 1979

Observe how consciousness is working on its own. Do not interfere in its working with your intellect. Keep watching. You think you know, but you are not what you know. You are That to whom knowingness happens. That alone IS. It is the beingness. Whatever happens is to the beingness only. First there must be a conviction that you are not a human being.

There is no such thing as time. It is your concept of time. If this is understood, body-consciousness will not affect you.

Consciousness is the seed. It has sprouted and grown. It has become the world. In the beginning the devotee worships God. Later he lets Him go. Consciousness cannot be thrown away, nor can it be held onto. It is 'you'. If everything is your Self, what do you throw away and what do you keep? So who will hold onto whom? Parabrahman is beyond delusion. It is the secret among secrets. It is known through a thought-free state. If one thinks about Him, one gets wrapped up in concepts. One wants one's consciousness to be satisfied and happy. However, one's true nature is obscured due to body-consciousness. Perfection comes only with Self-realization. Body-consciousness brings death closer day by day. Human beings suffer from the false concept of birth and rebirth. Once Truth is understood, there is no need of concepts.

Atman resides in the body. He is beyond concepts. (Paramatman does not know whether He is or He is not.) A person has only to understand that he is not of the nature of a human being. He is only consciousness that lives in the body. The picture of the universe is painted out of the light of consciousness. It is our true nature. It does not need any rituals. We must behave in a dignified manner after knowing our worthiness. Actions, however carefully executed, are imperfect as long as they are based on body-consciousness. They are based upon the desire of having a better life. All that is, is the nature of the Atman in the body. It is beyond memory, beyond words. Forget that you are a human being. If you consider yourself a human being, all the laws of mankind will apply to you. Have the conviction that you are the perfect Atman.

Devotion is naturally there. It is original and self-luminous. It is consciousness. It is the love to be. Do not identify with the body. Do not say, 'I am like this', etc. It can never be compared to any objective knowledge. Hold onto the Guru-word. There is no need of light and darkness, wakefulness and sleep, accompanied

by thirst and hunger. This should be absolutely clear. You
have depended on these things since the concept arose in
your mind that 'I am a person'.

When there was nothing, the knower of the nothing
was Paramatman. He never had any desire. Why then is
there a need of something? Is it not for the protection
of the body? By all means protect the body. But it is a
great sin to consider yourself to be the body. That sin will
be washed out only if you believe you are not the body.
The knower is not created. The conviction that you have
no death is the experience of immortality. One who has
not cognized the Guru in the body will have a miserable
death. Conviction must come without uttering a word.
The time of death is the time of immortality for the one
who follows the word of the Guru. That occasion can
never be described in words.

Keep on with rituals that keep the mind of the
common man happy. Otherwise, they may excommunicate
you. Yet, do not allow the impression on the heart to be
effaced. Think of that aloneness without using a word.
The idea of body-consciousness is that 'one who is born
will go'. Even while fighting a war, Arjuna did not lose his
state of samadhi.

Remembering the mantra is necessary to destroy
wrong thinking in the mind. After impurity drops off,
consciousness will be clear like a jewel in the palm. After
dismissing all words, the true nature, which is formless and
nameless, will become silent. When the mind is purified,
consciousness is seen clearly. Consciousness means Sattva
guna, which is self-sensing.

The qualities that sport in the five elements flow as the mind through your pure consciousness. All human actions are through the five elements. Earth is the storehouse of the five elements and, hence, life sprouts from her. The essence of the earth is the subtle body, which is your sense 'I am'. Without food there is neither prana nor consciousness. Observe your body to see your true identity. The knower of the five elements is Paramatman. He is beyond the five elements. He is beyond thought. He has no needs.

When you see yourself as the supreme Self, the colossal creation with the five elements will reduce to the size an atom. Meditate on how you were before the body-form. As long as what you see and feel affects you, you have not achieved knowledge of the supreme Self. To be perfectly free means not to have any desire and expectation for one's betterment. The supreme Self is not the consciousness, but the knower of consciousness. One who understands this secret becomes the supreme Self. The body will fall. Then why lose our perfection by identifying with it? The tenure of life is limited. The season will end along with life. This experience will go. What is known must go. The knower cannot be known. 'You are not that' must be the conviction. Keep firmly in mind that what is forgotten is not you.

Nirupana 86
Sunday, January 7, 1979

If you feel you have understood what has been said here, what do you think about yourself? This body is made of the five elements. The word associated with the body is of the nature of space. If you understand this, your misery and happiness will come to an end. But every habit dies hard. The habit of body-consciousness is like that. Once it is given up, the work is done.

The picture appears and then disappears. Nothing lasts, hence it is called maya. Your consciousness is a flame that depends upon food. It is like burning incense that depends upon its ingredients. The incense gets extinguished after the ingredients are burnt out. The fire dies. Did it go to heaven or to hell? Your present condition is due to body-consciousness. This must be understood. Whatever comes to you is through the five elements, and it will merge into the five elements.

Can there be questions when one is beyond the body and the mind? Do the thoughts belong to you or to your mind? They are not 'your' thoughts. When you quarrel with somebody, is it not the mind that quarrels? If you do not identify with the quarrel of the mind, it means the quarrel never happened.

Brahman realizes Brahman. The human being cannot realize Brahman. When you become one with Brahman, you will not be able to talk. For its sake, at least some duality is required. This separateness is the mind and its modifications. A person caught in a whirlpool suffocates and drowns. One who dives to the bottom of the vortex gets out. We are caught in the whirlpool of the body-mind. Dive deep into the mind to get out of it.

All the metaphors and classifications are for convincing the mind. They belong to the five elements. Truth is beyond metaphors. First comes maya or the self-love. Out of this is created the world with its five elements. Then we can say, 'we are'. Truth is beyond. Consciousness is spontaneously created. It is not to be identified with a particular person. It needs support of the body. Consciousness is self-love. It is atomic and yet it becomes as large as the universe. The world arises with consciousness. A rare one thinks about how consciousness has arisen. A true devotee sees through his beingness.

As long as you have not become quiet, there is no experience of the mindless state. On realizing it, even a fool becomes a great sage and is worshipped by people. You become attached with the known and, hence, you do not notice the knower. He is beyond consciousness. He is revealed by the recitation of the Guru-mantra. When you realize consciousness, you will know that you are beyond it. Mind is maya and mind is thoughts. The *samsara* (daily duties and activities) that is so fearful for common people, serves the true devotee. Where there is consciousness, there is energy. It serves the seeker. The body is the food for consciousness. Make it happy with unwavering devotion and you will realize your true nature. Then there will be eternal peace.

Your worries harass you. If you want to end that, worship your consciousness. It sets at the same point where it arises. When you repeat 'Guru, Guru', the Guru-hood inside will be pleased and reveal itself.

Nirupana 87
Thursday, January 11, 1979

We are all born into the same species, but our characteristics at birth are different. It is because of the combination of the five elements. Therefore the style of language for each one is different. We suffer the programs of the five elements as destiny.

The goal for each one is the same, yet there are different opinions. In deep sleep we are all the same. As soon as we wake up the differentiation starts. The feeling 'I am' is the characteristic of consciousness. When the shape comes into being, the essence of the five elements is prepared in it. It means consciousness is generated. It becomes extinguished when the end comes. It is not our end. The jnani is separate from consciousness. You know a jnani by his name, his body and what he tells you. But to know him directly, you have to go beyond your consciousness. So long as the mind with its modifications keeps wandering, you are not ready for Self-realization.

To believe that the body is myself is ignorance. Our identity that we are without the body is boundless. Consciousness considers itself as the body. This is the sin. The body has prana and there is consciousness as a characteristic of prana. When prana leaves the body, consciousness disappears. The ignorant one says that a person is dead. The body is the food that supports prana and consciousness. Consciousness is the Guru. Prana implies the word, the speech. They depend upon each other. Together, they are called prakriti (creation) and Purusha (the observer) respectively. The Guru's word itself is prana. Consciousness is the Guru. Having understood this, how do you see yourself? You think you are the body, don't you? Your conduct is the result of the five elements. The behavior of the five elements is called your destiny.

Whatever happens is like a dream. There are desires until consciousness and prana are realized. Desire is the root of bondage. After realization, one goes beyond needs. Carry out your worldly dealings in the best possible manner. Serve your family members by treating them as God. Expect no benefit out of it. You have to realize prana and guna very clearly. Then you will immediately transcend consciousness with its qualities. You will be truly content. The greatest desire is the desire to live. Consciousness in the body is the king – the Self. The vital breath or prana is the servant. Practice makes anything possible. Make a habit of saying, 'I am not the body'. This will not happen suddenly.

Nirupana 88
Friday, January 26, 1979

In the incense stick there is fire, there is smoke and there is fragrance. It is the same with the body. The body is the stick, prana is the fire, and consciousness is the fragrance. Prana is the vibration of the essence of the body, which is the essence of food.

Because of body-consciousness, a wife requires a husband and vice-versa. The body is temporal. The knower is not. You may give them names like Purusha and prakriti. The goal is the same. It is the feeling 'I am'. What actions did you perform before you cognized your body or your mother? What conscious actions did you perform to become the way you are? What sort of sadhana are you going to perform? What is your personal identity? For which identity of yours should God offer His blessings? Is there a form that you can strictly call your own? You will go back the way you came. Remain as you are. Just observe what has been accumulated.

Does anyone lament over a clock that has stopped? It just means that time has stopped. Should the ending of this time make you miserable? When a person dies, time comes to an end. Should you grieve over this? What gives you beingness is with you right here. Then what is the use of wandering about? Is there a special place in the world where it can be found? Stop here and think about this.

Krishna says: 'With the rise of the feeling 'I am', I saw that I was all'. Without consciousness, there is nothing. An infinite number of universes dwell in consciousness.

However, even one cell of it is not true and eternal. By identifying with the body, do you expect to get the knowledge of Brahman? You quarrel with the words you hear. Your true body is the all-manifest subtle body of your microscopic consciousness. The world will cease to exist when your consciousness comes to an end.

To continuously observe this consciousness is to surrender to the Guru. It means to focus one's energy. To surrender to the Sadguru is to give up body-consciousness, to let go of individuality. Remembering our consciousness is meditation. It is the same as the feet of the Guru. It leads to Self-realization. That which realizes is the same as the holy feet of the Sadguru.

Atman is awareness, self-luminosity. The light appears and then disappears. Is there truly any birth or death? You say you know yourself. Is it not because you already know 'you are'? So think only of consciousness. Where you, yourself, have no existence, who can say that the world exists?

Do you know that your consciousness is continuously taking pictures through word, touch, form, taste and smell? It is automatic. You do not know how this happens, therefore you take false pride in your actions. Everything is happening spontaneously, so do not take any pride of doership.

Nirupana 89
Sunday, January 28, 1979

No knowledge in this world is honest, because it is ever-changing. The whole worldly experience is dishonest (transient). You may have taken yourself up as so-and-so, but that identity will not remain the same. I know myself through my Self only. That which is known is not honest (lasting). Even that, by virtue of which it is known, is not honest. You will understand this as time goes on. The knower was never born. God is created from the material of the devotee. How does He incarnate? He takes His form through the consciousness of the devotee. No one will tell you this. Do not get entangled in the modifications of your mind. Just be in the company of your consciousness, the feeling 'I am'. It has come over us unexpectedly. It nourishes your Self, as well as the world. Are you still wandering about after listening to this?

Once faith becomes firm with one-pointed conviction, then all miseries become tolerable. Consciousness in the body is the Guru. Non-dual devotion is very difficult for a common man. Hence, consciousness has to be worshipped as the Guru. No other Guru is necessary. It is of the nature of love. It has come without asking. First I know 'I am' and then everything else comes to be known. All dealings in the world are conducted for the love of the Self. To act and conduct worldly business is Rajo guna. To register it as done by 'me' is Tamo guna. The movement of the universal Self is playing as maya. The Guru is consciousness which has come to you unknowingly.

You have not cognized the Guru, so you love your body. His vital energy protects the body. It does everything for love of the Self. It is the source of the light. It is consciousness. Take it as the Guru and worship it. You will not be able to worship your Self because of your conditioning. Therefore, worship the Guru. Faith in your Self is the faith in Paramatman. That is non-duality.

It is only through practice that one can stay without the chattering of the mind. When a thing is seen, its photograph is taken automatically. That is the skill of maya. Pure consciousness is the passive witness. Everything is known to it. It is your Self-love. Worship that love as the Guru. Then the realization will sprout in you just as a bud sprouts and becomes a flower. You cannot follow the Guru-word because you are the slave of your mind. It is possible to be silent without words, slowly through practice. When the word becomes silent, it is the *Sahaja* (natural) samadhi.

Your nature is that of the Self in all beings. They are all your manifestations. At first the dream space emanates from you, then you move about in it as an individual. All this happens spontaneously. The Self of the universe is the 'I am-ness' or the state of wakefulness that has come over you. Worship the knowledge that listens to the word of the Guru and surrender to him.

Nirupana 90
Thursday, February 1, 1979

People repeat God's name in various ways, as they are taught. According to my experience if the mantra is recited with proper breathing, the mind becomes silent and samadhi ensues.

Even when Arjuna was fighting a war, his peace was not shaken. Without peace there is no samadhi. The peace that results from Self-realization is the real samadhi. The rest are mental constructs. Know that you are not the body or the mind or prana, and be quiet. Then the actions performed by the body-mind will not affect you. To whom has birth happened? To whom does old age come? Think about that. All good and bad habits come with the body, and go with the body. But you are not the body. As long as you take yourself as the body, there will be a sense of being a man or a woman with the accompanying pains and pleasures. All attributes depend upon body-consciousness. Our true nature has no attributes.

The ultimate Truth, Paramatman, has no caste or creed. The one who is the knower recognizes this and keeps silent. If I tell you to do some ritual you will do it, but it will not be of any use to you. Your miseries are because of your consciousness, not because of the world. Knowledge that can be spoken is of the nature of ignorance. Any action in the world is just entertainment. Unless you forget this entertainment, there will be no peace. The real jnani does not see the world as true at all. A jnani has no problem of whether to act or not to act. Hence, nothing can be said about his household. Just saying, 'I am not the body, I am not the mind', is not sufficient. It should be known whose attributes are the body and the mind. Only wordy knowledge will not do.

Consciousness in the body is the characteristic of the essence of food. It will last as long as the essence is there. All things are contained in consciousness. Prana and consciousness arise out of the food essence. How long will they last? Consciousness through which you experience the world is not everlasting. Actually, nothing is really created!

Break away from the concept that you are the doer, and then do what you please. As a diamond cuts diamond, similarly, one has to use consciousness to go beyond consciousness. No other instrument will serve the purpose. Hold on tightly to that through which you experience fear. (Consciousness creates duality, which causes fear. To get rid of duality, one has to be one with consciousness, resulting in Self-realization. Then who is there to experience fear?)

After listening to this, perhaps you will not see my face again. However, if it gives you realization, you will come running from afar and prostrate. You may wander all your life in search of Truth, but only your consciousness will liberate you. It will free you from all your needs. Afterwards, there will be no need for God.

You have to be free of consciousness. It is the primordial maya. It is not the permanent state. If one has the understanding of time, fear will go away permanently. To eradicate miseries, embrace That through which miseries are known. That through which you know everything is the feet of the Guru. Meditate on that. The three gunas are working, but you as an individual claim doership. This individuality must be dropped. You think you are acting, but it happens automatically. You will know that everything happens by itself. You do nothing. It only appears that way to you. What is not accomplished through meditation will be known through discrimination.

One who has created the body knows the remedy. What can doctors do? Without taking any support of the name or the form, just be one with your consciousness. In fact, nothing has happened and yet you see the world-phenomenon. It is a characteristic of your consciousness. Be aware of that.

Nirupana 91
Thursday, February 8, 1979

The nature of the Self cannot be thought of. We can never contemplate on ourselves. A simple remedy for this is to treat your consciousness as the Guru. It is pleased when it is worshipped this way. Convince yourself by saying that you are Brahman. Follow that as the Guru's word. There is nothing as perfect as Self-realization. There is nothing as imperfect as body-consciousness. The Guru's word is 'I am formless, sinless, pure consciousness'. A true devotee should never give importance to what people say. He should be firmly rooted in his Self-realization.

Nirupana 92
Sunday, February 11, 1979

You are prior to thought. How can thoughts arise if you are not there prior to them? You are prior to the wakefulness. It comes over you in the morning, works through the day and sleeps at night. One day that wakefulness will sleep forever.

My teaching is unique. It is of no use to the one who treats himself as the body. What you are listening to is the highest type of meditation.

What is the meaning of life? It has none. It is there without any reason. It is like urinating. Just witness. Even if life is understood as knowledge of the Self, the knowledge gained is untrue. There will not be a vestige of it left. As soon as prana leaves, you will be as if you never existed.

The Absolute is there forever. The knowledge 'I am' comes over the Absolute. It is the source of misery. This 'I am' itself is the knowledge. Your beingness is untrue. This is the essence of spirituality. Most people are interested in the affairs of others. No one thinks about himself. One is searching for God who is limitless. However, the seed of the world is contained in the tiny consciousness. No one thinks of that.

Consciousness is called chidakash (the space within). The knowledge of the world is not outside of consciousness. Sleep, trance, and death imply forgetting our consciousness. Death is dreaded. Forgetting is the nature of consciousness. The source of both the worlds of wakefulness and dream is your beingness. Yet your consciousness is seasonal. What is beyond it is true and eternal. Do not hurt anyone by your words. Do not slight anyone. When it is all untrue, what expectation can one have from it? Or for that matter, why should it be neglected?

Nirupana 93
Sunday, February 18, 1979

Because of the influence of maya one says, 'I am the body'. In fact there is no such thing as maya (it is illusory). It makes an individual take pride in the body. Both the body and its actions are transient. Because the mind takes responsibility, this worldly life has to be suffered. The company of the body and the mind was not there before, and will not be there in the future.

The body contains pure, self-luminous consciousness. It has no bondage. Under the influence of maya, consciousness has identified with the body. Prior to such a belief, it is formless, thought-free Absolute. After believing otherwise, whatever happens is delusive. Consciousness is the undifferentiated Absolute. A slight modification in it creates the world. The Self sees everything, senses everything; yet it cannot be seen or sensed. It knows the actions of the mind, but it is not the mind.

If there is conviction that you are not the body, you will understand that the whole world is motivated by your own knowingness. A concept arose in the Absolute and that is maya. If there is an experience of misery, there is also a need for happiness. With the conviction that you are not the body, there is no experience of misery or happiness. As long as the mind is there, the need is there. The Paramatman has no wants. When there is no experience of the mind, one is truly silent. Are people who take a vow of silence truly silent?

Remember in your heart that there is no other God except for your consciousness. Then externally, you may behave as you like.

Nirupana 94
Thursday, February 22, 1979

Consciousness is in bondage so long as it is identified with the body-mind and prana. When it realizes itself, it is no longer in bondage. The one who says, 'I am not the body, I am not the mind, I am not prana', is not bound by the same. One who knows prana feels very joyful at the time of death. Whatever is known goes away. The one to whom it is known neither comes nor goes.

One who understands this knows what 'birth' means. One who has rightfully discriminated the concept of birth does not suffer from it. Now tell me who is born, whether it is you or the desires? A jnani knows the answer. The jiva in bondage also knows this; yet he is caught up in the concept that he has to undergo more suffering. The jnani cannot be described through words. He is neither a man nor a woman. He has no form. The one who knows this cannot be comprehended.

The concepts of birth and rebirth are for ignorant people. Desire is of the nature of space. Then who is born? Prana comes from space, mind arises from prana, and you identify with the mind. When it is understood that 'I' am not an object, one knows that whatever is seen is not 'I'. Everything is in space. It will take the shape of concepts that you give to it.

The primordial maya is of the nature of space. Therefore what I tell you is all ignorance. You may still say that it is of the nature of true knowledge. (That means ultimately it is beyond words.)

During sleep there is no mind. There is only prana. When mind arises and becomes visible, you call it a dream. The mind can never say anything new or original. It can only repeat what it has learnt. You have put the noose of the mind around your neck. A jnani does not do that.

We have to find out who creates concepts. Give up all loose talk and chant 'Jai Guru, Jai Guru'. There is no knowing what He will grant you.

Nirupana 95
Thursday, March 1, 1979

As a matter of fact, prana is the upholder of the Sattva (beingness) quality. Food is necessary for our beingness to keep the flame going. The light of this flame is our consciousness.

In meditation, a point of Sattva becomes visible. Once it is seen, all sins come to an end. That is the sign of Self-realization. When it is seen, all the impurities (sins) are washed away. So long as there is the union of food, water and vital breath, you feel 'you are'. It will not do if one of them is missing. To understand all this, it is of no use just to have a philosopher as a Guru. It is necessary to have a Guru who understands the nature of the Self.

Mind cannot reach the Atman. Mind is limited to the body. Experience of the body and the mind arise simultaneously. The Atman reveals Itself when the body is forgotten. Man becomes free by removing body-consciousness.

Where the Sattva quality is impure, body-consciousness must be there. Body-consciousness goes when the Sattva is purified.

Nirupana 96
Sunday, March 4, 1979

Mind depends on thoughts. Consciousness is beyond thought. Consciousness arises out of ignorance (the primordial state – the Absolute). Ignorance becomes knowledge. When one leaves the body, the knowledge recedes into ignorance. One who recognizes this is a siddha. (Here, the word 'knowledge' means consciousness and the word 'ignorance' means the Absolute – prior to manifestation.)

Due to contact with maya, this delusion is called God. He too is maya. There is not an iota of truth in this world. Many people study yoga, which is the joining of knowledge and ignorance. In the end, all is ignorance. It has to be realized that consciousness itself is ignorance.

When there is no consciousness there is no time, and vice versa. What is the meaning of time? If there is no consciousness, can one recognize time?

You are the power that takes continuous photographs of the five elements. You do not make any effort there. Therefore there is no doer. You may say that you own nothing, but do you even own yourself? Knowledge is the source of ignorance, and vice versa. The recorded tape repeats itself. Does it have any intelligence? Exactly like that, the impressions that have been recorded in your consciousness since childhood do the talking. Is this understood? The tape and your consciousness are of the same category.

The fact that we remember ourselves is the main

ailment. It results in thought and carries out all mundane dealings. Time, maya and Brahman (the manifestation) are the same. Paramatman is not of the nature of consciousness. It is the perfect, pure vijnana, prior to consciousness. It is not born out of a womb. The experience of the imperfect state has needs like hunger, thirst, etc. That is how it is recognized. Enjoyments are there so long as there is maya of the form of consciousness.

Nirupana 97
Thursday, March 8, 1979

Jiva means consciousness. One is restless because one believes one is of the nature of the body. The body is a doll made up of food. The mind has taken to the belief that one is of the nature of the body. As a result, it has to suffer all kinds of miseries. Really speaking, the mind has no individual existence. By taking yourself as the body, you are retrograding yourself day by day. Even that deterioration is not real. All this is called maya. The fact that you experience fear should make you find out who you are in all this. There is no person in the body, as such. There is prana in it, there is consciousness in it. Your true nature is the Self, not the body.

The Guru is not an individual, he is the manifested all-pervading consciousness. Take up the identity as formless consciousness and carry on your activities. The reason why devotion to the Guru gives liberation is that one comes to know that he is free. The mind can never cognize the Self. When the mind steadily attempts to find the Self, it disappears in the process. Maya has compounded the body with consciousness. What is visible has form and color, but the seer has neither form nor color.

Why does memory fail in old age? It is because consciousness, one's quality of Sattva, starts dissolving. We must have the knowledge of what we were before we hear about how we are now. Our behavior is the result of characteristics of the essence of food. Please remember that the mind flows according to the quality of food. You have a great attachment to your consciousness. Worldly activities are carried out in order to tolerate our beingness. The one who has the conviction that he is the Atman will never feel anything, even if a thousand miseries are heaped upon him.

Nirupana 98
Sunday, March 11, 1979

The jnani knows what is eternal and what is not. It is to be understood by discrimination. What is understood by the mind has to be further discriminated. In this process one understands the gross body and the subtle body. The jnani thinks of the Sattva, the 'I am-ness' or consciousness with discrimination. He then becomes stabilized in his true nature. The gross body is made up of food. Consciousness flows from the essence of food and the feeling 'I am' arises from consciousness. It is the instrument for right discrimination. The jnani knows that it too is transient.

One who discriminates about time is not bound by time. He is the knower of time. He is prior to what he knows or senses. As long as you think that death is real, you have not come out of the cocoon of consciousness. The seeker has to convince himself first that he is not the body. Until then he cannot discriminate.

How can he, who is not the body, ever be stained? With body-consciousness, one suffers misery even if there is apparent happiness. Without body-consciousness, one is happy even in misery. He is liberated. Ego means identification with the body. As space does not go from here to there, the Self does not go places. It is everywhere. Where there is no discrimination, death is real. It is not real for a jnani. It is the ego that performs actions taking the body as its nature.

If a man is told that he will deliver a child in two days, he will not be affected (as he knows it is not possible). Similarly, one who knows that he is not the body is never afraid of death. Parabrahman neither comes nor goes. He is infinite. Brahman (with qualities) has to come and go through it all. The jnani discriminates as to what it is all about. His being in the body is incidental. As the Self, he pervades inside, outside, and everywhere. As an example, the vessels may be big or small but the space in them is the same. Think properly about this while prana is still in the body. As long as the body and prana are united, there is experience. A jnani knows that he is not what can be known. He is the knower. A jnani knows that. You are not consciousness, nor what is experienced through consciousness. Discriminate properly to understand this.

One who identifies with what the mind says is a sinner. He is in bondage. Parabrahman has no identity. He is beyond everything. The company of consciousness will end just as the sun sets, just as childhood ends. Observe consciousness. Worship it with love and give it the status of God. In the end you will be convinced that you are the Self. This only is the spiritual path, the ultimate Truth.

Nirupana 99
Sunday, March 18, 1979

You have accepted bondage of the body and, hence, you are bound by its actions. Paramatman is without bondage. You have accepted concepts since the birth of the body. You are holding onto these concepts very tightly. The original concept is 'I am' or 'I am awake'. Because of this concept there is a sense of time. Once the original concept 'I am' is proved to be untrue, you will realize that you are birthless and deathless. There are millions of incarnations of consciousness every moment (what we see, visualize and imagine are the incarnations of our consciousness). It is said that the thoughts at the last moment decide the future of the one who is dying. This is true for an ignorant person who believes he is the body.

What is a jiva? What is a person? It is the beingness. It is formless. Consciousness is born; it has the characteristic of matter. It is the essence of food. It is pure as such. Because of the body, it seems to be polluted. The simple meaning of Parabrahman is That which is beyond everything seen or felt. He is eternal and true. Is there any experience of His association? He is beyond space. He is changeless. Does one experience space in deep sleep? The one that changes is the one consumed by time. Whatever happens is due to the quality of consciousness. Paramatman cannot do good or bad. In my true nature, there is nothing that can be changed. Paramatman is neither knowingness, nor non-knowingness. He does not have an iota of information. One who practices devotion is of the eternal nature of Parabrahman.

If there is sunlight, there is no need to look for the sun. Sunlight is not separate from the sun. Similarly, everything comes into being from my consciousness. I, myself, am Parabrahman, the Perfect One. All things happen in the space of consciousness. Expectation, desire, fear, birth, death exist along with the mind. They arise with the sense 'I am'. It wants to continue. Consciousness creates the great sky that we see. The space of consciousness has come by itself. However, I am Parabrahman. I am complete.

You think about your body. Worship your consciousness. Imperfections abound when you worship the body. One who becomes one with his consciousness must get an experience of the all-witnessing state of being (the fourth state). The world and your consciousness are not separate. Your wakefulness and the nature of the world are the same. Remember well that the Atman, knowingness, and the world are one and the same. Ruminate on the fact that our consciousness is seen as the world.

Importance is given to the birth of the body you call yours. Does anyone have the courage to say, 'the whole world is my own form, my nature'? Due to the quality of Sattva (consciousness), wakefulness comes as 'I am'. Due to the fact that it is seen for a long time (one's life span), one gets intoxicated. Eventually, wakefulness becomes difficult to tolerate. To know the secret of consciousness, one has to become very familiar with it. Consciousness during dream and wakefulness is the same. It is a material process. After properly knowing all the three states i.e. wakefulness, dream and sleep, one who lives in the fourth state is pure Brahman. It takes total dedication to realize it.

Nirupana 100
Thursday, March 22, 1979

One who has the unshakable conviction that the Guru is the Paramatman realizes his eternal nature without any effort. Humility and surrender make you realize your inner nature. When your attention is diverted towards your true nature, the mind disappears. You may bow down, but remember that you are That which is prior to the act. Your sense 'I am' is prior to that. The sense of individuality will vanish; the pure sense of beingness will remain. You may be practicing devotion, but it should be directed to the One who is the knower of consciousness. When our mind disappears, while awake, the knower of consciousness is revealed. Thousands practice devotion. One who reaches the target has a single-pointed aim.

When there is no knower, how can knowingness work? You are consciousness. Its support is the Sadguru. He is prior to consciousness. He is all-pervading. Without Him, who will know consciousness? When body-consciousness goes, individuality goes. Under guidance of the Guru the devotee realizes that he is not the mind or the body. He is the knower of the body-mind. He attains Godhood. The Guru may worship like a common person, but he is free of delusion. He sees no difference between himself and God.

There is fear of death as long as there is the connection to the body-mind. There really is no death for you. Then why should there be any fear? The highest form of devotion is to remember what one hears from the Guru. One who loses the nature of his jiva gains the nature of Shiva. Even if he leads a worldly life, it is in his Guru's service.

It is a sickness to call your body as your Self. Your entire worldly life: children, wealth and desires are mere entertainment where there is nothing to gain and nothing to lose. If you are a true devotee, maya will take different forms and serve you. With devotion, doubts are eliminated. Without consciousness in it, is the body not a corpse? All the activity belongs to consciousness and not to Me (the knower).

The word is there because of the sense 'I am'. The tongue has a power to taste because of consciousness. Be a devotee of the nature of knowledge of the Self. What meditation are you going to do? The meditator and the One who is meditated upon are the same. Listen properly, keep it in mind and ruminate over it. Understand your attachment to worldly things.

Nirupana 101
Sunday, March 25, 1979

We are meeting here because of the blessings of the Sadguru. This cannot be understood with body-consciousness. To serve at the Guru's feet (one's own consciousness), the aspirant has to be holy and purified. One who lives in body-consciousness will not get to drink the nectar of the Guru's feet. (He will not realize his own consciousness.) The aspirant has no form. Yet, because of his light the world becomes visible. When you see a dream, which light do you see it by? The seeker's consciousness is the same as the holy feet of the Sadguru.

Your consciousness does not have a birth. Your existence as pure consciousness is the state of the Guru. When the disciple accepts it, he is born as God. Prior to that it is a birth of the body. When the Guru initiated you and told you, 'you are not the body', at that very moment you left off your human nature. Now, you will have no birth. Everything is known through your consciousness. It is the center of the universe. Without the Guru, consciousness cannot realize itself. If you have no time, remember the Guru-word at least while going to sleep. You should worship consciousness as the feet of the Guru. All things in the world are created for the love of the Self.

Nirupana 102
Wednesday, March 28, 1979
Gudi Padva, Maharashtra New Year's Day

We are aware today that 'we are', but what happens to that awareness in the future? Those who die while identifying themselves with the body have to take another birth (according to the scriptures). Whatever concept there is at the time of death, it happens accordingly. This is not the case for one who is enlightened. It is not my experience, so I do not talk of rebirth. One who has realized the totality does not have individual birth or death. As totality, the Atman does not have beingness. The beingness comes with the body, which is food. The cause of the existence of beingness is trivial. Yet it is responsible for rebirth. The jnani knows this.

One does not have the experience of one's own birth. If he speaks about another person's birth, will it be true? This knowledge is to explain how the bubble is formed. All other acquired knowledge is false.

Maya arises out of body-consciousness. The love 'I am' is the maya. Some people find it difficult to listen to this type of knowledge. It requires a great deal of inner strength.

Pure consciousness is everywhere. When it is not in the body, it has no knowledge of its existence. Can space have the experience of breathing? Words and their meanings create a variety of desires. Instead of looking outside if one looks within, one will be freed quickly. Do not ask others about it. One has to discriminate. When there is discrimination, there is detachment.

You work hard for a living. What is living? Is it not an attempt to continue the beingness? Why does man suffer so many hardships? Is it not to perpetuate his beingness?

Consciousness is unbearable. With that comes the fear of losing it. Therefore there is both misery and fear. All worldly things are created in order to make consciousness bearable. There is a need to have a husband, a wife, a child, food, etc. Hence, the love for our beingness itself is improper. The love for the self wants to continue. That is the great illusion – the love for the self has become the cause of creation of the universe. When life comes to an end, will we care about what happens to the world? If you feel the urge to understand this, you will definitely understand.

Basic spiritual knowledge is simple, but people unnecessarily get involved in painful rituals. When there is no beingness, the body is a mere corpse. Your true nature is beyond description. It cannot be known, yet it does exist. It is the Source of everything. Consciousness has appeared, and it will disappear. That is all. What else do you want to know?

If you stabilize yourself in your true nature, the basic needs will automatically be provided for you. You will have to make no effort for them. The Guru reveals to the disciple his own worthiness. He initiates the one who has surrendered. The meaning of the mantra is 'I am Atman, I am not the body'. This is like the name-giving ceremony for the newborn. Parents give birth to the body. The Sadguru gives birth to consciousness. He sows the great seed into the heart of the disciple. One who perceives the Guru-word becomes God.

Your tongue does not have a taste of its own. Hence, it can recognize other tastes. Similarly, consciousness is without concepts. It is simply an illumination. The only honest thing in the world is the Guru-word: 'I am Brahman'. There is something in the body by which you know 'you are'. This cannot be understood without the grace of the Guru. You strive to comfort the body. When you redirect your efforts to realize the Self, you will become immortal and imperishable.

Nirupana 103
Thursday, March 29, 1979

The nature of the Sadguru is eternal and infinite. Rama, Krishna, Hari, etc., are all His ornamental names (these names belong to consciousness in their body-forms).

When the concept of birth is proved to be untrue, everything that comes with it is also proved to be untrue. The Guru is Parabrahman. After understanding this, one holds onto it within himself and becomes of the nature of the Guru. Once the subtle body is effaced, there is no longer any concept of death. Then what remains is the birthless principle. Body-consciousness and the sense of doership vanish by the grace of the Guru. Once understood and imbibed, one never loses it.

The grace of the Sadguru means the manifestation of His consciousness. Consciousness has a sense of individuality because of the body. This sense goes away and what remains is the totality.

The nature of Brahman is consciousness. As long as there is a subtle body, there is ego. When that is wiped out, there is no birth. Body-consciousness is replaced by the universal Infinite. The state of Parabrahman and the grace of the Sadguru are one and the same. It means realizing one's own nature. You become That according to what you have heard. Then the grace of the Sadguru will descend. We are nothing else than the nature of the Sadguru. Consciousness in the body is moving about accepting various concepts in the world. One who has kept his attention on the word of the Sadguru will surely get His grace. The Sadguru's nature will become open and clear. You will know that you and the Guru are the same.

The experience of the world and the dream come through the body. What is there, after all, in the body? With that knowledge, one's subtle body drops off and what remains is true nature. Now the seeker has no individuality, no birth concept. One who has not realized this has to behave in accordance with the nature of time. The life-term from birth to death is a passing season; it is time. All your experiences depend on time. So understand this once and for all before your life comes to an end. The jnani takess the day as only a moment. All things are being done by the measurement of moments.

In what form do you want to preserve yourself? What you are now is only seasonal and, therefore, temporary. If you understand the nature of time, you will transcend time. All this will be clarified through the Guru-word.

The continuous whirring of consciousness is going on within you. Just observe it.

During the period of ignorance, liberation was necessary. After one gets knowledge of the Self, that liberation serves you. This is so as long as there is a slight trace of individuality. Individuality depends on time. The knower of time is the Sadguru. One who depends on time does not ever become free of worry. The knower of time does not need a term of life. Bliss means the realization of our timeless true nature. Your experience of time is between the dawn of consciousness and its setting.

The Sadguru is one's own true nature. What a person takes himself to be is of the nature of time. It is the sense of you and yours, and nothing else. And yet there is no such thing. Be very quiet. Do not take the trouble to acquire or renounce anything. Only the mind is born, not you.

Nirupana 104
Sunday, April 1, 1979

Ordinary people cannot get Self-realization. They see themselves as bodies. Unless body-consciousness is eradicated, Self-consciousness cannot arise. The fact is that impurity of the gross body cannot affect consciousness in the body. Yet the same consciousness is moving about in the form of the body. Whatever apparent happiness one enjoys also becomes the source of misery.

The Self identifies with the body and loses its perfection. So long as there is a concept of birth, there is misery. Consciousness is formless, pure and holy, but it is laden with the concepts of ego and birth. One who is disgusted with worldly affairs becomes detached. Because of body-identification, it has got mixed up with the five elements. The knowledge in the body is the holy sight of God. It is He who makes one understand that the idea of birth is false. He crushes the sense of individuality.

Consciousness is busy with many thoughts. With the Guru's guidance, you have to turn it back onto itself. One who understands that there is no difference between his consciousness and the Guru, becomes enlightened. When one believes that he is not the body, he gets the grace of the Guru. Consciousness is infinite and unlimited. Then how can it have death? By the Guru's grace, the birth of the body becomes the birth of Brahman. Then the seeker forgets that he is a particular individual.

Even when the jnani is all-pervading, he still has one desire. Knowledge should continue to progress.

He keeps looking out for someone worthy of receiving the knowledge and to pass it on. As such, all are devotees of God. Devotion to God is devotion to the Self. Everything is done to perpetuate the sense 'I am'. According to the Guru-word, if you worship the formless consciousness, you will be immortal and indestructible. You will understand that your true nature is Parabrahman.

Does the Self have needs such as food and wife and children, or are they for the devotee? The Self is mistaken for the form of the body. Those who have knowledge of the Self have pervaded the manifestation and transcended it. They are Parabrahman – beyond form and qualities. If you have realized the Self, rituals, religions, black or white magic, curses or ghosts, are of no consequence to you. Instead they turn back and strike those that direct them upon you. One who plays with a jnani brings misery to himself. If you believe the fortuneteller, you have not acquired knowledge of the Self.

In the dream, the world was seen. In the dream there also appeared your own body. The dream eventually ended and the world disappeared. Then what happened to the One who saw the dream? Did He see His corpse lying there? He never came and never left. Atman is not prana. Recognize this fact. It will not be enough if you just memorize it. What is there in the body due to which we know 'we are'?

You must practice devotion to the Guru (non-dual devotion). Be vigilant. Prepare yourself to see the bliss of the last moment. For others it is a dreadful event.

Nirupana 105
Thursday, April 5, 1979
Birthday of Lord Rama

When Rama was born, he had no knowledge of Parabrahman. His Guru Vashistha taught him that he was Parabrahman, without beginning and end, and he was not the body. You must cognize Rama's birth through direct devotion. Your beingness is the incarnation of Rama. All living beings have beingness. All worldly activities are for passing the time. They are of no use to you. The one who says, 'I am dying' is making a great mistake. The one who talks about Rama is your own consciousness. The one who realizes the birth of Rama is not stricken by death.

That which is prior to any memory, That which is Self-sensing, is the true nature of Sri Rama. Your feeling that 'you are' is the holy sight of Sri Rama. That due to which we know 'we are' is the yoga (union) of Sri Rama. Parabrahman had forgotten Himself, but by the grace of the Guru, He realized Himself. The holy feet of the Sadguru are the same as Sri Rama. Atman, the Self, is not pleased without contemplation and devotion to the Guru. Rama, whom Sri Vashistha taught, was the Rama whose physical presence was acting in the world. The one who made him cognize Parabrahman was his own Self. Your consciousness is the Guru's feet. Please remember this. If you are fearful, just repeat 'Guru, Guru'.

Prana provides consciousness with everything and nourishes it. Prana is Maruti (Hanuman, a devotee of Rama) and consciousness is Sri Rama. If you want to see

Rama, please your prana. For that, keep on repeating the mantra constantly. The source of mind is prana. The source of prana is consciousness. The fact that you know 'you are' is Rama Himself. Prana provides it with everything.

Your beingness has suddenly come to your awareness – that is the birth of Rama. For understanding this, discrimination is necessary. It might be that one is polluted by many sins. Even then, if one's faith in the Guru is strong and one has been initiated by the Guru, his sins are absolved and reduced to ashes. You must be anxious about contemplation of the Guru. To remember the birth of Rama, treat your consciousness as the holy Rama. There is no metaphor for the Guru because there is nothing that can be relatively compared to him. The cognition of Rama is the recognition of your pure consciousness. It is praised with an infinite number of names. They are the names of our own Self. This conviction is necessary. Parabrahman is absolutely open and clear. See that with determination.

If you have seen the state of deathlessness, you will always be at peace, even when others criticize you. Do not tell others but repeat mentally, 'Am I not Rama Himself?' You are experiencing this tape (of consciousness) for a few days. It will go away. Whether the body goes or stays, do not let go of the Guru's feet. There is no effort for that. A rare one gives his consciousness the status of the Guru. It is a great fortune. Keep yourself in awareness but not as the body, or as the mind. One who gets the Guru's grace requires nothing else to meditate upon. What is required is faith and trust. With that you become immortal. This will not be understood without devotion.

The Guru is prior to words. The one who speaks the word is prana. Without concepts, just see what you naturally are. Then all that you have believed so far will spontaneously go away.

Since birth, there have been desires. They are pacified only through knowledge of the Self. Those who prattle about Self-realization are making themselves cheap. Remember this well: going around naked is not detachment. It is detachment when one becomes aware of the fact that everything is transient and is going to perish.

Nirupana 106
Thursday, April 12, 1979
Maharaj's Birthday (Hindu calendar – Hanuman Jayanti)

When consciousness realizes consciousness, it is called Self-realization. Consciousness has no form, then how is one to recognize it? How does consciousness know itself? Consciousness identifies itself with the body, which has been changing since childhood. Consciousness is aware of itself, but it has not recognized itself. Consciousness should keep the body aside and look at itself for a moment, then its knowingness disappears. Consciousness forgets itself and samadhi ensues.

Consciousness is by nature universal. The body may pertain to a worm, but its consciousness contains the universe. This will be understood when consciousness realizes itself. All the names pertain to consciousness.

The worthiness of consciousness differs according to the different types of bodies.

You experience time. It means you are the witness of time. It also means you are not time. The luminous, all-powerful consciousness has taken itself up as the body. It has become weak. The body is only the food for consciousness. Consciousness is a non-doer. It only witnesses. It has taken up names like Brahma, Vishnu and Shiva. It has no birth or death. If there were birth and death, it would have told you stories of thousands of births. But does it remember even a single birth?

You cannot hold onto consciousness as it is free and all-pervading. Be true to your consciousness. In the beginning you may feel restless, but it will not fail you. Surrender to it, as it is God.

Our true nature does not know that 'it is'. Out of this, the feeling 'I am' developed, followed by the world. When one is in a state of everlasting Truth, one is beyond experiences. In this state nothing is known; we do not know ourselves.

In the state of ignorance, one gets involved in worldly activities. They will not last. You have nothing of your own that can be protected. What is the sum total of our spirituality? It is to find the truth and untruth about us. All that can be found is the untruth.

It is due to the quality of Sattva (the knowing faculty) that one experiences beingness. As sweetness manifests itself in sugar, like that the knowing faculty, Sattva, manifests as the mind. And you are not the mind. Consciousness may expand itself to any extent but it has to become unmanifest again. That is its true nature. You want your beingness. But how are you going to fulfill that need? That which is prior to knowingness knows that the quality of Sattva will not last. Then who will inherit what the knowingness does?

Nirupana 107
Thursday, May 3, 1979

Krishna says: 'That which is in the heart of a human being prior to any experience, is My true nature'. The world is known through it. The knowingness has been created unknowingly, as our consciousness has come over us unexpectedly.

Witness the consciousness. It is self-luminous. It is the seed of the world – the same as Hiranya Garbha – the golden womb mentioned in the scriptures. Everything is hidden in it. Krishna says: 'Jiva implies consciousness. The totality of consciousness is My true nature'. Focus your attention on That by which you know 'you are'. Whatever is, is consciousness. It has forgotten its true identity. Therefore it believes itself to be the small body. Do not ill-treat the body but observe consciousness that is in the body. 'That is the holy sight of Me, the supreme Self', so says Krishna. This is His true experience.

There are many Gurus in the world. A rare one tells you to pay attention to the consciousness in the human body. Meditate on your consciousness. Do not pay attention to things known through consciousness. Your in-built love for yourself is the highest devotion. Be devoted to the love ('I am') which is now listening. It will bring you contentment. The body is just a happening – a condition. The experience of immortality means there will never thereafter be the experience of death. Worship your consciousness as God. Rituals are only for passing the time.

Devotion of this kind is prescribed for steadying the consciousness. Do not entertain any idea of your gender, whether male or female. That is only an incidental condition, a temporary phase. The body may go on or come to an end, but you are the luminous consciousness. According to the Guru-word, one who merges with his true nature is a yogi. It means that consciousness has realized itself. Worship consciousness with consciousness. One who sees his consciousness as all-pervading, his every action is an offering to Brahman. The self-sensation 'I am awake' is the holy sight of God. Everything is seen through Him, but He is not seen. Who is He? He is your own pure consciousness. All the fourteen types of learning and the eight spiritual powers belong to Him. The body is the food for consciousness (God), it is not His nature.

You may be working, you may be young or old, but you never forget whether you are a woman or a man. The unbroken contemplation of one's own nature should be like that.

The devotee's consciousness is the same as the Lord's feet. By its virtue, the whole world moves. Krishna says: 'I am the consciousness in the heart of each human being. My incarnations mean the incarnations of consciousness'.

Nirupana 108
Sunday, May 13, 1979

As water is the support for moisture, so Shiva is the support of the jiva – the individual being. Shiva is consciousness. Because of delusion, your consciousness has identified with the body. Therefore you die in the end. I am not talking to the body, but to consciousness, which hears through the ears. Consciousness that goes about as the body, with its name, is called an aspirant; one who is desirous of liberation. Almost all devotees in the world are aspirants (*mumukshus*). The devotee who has given up bodily identification is called a seeker (*sadhaka*). Aspirants may be great scholars, but they are not seekers. Once convinced of his true nature, beyond any doubt, one becomes a siddha – the liberated one. An aspirant is male or female because of identification with the body. The seeker is neither male nor female. The listener is formless. That which acts and carries on worldly affairs has a form. But if the energy that is without body is not there, does the form have any value? The consciousness that listens is God. This fact should be imbibed thoroughly.

If you do not understand your worthiness, you will have a fear of death. You have given a life-sentence with hard labor to the One who is free by nature. The nature of the Self is consciousness – not that of a person. The jiva has a sense of duality – separateness. Just through concepts, visions arise without any substance. Whether there is form or formlessness, consciousness is infinite and unlimited. It is both manifest and unmanifest. Only to give it meaning, it is expressed in words in this way.

Unknowingly, you came to know 'you are'. This understanding has no form. Things are seen only when the mind gives them a shape. There is no difference between the speaker and the listener. The nature of mind-flow is according to the worthiness of one's form. For one who believes himself as formless, the mind will flow accordingly (he will be thought-free).

To carry out action is Rajo guna (the quality which makes a person restless and forces him to act). Tamo guna (ego) takes the credit of it and says, 'I did a good or bad thing'. Consciousness is pleased with its own quality (Sattva guna). All activities arise in the manifest. It is transient. There is no such evidence in the unmanifest.

Because of the vibrations of prana, the basic consciousness has become vast. It is transient, so it is called illusory. When it goes beyond consciousness, it becomes unmanifest even when there is a body. So how can there be death? It is like the heat, which is manifest and yet unmanifest. The heat in hot water disappears when cooled. In the same way, the knower of the Self disappears at the end. When prana leaves, so does the heat-fire. The jnani neither comes nor goes. He is, by nature, unmanifest. The thoughts of worldly affairs keep flowing in the mind of a householder. Similarly, the seeker always thinks of Self-realization. Make friends with your consciousness as if it is God. Worshipping it will make you happy.

Nirupana 109
Sunday, May 20, 1979

One says that he was not there prior to birth. Consciousness now says that it was not there. That is the puzzle. The one who *knows* he was not there, says it. Who was there as a Witness prior to consciousness?

Where there is no experience of the body, there is everlasting Truth. *It is.* One who experiences is transient. Have you understood your present identity? You worry for yourself, you look after yourself, you are anxious about yourself. Yet, do you know for whom it is? We do everything for the 'I' that we try to protect – what and who is that 'I'? You are worried. But for *whom* are you worried? This experience has come unexpectedly. Do you understand it? Consciousness is an illumination due to the experience of the Self. Please understand that the one who speaks is the knower of consciousness.

You consider yourself as the body, hence you believe in parents. But you are self-luminous; you have no parents. Your sense 'I am' that has the memory of meeting me is the Guru. Do not treat it as the body.

Whatever knowledge you are hearing is all a modification of the mind. It is a tool, a device. It is only an aid. The temples, devotion, etc., are devices, ways of thinking (aids to realization). In order to live happily, one should use such devices together with right discrimination. This is the meaning of spiritual science. Using such devices and rituals, one has to untangle the knot of maya. The cause of this is consciousness (as gunas). The body is a doll of food. The essence of the body is consciousness. It is created along with prana, which carries out all the worldly action. Consciousness stays as the witness. It is the knower. Yet, consciousness is of the category of maya. Because of consciousness, we know 'we are'. Due to maya, it considers itself as the body. This misidentification is removed by the grace of the Guru. The one who knows that consciousness was not originally there is eternal. Consciousness has no support, hence it takes itself as the body.

Maya is a covering that has come over the true nature of Paramatman, the Absolute. First comes consciousness and then the body is known through it. To feel that we are the body is maya. This itself is the delusion. The Absolute says (as if), 'I have been covered all over by maya and I do not know Myself'. This is the guna-maya (delusion due to consciousness). The Self has no wishes or desires. Under the influence of maya, the self says, 'I am sinful'. Most importantly, one must know that the body is not one's identity.

When there is no experience of the mind, consciousness becomes luminous. The One who is prior to consciousness observes this. The One who knows guna is prior to guna. Guna (consciousness) means maya. The knower has no connection with consciousness. When a person says, 'I am the doer', he is influenced by maya in the form of his consciousness. No desire in the world is satisfied completely. Because of guna-maya (manifested consciousness), our wants never end. When one understands maya, desires and expectations go away. What is the sign of Self-realization? There is no fear of death. To achieve this, one has to follow the Guru-word: 'I am formless, without body and of the nature of pure consciousness'. This cannot come through rituals. Such means are of the nature of maya. Hold onto the Guru-word, change your false understanding and the blessings you look for will come through.

Many highly learned people come to see me. They can recite all the scriptures from memory. However, they do not say a word. They wonder why they never get such an experience. Their capital is what they know after the rise of consciousness. They are knowledgeable about many things, but there is still something lacking. They do not know their own Self. They call themselves knowledgeable based upon the strength of the information they have gathered. Without the Guru's grace, the Self cannot be known. What has happened and due to what – the scholars do not undertake this search. (They do not inquire why they know 'they are'.)

So long as there is consciousness, there will be memories. But when consciousness itself is rooted in ignorance, is the world true or false? The ignorance was transformed into knowledge. Still is it not ignorance that is at the root?

The Sadguru is the Witness of both the manifest and the unmanifest. He is perfect Brahman. He is ever present. You will be perfect Brahman by following His word. Water, fire, air, space – do they ever die? They only appear and disappear – similarly, can there be any death for you?

All the worthiness, all the importance, is present in wakefulness. Once wakefulness turns into deep sleep, knowingness becomes zero. Jiva, jagat and Brahman are forms of your consciousness. Wakefulness and deep sleep are two stages. The jnani knows that one is converted into another. He is the Witness of the two stages.

Nirupana 110
Wednesday, May 30, 1979

The jnani cannot be recognized by bodily appearance. The image created by your intellect is absolutely of no use. The reason is that the Self is prior to the intellect. Then how can the intellect assess It? If you do not know yourself, then how can you ever know other people? Words have no impact on the jnani. Mind has all the experiences. Therefore the various states of being do not transcend the mind.

Can another person have a dream that is exactly like mine? Each one's experience is different. Does even the best of men enjoy his knowingness? Everyone is valued according to his body and his behavior. The dreams that people dream, can they ever be the same? Similarly, everyone's knowledge is different. The experience of beingness is the same, but can the behavior of the mind be the same in all?

I would prefer an atheist than a spiritual seeker who is unsteady. You may reject God claiming that you have no direct knowledge of Him. But do you not have the awareness that 'you are'? What about that?

The Self is of the nature of the Self. It cannot be

defined. It is not of the nature of the body. You take responsibility of all your actions because of your body-consciousness. First investigate as to how you came to know 'you are'. Nothing can be avoided; however, it can be understood. If it could have been avoided, one would not have taken the form of the body. When a concept arises, how to avoid it? Be free by saying to yourself, 'I am not the concept'. When the food is bad, does anyone need to be told that it should not be eaten?

The knower of the Self has got only one posture i.e. knowledge of the Self. The rest are traditional concepts. When and how did you get the thought that 'you are'? Follow this thought assiduously. In order to eradicate the concept 'I am the body', bring in the concept 'I am Brahman'. It is like cutting a diamond with a diamond.

Consciousness has to be realized. One has to understand who he is, what the world is, and where their joining point is. What does it mean when we get the information that 'we are'? It means we love ourselves and, hence, we are compelled to love others. If you have no need of yourself, there will be no need for others. The real meaning of 'I am That' is 'I am everything'. Do not dwell on the memory of others. It is the source of bondage. You worry with the memory of your children, etc., but when they were not there, did you have their memory? As relations grow, misery also increases. Therefore you are miserable due to the memory of your bonds with others. You are a jiva because of your attachments.

Shiva is manifest and all-pervading. He dwells even in insects. You are bothered by the memory of 'me and mine'. If your prana leaves you just now, what connection shall you have with these memories? Why shouldn't we be as we are after prana leaves us, this very moment? Why should we go on worrying unnecessarily? There are infinite number of memories. Which of them shall I hold onto and experience misery with? After death, all relations come to an end. Then why not experience the same condition right now?

You believe you have parents, but they are not separate from you. What they call *chit-ananda* – 'bliss of consciousness' – is only an entertainment for humoring the Self. I have no memories. I have roasted myself without fire and have eaten myself up.

Nirupana 111
Thursday, May 31, 1979

Krishna says: 'I reside in the hearts of all beings, but I am especially manifest in the heart of a human being. I am directly present there. Bhagavan means the Luminous One. Therefore consciousness, which is also luminous, is My manifestation. The love, which has come without asking, is also My manifestation. One who realizes it becomes like Me. I am the beingness in all living things. My manifestation means My own true nature. A particle of gold and a heap of gold, both are gold. My special manifestation is the consciousness in humans and the one who realizes it becomes Me. Then he understands what this movable and immovable world is, through his own consciousness. I am prior to intellect and those who are trying to search for Me through intellect will not find Me'.

One that is prior to memory cannot be remembered. Nirguna is prior to consciousness. That which acts is the mind. When the sages talk, it is the knowledge of their minds. Consciousness cannot be shown, but it acts through the mind. The body is the food for beingness as consciousness.

As there is warmth in hot water, so is the Atman in the body. When hot water cools, does it mean that warmth is dead? Did it get extinguished? After prana leaves, its characteristic disappears. That which never came, never went away. Consciousness is knowledge. The knower of consciousness is called Parabrahman. He is beyond self-sensation. It is because of the memory of your relations that you have forgotten your true nature.

The One without a second became aware of His beingness and that gave rise to so many bodies. Which particular body should He accept as His own? Is any single body comparable to Him? People give great importance to Self-realization, but Paramatman is beyond it. One who is proud of his realization has not yet ripened. Nothing can be done; just observe. Actions bring misery because one accepts doership. God nourishes us all, but not through intellect. Just see. His five limbs: earth, water, air, fire (heat or luster) and space have no need of any intellect. The sixth is consciousness. It also has no need of intellect. The jnani may appear to be a doer, but that does not affect his bliss.

Do not do anything. Understand what you have heard and then give that up also. Do not take yourself as someone special. If you realize your consciousness, you will not be affected by your thoughts. Then the body may behave in any way it pleases.

There is none other than God, so whom does He oblige? Is He not experiencing only Himself? Once you reach the point prior to consciousness, you become all. Remember this simple thing. Consciousness is the thief. The same is God. It is the donor and also the beggar. It came unasked for. When God showers his Grace upon you, is it for Him or for you? If you are not, is God there? Means or methods will never help achieve Parabrahman, the Absolute.

Nirupana 112
Sunday, June 3, 1979

Millions of gods have come and gone. You are the root of them all. You want to go beyond, but you are at the root. Be one with It. You know the word, and not the other way around. So why do you want to be free of the word? (You already are beyond words.)

When there is no sense of 'I am', is there any God? He is the luminous form of my consciousness. You will only behave according to your likes and dislikes. After leaving this place, if you go on ruminating over what you have heard here, your likes and dislikes will vanish. So long as I am drinking the juice of the body, the breath continues. You worry for yourself, but before your parents saw you, who gave you air, water and food? Who made the body grow? The body is the food for consciousness.

Spiritual rituals are given as a punishment of hard labor.

There are no intentions in the mind of a jnani. We say that you must get knowledge. Then what should happen to you? Just know that animals, birds, insects, have all been created out of you. If you understand this, then is there a need to love the whole world? (Maharaj says, 'you are the world'.)

That which was not known has become known. The root duality is that you sensed your own beingness. Are you free from your desire to live? That is the real bondage. The very experience of your beingness is untrue.

You say the words, you hear them and you give a

meaning to them. The word and its meaning may be called the jiva. The knower of them is called Shiva. Jiva and Shiva are the names of one and the same entity. As Shiva, it is pure knowingness. Prana is energy. When that power leaves the body, Shiva does not complain.

Jiva and Shiva are names. Jiva and Shiva are due to Shiva alone. The true nature is prior to names. Shiva has no identity other than your pure consciousness. He has no sense of 'I-am-ness'. To have relationships is the sign of being in the jiva state. Shiva is prior to understanding. Before knowing, one says, 'I am the body'. After knowing, you will know that as many millions of bodies as there are, they are all yours. The one who is listening has no bondage. Recognize it. No need to try and free it.

Nirupana 113
Thursday, June 7, 1979

Sat-chit-ananda is experienced when there is consciousness. The bliss is felt by consciousness. It is qualitative and, hence, it is not the eternal Truth. One talks about Parabrahman, but the Absolute does not know Itself. For the sake of Parabrahman, you have to sacrifice Brahman, the manifest. Is time known through consciousness or is consciousness known through time? As long as there is consciousness, there is time. There is nothing outside the Brahma-randhra in the crown of your head. Whatever is seen and sensed exists in that aperture.

The name (mantra) given by the Guru is proof in itself of the Guru's word. The name given by parents is a proof of death. How do you get Self-realization? Do we make an effort for waking up? The one who follows the Guru's word does not have to make special effort. One who has accepted the Guru's word will not be controlled by time. Jiva means consciousness, whereas the Atman exists in the Sattva quality but is not affected by the quality. Because of Sattva, all our experiences are coming to us. They say prana left the body, but Atman neither comes nor goes. It is not bound by prana. The knowledge of the Self must be known by the Self.

There is no greater devotion than devotion to the Guru (non-dual devotion). It transcends the Vedas. There should be the conviction that the Guru's word itself is 'I'. When you go about as a body, it is like stirring up the reflection of something in the water. Use the body but do not allow body-consciousness to stick to you.

Nirupana 114
Thursday, June 14, 1979

Rarely does anyone deliberate on why consciousness has been created in us. One amongst a million might ponder on it. Consciousness means our sense of 'I am'. Only a rare one holds onto consciousness as taught by the Guru. During the practice of meditation, many experiences come. Seekers get stuck when they get spiritual powers and people honor them. Only the one who continuously discriminates is able to progress.

As a spark is emitted from an electrical short circuit, similarly, consciousness has also come out of a short circuit. We have heard words like jiva, Paramatman, etc., but what was there before these words were heard? How was the listening created and from what? Do we have any identity apart from consciousness? The period for which consciousness remains is called the span of life. The one who becomes one with his true nature is a jnani. He observes how consciousness has come over his true nature. He is One without a second. He is not his knowledge, 'I am'. He is the knower of the source of consciousness. It would seem that the jnani also goes about doing worldly activities just as anyone else. But he is completely free within. He knows that no quality of any of the five elements can be used to describe his true nature.

Everything is created out of nothingness. There is no creator. Everything is happening spontaneously. There is no design with which to identify a jnani. Through meditation, merge consciousness into consciousness. The Guru-word is your true identity. You are pure consciousness. Everyone knows this truth. Yet one identifies with the body. When the essence of food dries up, consciousness disappears. Go to the subtle. Unless you realize the subtle, you will not realize the gross.

When prana leaves the body, consciousness disappears. It does not die. When consciousness (guna) forgets itself, it is called nirguna. What you have heard and believed to be true has to be suffered or enjoyed. Therefore believe everything as untrue. The knower, in spite of having consciousness, having a body and a view of the world, is still nirguna – without quality. The reason is that He is the knower of all of these. The whole world got created in the void of the subtle consciousness. Then it was felt that we are in the world and the misery started. But when this 'I am-ness' goes, we are free. It is all enacted in the cerebral aperture. One feels one is awake in that aperture, and the vast world is created. When there is a change in that aperture, the world also changes. Therefore give up body-consciousness, your ego. The attachment to the body is the impediment.

The root of the five elements is atomic consciousness. The whole world is contained in it. How can the jnani take the world to be true? The ignorant one believes it to be true, therefore he experiences misery. One who identifies with the body is the sufferer and the enjoyer, not the jnani. Recognize the Truth. Leave aside all concepts. Recognize the creation of your consciousness. One who recognizes it goes beyond birth and death. He never comes or goes.

It takes time to accomplish good work. Bad work can be performed immediately. Good work brings well-being.

Nirupana 115
Thursday, June 28, 1979

It is not possible to keep your identity permanently. What is your true situation? Before all this became visible, you were in existence and will always be so. However, the identity taken up by you that 'I am so-and-so' will pass away. All your associations will not remain with you. You did not have any experience of the two states of wakefulness and sleep before. Now you are experiencing yourself and the world during these two states. When these states were not present, the five elements (the visible universe) were not there. You did not have knowledge of your beingness. Then what was there? There was only perfection without any need of your beingness.

Wakefulness itself is the universe. Sleep gives rest. That means there is comfort and rest for the being. Any state of being is transient and, therefore, imperfect. The whole experience is imperfect. Yet you stick to it. You have no experience of wakefulness in your sleep. There is no experience of sleep during wakefulness. The dream experience is in between. The experience of beingness is only in these stages. The seer who knows that all experience is untrue is immortal. When you were without the two stages of wakefulness and sleep, did you ever feel the need of your beingness?

The phenomenal world spread out of the primordial illusion, 'mul-maya'. No one created it. It has no creator nor destroyer. Only wakefulness has come over you. Our consciousness automatically takes the form of the universe. Where is the seed of the universe? The feeling that 'I am awake', accompanied with the expectation to continue, is the seed. This itself is the dream. One sees the dream world, but how many recognize the seer?

You have constant worry and fear. The beingness has come over you without your asking. When it vanishes, where does the world go? When awake, wakefulness is infinite; in sleep it rests in the seer. It does not go anywhere. The two stages (sleep and wakefulness) were not there, so how can they die?

With good fortune, one meets a 'Perfect Man' and he clears your vision. With his blessing one may get the experience of immortality. Those who practice devotion to the Guru (non-dual devotion) become immortal. Presently, the beingness has no peace. Deep sleep is the only experience of peace. Wakefulness and sleep are a puzzle through which you realize your Self. But you have no connection with this puzzle. You go about with a name and a body-form, and say that you are alive. You earn and accumulate – only to die in the end. There is the illusion of grief, misery and fear. But you have accepted it as true! The scriptures say that you had an infinite number of deaths and births. These are only concepts. Have you had an experience of at least a single birth? When will you ever realize this mistake? Only when you live with the conviction that 'I am the self-luminous consciousness', as the Guru has unequivocally stated.

With the Guru's word you will see that you are immortal. Then you will understand that you are a distant seer of sleep and wakefulness. You have taken up the false appearance as true, hence you have to take birth again and again. This is what the scriptures say. That is the cause of suffering. Meditate on the Guru that is within. Then He will show you what is death and what is deathlessness. Whatever appears and is sensed is unreal. The entire five elemental world is unreal. One says for the sake of saying it that someone is realized and the other is not. One has to understand this. Do not curtail your worldly activities as a sign of detachment. If there is a perfect Self in this world, then see for yourself and recognize that it is You – your own Self.

Nirupana 116
Sunday, July 1, 1979

Why is this word Atman mentioned at all? Prana carries out all actions. Even samadhi is of the nature of prana. Atman is simply the onlooker. Atman or Self-knowledge means consciousness. It has no bondage. The only bondage is that our minds identify us with the body. When prana is separated from the body, consciousness vanishes but it does not die. This is death from the point of view of the ignorant. For the jnani, it is nothing.

The world is in your mind. 'We are not the body' means we are not the food; the food for prana. Consciousness is generated from the essence of food and the universe is created from consciousness. The action goes on. It is false when viewed as maya, yet it is true when viewed as

Brahman. Both are superimpositions on consciousness. All your dealings are done on the strength of the word. The first word was taught by the mother. All worldly experience has a limited duration. After life ends, is there any consciousness? Remain silent without uttering a single word. It may seem impossible, but make it possible.

One who transcends beingness is in a state of indescribable bliss. Maya goes about in many uniforms but not a single one is true.

Do not believe in any god or deity except your own consciousness. Though in the beginning, an aspirant may need to do this. The meaning of words lasts so long as the words last. Once the words go, the meaning also goes. When you achieve samadhi, you will know the secret of maya. The fear of death remains because we believe ourselves to be within the world. The fact is the opposite; the world is projected through us. Man's consciousness is vaster than the world. Maya is a tragic comedy. All these are concepts of consciousness. The knowledge 'I am' is proof of the Absolute. One who realizes it becomes one with the whole world. Perfect happiness is not possible at the level of consciousness. All this is imperfect. You have to know what is imperfect in order to get perfect bliss. It cannot be witnessed. When your time is coming to an end, do not forget to see how maya is ending. Then your true, eternal nature will be revealed.

Nirupana 117
Thursday, July 5, 1979

You want a lot of things but with what identity that you can call your own? Your present identity is of the nature of food. The body is the food for your consciousness. It is because of your consciousness that you experience the vast world. How long will it be with you? Why do you have it now, and why was it not there before? You achieve a lot of things because of the body. However, the body will not last.

It is a fact that you are going to die. Then what use is there of the world, the transient mundane household life, God and religion to you? People do all sorts of things to make the consciousness bearable. Yet, whatever is going to happen will happen. People feel that difficulties could be avoided if you perform penance or chant God's name. The only benefit is that the fear becomes less. Why are you anxious? It is to endure consciousness. If we keep ourselves occupied, we can bear with ourselves. When we are tired, we fall asleep. The fact that you know 'you are' is your consciousness. Because of it, you can know. You may call consciousness as Guru or God. Meditate on it and leave the rest aside. Do not ever equate consciousness with the body.

You do not get privacy because you are busy during the day, but who sleeps at night? Is it not your consciousness? Then at that time, at least, meditate on it. Your thoughts at the time of going to sleep continue to work. It is like when a seed is covered, it sprouts and becomes a tree. Surrender to your consciousness. Keep up the vow of surrender to the Guru's word.

On my path of spirituality, effort is of no use. Consciousness has arisen spontaneously. It is self-luminous. If you try to remedy it, it will only get worse. Whatever effort you do is through your identification with the body. What do you do with That which cognizes the body?

Does the faith that 'you are' come before or after you believe it to be so? Consciousness is prior to everything. Worship this fact. Was consciousness brought from somewhere else? It is self-luminous. You depend upon your intellect only. Do not get caught up in the cage of your intellect.

The easy remedy is to continue saying, 'Jai Guru, Jai Guru' (Glory to the Guru) without words until you sleep. Then it will continue during sleep. If you become a real devotee, you will transform from devotee to God. Saint Tukaram says, "I do not want the Atman. It is better that you are God and I am the devotee." But he said that after Self-realization.

A rare one takes himself up as consciousness. The rest worship it as Brahman or God. As long as memories are playing havoc, how can there be Self-realization? Someday you will realize your Self. Then you will understand that the world is a play of consciousness. The Self is your formless, blissful and true nature. It is neither male nor female. Body-consciousness is denial of the Self. Is not consciousness prior to words?

Forget the mind, think of the Self. When there is a meaning to the word, the mind is present. But if there is no meaning to the word, then where is the mind?

If the mantra 'Jai Guru' is constantly on, the devotee is happier than when he is asleep. Then there will be success in everything. If someone achieves Self-realization, then wherever he is will be a holy place.

Even for gods a human body is rarely available. Who has created this beautiful world? Is it not consciousness in the human body? Do as much worldly activities as you like but do not betray the faith in your Self.

After Self-realization it becomes clear that one is without any birth. The stars have an effect on the human body. As soon as the entity that is born from the parents gets separated, a picture of the sky gets stored inside the entity. The one who has taken birth has no intellect, yet an image of the parents is already captured. Whatever is recorded in that first picture is the destiny. After that it may be a boy or a girl. There are so many discoveries in the world, but no one knows how the images were taken in consciousness. Then the act of continuous recording of the word, touch, form, taste and smell continues. This fact is not easily noticed, but those who know its secret transcend birth.

All those who are worshipped as incarnations of God had a Guru. No one has become a mahatma without a Guru. He is convinced that he is the same as the Guru-word. It will happen only if consciousness gets inspired and has the desire, is it not? That is why I do not insist on anything for anybody. When it arises from within, after hearing it, one gets the worthiness of the One without birth. Will you say with confidence that you were never born?

The sight of the seer is not a physical sight. The whole creation is in his sight, but he is beyond the creation. Out of delusion, he believes that he is in the creation. The dream arises out of you, yet you say that you were going about in a dream. The influence of maya is such that a man desires to achieve perfect well-being, and yet he believes that he was born.

Consciousness is created out of Sattva and is of the nature of Sattva (vital life force). But the jnani realizes that he is not the Sattva. Out of millions, a rare one is not affected by all the action that happens in the world. Please be respectful to these words that you are listening to. It is your good fortune. Then your present will be happy. It will serve you and lead you to the Supreme.

Nirupana 118
Monday, July 9, 1979
Guru Purnima

Guru Purnima is believed to be the day of achieving perfection of one's own true nature. After Self-realization, the devotional activities continue indirectly. The Sadguru cannot be cognized through consciousness. The Sadguru cannot be known. With sincere faith, one holds onto the Guru-word and consciousness becomes free. Consciousness cannot describe the Sadguru. The Sadguru is eternal, perfect and free from desire. One should contemplate on Him.

In what do you keep faith as you deal with the world?

Is it not in your consciousness? Yet it is not everlasting. What is understood by your mind is unreliable. The Sadguru cannot be comprehended by you, yet He will grant you the treasure of His true and eternal nature as it is. One who is beyond description, beyond quality, is the Sadguru. The rest who just talk are not of the nature of the Sadguru. Recognize what is untrue. In this untruth, you will not find your true nature. Keep meditating. To understand what is the consciousness that meditates, and how it has become luminous, you have to hold onto the Guru-word. The idea of death will be destroyed only through Nirvikalpa samadhi (without any mental construct). It cannot be done through concepts. Be loyal to the faith in yourself. There should be no anxiety such as 'what will happen to me?' The whole world has arisen spontaneously. Go to the Source from where it has arisen. To understand this, devotion to the Guru without any duality is necessary.

Nirupana 119
Thursday, July 12, 1979

You can easily get wrapped up in rituals. That is bondage. What is your greatest concern? Is it not your body? So long as you make spiritual effort with body-consciousness, you will not get peace. You cannot put on an act for Truth.

There is no God other than That by virtue of which you know 'you are'. But even this will not give you lasting peace. When you understand its Source, you will become an ocean of peace. You do not have a shape or form. When you become convinced of this, you will become formless. When thoughts disappear, pure consciousness remains. Then right thinking arises in pure consciousness. Through right discrimination, concepts are destroyed.

You have to meditate on your consciousness without punishing the body and the mind. From the meditation, various discriminatory thoughts arise.

There is not a single thought without ego in it. By creating a thought to understand another thought, purify your selfish intellect. Where there is ego, there is bondage. Consciousness is pure love. Continue chanting 'Jai Guru, Jai Guru', even if it is done silently. By doing this we awaken ourselves. Guru means consciousness. To remember the Guru is a sign of great fortune. Your consciousness is the all-pervading Guru. The guna (consciousness) does so many things, but after Self-realization it becomes without quality (unmanifest). Consciousness becomes pure and holy by chanting

'Jai Guru'. Then it becomes without quality.

Krishna did a lot of dealings in the world, but no quality ever touched Him. While dealing with life's affairs, who can claim to be quality-less? (Only a jnani can.) All chaos is due to a concept ('I am the body'). The affairs of the world are going on by the strength of a concept. Do not renounce anything. You have only to understand.

Rajo guna will not work without expecting the fruit of action. What is painful? Is it your desire to continue your beingness? Rajo guna is involved with identification with the memories.

Consciousness, the knowledge 'I am', is the vision of *Narayana* – God. In Narayana, there is both male as well as female. Pure consciousness is called Narayana. Beings do not know it, hence they suffer misery. Those who have recognized that consciousness is without quality (guna) get tired of staying on in the world. They go to a lonely place like the Himalayas. The universal consciousness is very vast, but it is unmanifest by nature.

You should be close to the Guru so that you feel that your consciousness and the Guru's manifestation as 'I am' are the same. Is any action possible without prana? Is the One who knows prana affected by it? Simply remember that your form is like space.

Nirupana 120
Thursday, July 19, 1979

Our behavior through body-consciousness is like the condition of a patient in a hospital. During sickness one feels the need for oneself. So long as there is sickness, one has to look after oneself very carefully. (Sickness means our beingness.) You might not understand this, but it is important to understand the same.

Identification with the body is like a sickness. Therefore it needs to be taken care of throughout the day. Why? It is because we do not want to lose ourselves. Consciousness is doing all this to protect itself. Yet it eventually has to go. You look after yourself so that this experience of sickness should not pass away. Since the experience itself is that of sickness, it will come to an end. The Absolute is the true state and it cannot be known. The known cannot affect the unknown.

Why do we do japa and meditation? Is it not in order to protect the consciousness? However, this quality itself is of material origin (it is created through the essence of the body, essence of food). Because of body-consciousness it has expectations, desires and passions.

The parents are dead. What use are they now? Then what is the use of even the knowledge that they are gone? Like that, the jnani has also no use of his Self-realization. With such discrimination, one goes beyond consciousness.

Every being is protecting that which can never be protected in spite of all efforts. All that is desirous of protection will not last. What will you call Him in whose association nothing remains? He cannot be given any description at all. How many loaves of bread of the knowledge of spirituality can one bake after all? Can the Self be identified with any characteristics? You aspire to get physical and spiritual well-being through your body-consciousness. But the body is not your true nature. The One that makes the body function has never been seen dying by anyone. Body-consciousness takes all the responsibility and pride. As a result, it becomes a source of misery.

The One who is forever awake is the Sadguru. He gives you wakefulness. Take that wakefulness and be awakened. Then you will get the true nature of the Sadguru. One who follows the Guru-word does not have to make much effort. Atman means 'I am – I exist'. When prana separates from the body, the Atman vanishes. Where there is consciousness, there is also time.

There is no other. Whatever is, is you alone. Yet you create duality and expect well-being with the support of that duality.

Nirupana 121
Thursday, July 26, 1979

Millions of Krishnas and Ramas have come and gone. Has any one of them made any change in the nature of consciousness? Consciousness is a quality that arises with the combination of the essence of the five elements and prana. It is said that some people can recall up to 10 or 12 past lives. But why do you not understand that all the births have come out of your consciousness? You say you have had many births but why and how were you accused of your first birth? When you were not aware of any individuality, did you remember yourself? In order that the manifest should appear, support of an object (matter) is necessary. How is the manifestation of an individual made up? Who was there prior to manifestation and where does he want to go by making some effort? After listening to this, you will understand that your consciousness is the quality of the vital life force; it is not you. Only see how consciousness has come over you. Leave off the rest. All complications have started with consciousness.

That which has to experience consciousness has no name or form. Hence, It has identified Itself with the body. Consciousness depends upon food. You have to find out the ultimate meaning of spirituality. You have to see how the knowingness of your consciousness has arisen. Why does the jnani become free? Because he has understood how consciousness arises and undergoes dissolution. You meditate, but what do you have in your meditation except your body? If you give up your body-consciousness, then what will you identify with?

How and through what has the birth taken place? You are the quality of the essence of the body. Then how will you go to heaven? Until you get the full understanding, observe how consciousness has arisen. In this five-elemental vision, have you got a particular identity? When this becomes clear to you, you will understand that you yourself are moving in the form of the whole world. That child of a cowherd (Krishna) said: 'I am All'.

Q. Maharaj, it is said that Parabrahman has no movement. Then why does He create consciousness and through it the rest of the world?

A. This is all your concept. Parabrahman does nothing.

Q. Maharaj, how long will it take for us to get our realization?

A. Until such time when your concepts come to an end.

Wakefulness is the primordial illusion, the root-maya. God is also born of maya. All this trouble is due to consciousness. There is deep peace at the bottom of consciousness. There are millions of states of the mind. Pay attention only to the Source. Once the marriage (union) has been celebrated, you can do what you like. Does anyone need to be taught further? Like that, find out how and why consciousness has arisen. Then you will solve the riddle. If there is no memory, there is no question of forgetting anything. Therefore, there is neither memory nor forgetting – neither exists. There is no jnani of the Self; there is only Self-realization.

Your bondage consists of your concept. Therefore, liberation from the concept is required. There is no source for any experience. Everything is perfect and filled to the brim, which means there is nothing. This is the realization of the jnani. The Absolute has no sight of its own.

Nirupana 122
Thursday, August 2, 1979

What is thought? It is something that is sensed and can be acted upon. The Sadguru is beyond thought. He is the eternal-Absolute. Body-consciousness has concepts like big and small. The devotional songs we sing are not dedicated to any outside entity. They are for the Self, our true nature.

A man's behavior depends upon the faith he has accepted. The word of the Sadguru is as easy as it is difficult. The problem is that you cannot analyze the meaning of it by comparing it to something. The true nature of the Sadguru has no beginning, middle, or end. His existence is true and everlasting. It cannot be experienced through practice.

The body is the root cause of everything. People practice devotion because they want comforts. It is not because they want God. The nature of Brahman is such that it cannot create any obstacles in anyone's path. Hence, you get it if you wish for it. When you become like the meaning of the Guru-mantra, you will know what the

Guru is. No one can achieve perfect yoga (union) through body-consciousness. Nobody creates obstacles in others' paths. Everyone creates an obstacle for himself through his own concepts.

First there is consciousness. Then comes the sound followed by the word (manifestation). That union is called Brahman. It means our sense of 'I am'. Every human being behaves according to the meanings of words. This is called the mind. Because of your mind and words, you say, 'There is Brahman'. When consciousness is stabilized at the Source, the word dissolves. Consciousness is prior to what is seen and felt.

Consciousness in the body is the characteristic of Sattva (vital life force). The body may be male or female, but prana and consciousness are neither male nor female. The jnani has no death. Time has an end, not the jnani. When prana goes, consciousness disappears. So, who comes and who goes?

You practice, but do you become like the word of the Guru? Your faith depends on identification with your body and the mind. They may call him a sage who claims, 'Today I am going, or I shall leave (die) after ten days'. But where is he going? To say such a thing is also ignorance. Only an ignorant one projects a future in his mind. The jnani has no future; he is neither the body, nor prana or consciousness; he has no enlightenment. I have no name, no form, no color, and no design. This is the result of the grace of the Sadguru.

Nirupana 123
Sunday, August 5, 1979

That which knows is formless. It is simply the knowingness. Having no form, It performs no actions. It is the seer. It sees everything. If one is convinced of this, there will no longer be any desire.

You see the sky. It has limits. However, you are unlimited. You must be convinced of this. So long as you consider yourself as a visible form, you will have to face death. You wander all over the world because you consider yourself to be a visible form. Until this ends, there will be no peace for you. If you like to listen to this, pay attention. By listening to this, the visible form will disappear. *You* will not disappear. Do not try to search for the nature of Truth (your Self) – only be aware of the fact that you are taking the untruth as truth.

It is a fact that ultimately consciousness is of no use to you. In the company of the Sadguru it gets purified. When that happens, people will come for your darshan. Even if you know that you are not consciousness, people will still come for the holy sight of your consciousness. You may become extremely learned, yet your body-consciousness does not go. It *must* go. The house is mine, but I am not the house. Similarly, consciousness is mine but I am not consciousness. Each visible form has a time limit. You say it died. As long as you use that word 'I', body-consciousness has not left you.

Maya is the combination of name, form and consciousness. But you are the knower of these. The knower is there, but he has no sense of being a knower. Find out what that means. One who has knowingness also has an end. One is called the knower because One cognizes the knowingness. He is not known to consciousness. He feels 'He is', but He is not that feeling. He is the knower of That.

A mother feels sad when she sees the pain of her child. She understands the pain of the child, but she is not the child. Similarly, the knower is unmoved. He is not the vital energy, hence he cannot interfere with consciousness. You want knowledge that would fit into your consciousness, but consciousness is the essence of the five elements. Knowledge does not remain when consciousness goes. You say the knower does not remain, but who is the Witness of that? You say that nothing remains after consciousness leaves, then who is asking the question? If you deny all this, what will you gain? The fear of death will still be there.

You go on living, accepting a personality – ego – 'I am this', 'I am like that'. Without that you are not comfortable. It is very rare that someone lives without an ego. When you are nothing, you will still be able to say, 'I am Brahman'. When I say, 'I am the knower', it is only for your understanding. Consciousness is the root-maya. She is the mother of the world. She stays with the knower as his shadow.

Once one gives up body-consciousness, who is the husband and how is he related to the wife? Consciousness is very cunning. There is no telling what it will do and how it will act. But with a jnani it is like his shadow. Wakefulness, sleep, pain and pleasure are due to consciousness. The one who has realized that he is not consciousness, can pain and pleasure affect him? I have nothing to do with consciousness itself, then what can be said about the things known through it? If I accuse someone of being a fool, it is accusing my own consciousness, as there is only one consciousness.

By listening to this, you are going to be empty. If you want to keep your consciousness intact, do not come here. Is that not bondage? That which sees the body is within the body. It is consciousness. The knower does not take any visible thing to be true. The world is known through ignorance. Nobody understands this fact. The birthplace of consciousness is ignorance. First ignorance got created. It was confined for nine months. Then it came into the world. When ignorance goes, knowingness disappears. (The ignorance implies unmanifest.)

Only through meditation will you realize how exactly you are. When consciousness becomes pure ignorance, it is called samadhi. Even great sages have not thought about the one who was closed in for nine months. Who sees? Consciousness sees, but its behavior depends on the vital life force. That which takes the picture as true is also the ignorance (the ultimate Source).

Guru is the most important word of all words. He is not an individual – a personality. That through which the manifestation has arisen is the Guru. In the beginning, take yourself as 'I am not the body, but I am consciousness in the body'. It is difficult to stay like that. Therefore they identify it as Rama or Krishna or Brahman. The best way to worship consciousness is by treating it as the Guru. That is how it is pleased. Then devotion and the devotee become one, and his knowledge becomes of the nature of God. Consciousness is the knowingness. One who is the knower of consciousness does not have a sense of being the knower. Consciousness is many-faced. It has been created. Its Source is ignorance. One who has recognized this has no sense of being the knower. Everyone is convinced that whatever he knows is quite correct. How peculiar it is!

In prison for nine months, along with ignorance, were also created wakefulness and sleep, as well as thirst and hunger. Consciousness in the body is the main hindrance. To tolerate it, one has to do so many things. In order to understand it, devotion to the Sadguru is necessary.

The world is created through pure ignorance. The feeling 'I am' is also untrue. Because of it, you suffer. This knowledge is actually easy and open, therefore there are not many takers for it. People are attracted to what is difficult and complicated.

As a deer has a fragrant substance in the navel, similarly, you recognize a fragrance within your heart. Consciousness in the body is the essence of food. It is the fragrance. That fragrance starts diminishing if the movement of prana starts fading by reason of absence of food and water.

Pay attention to the listener. Whose information is he listening to? Then the Sadguru's grace will descend upon you.

Nirupana 124
Thursday, August 9, 1979

Chit means consciousness. It is known to us and that is the chidananda – the joy of knowingness. Does the joy come from outside or is it there spontaneously? Then why are we looking for it out there? The source behind all this is our consciousness. It is perfect and has no beginning. It has come unasked for. You are listening to this as if it is someone else's information. But I tell you that it is your own information, and that means my information as well.

Q. Maharaj, does consciousness have a beginning? If it is there then does consciousness know it?

A. When you are stabilized in consciousness, you will come to know this.

There is only the One without a second, then how can It get realization? (The word Self-realization is also incorrect.) Our consciousness needs a means of entertainment, otherwise it is unbearable. When can it be bearable? It is when you perfectly realize the same. Get merged into your consciousness. Then you will understand how it rises and how it dissolves, and you will be at peace.

The root of the mind is prana. The source of beingness is also prana. How can you go beyond the mind? You believe yourself to be the body, therefore you wish to go here and there. The Absolute is prior to everything. Consciousness is within the Absolute and everything is contained in consciousness. It is a big mistake to think that one has to go beyond something.

The body is food, which is perishable. One likes the love (consciousness) in the body. Therefore it is chidananda – the joy of consciousness. Yet it is perishable. The Absolute that is the prior-most is called Parabrahman. Consciousness is called Brahman. It encompasses everything. While you live, what do you live as? And with which identity are you going die? Our nature is in the form of chidananda. It is not something that comes through effort. It is the spontaneous bliss.

What is it that gives worthiness and beauty to the body? It is consciousness. If it were not there, the body will decay! What is the important factor? You are alive because of the essence of the body. You have been created out of that essence. Have you come from heaven? What do you wish to gain by practicing spirituality? That which is the root of all, is true and everlasting. If you have realized this fact, then what is the need for spiritual practice? Is it not entertainment? You learn arts and sciences, that is also entertainment. What is your motive for coming here? Is it not to understand that all this is 'I'? (Non-duality).

You ask questions due to the influence of body-consciousness. Otherwise, what is the necessity for talking? Your every word is a means of passing the time. The words are means of entertainment, but they can also bring us trouble. There is no danger to the One who is prior to the word. You might say, 'Then what is the use of listening to this?' That which expects benefits is short-lived. Anything you honestly believe in will not remain with you forever. If someone lives longer than others, what special benefit does he derive? That which is created out of the essence of food and which lives on food, how lasting can it be? Understand all this and love all.

Do not think that such talks encourage you to give up your worldly life. Just remember that nothing of this will last. Male or female is the name of the shape made of food. Hence, it is false to say that one is a woman or a man. Listen to this and keep it in mind. Understand that the one that comprehends will also not last.

Whatever is happening spontaneously is all right, as it *should* happen. Out of mercy, if you interfere in the situation it will be troublesome. If you increase the life span of people, the population will grow limitlessly and food will become scarce. Does mercy make anyone happy? Suppose you show mercy to someone and make him a king, does he really become happy? How much fear does the king have? The greater the prominence, the more trouble it brings. Hence, Saint Tukaram wished to be the smallest of small. Some devotee may ask for the ultimate poverty of Parabrahman – the Absolute. It has nothing; yet there is no one as full and prosperous as the Absolute.

With the grace of the Guru, name and form are transcended. The Sadguru means the Absolute. People name it such. However, at the level of the Absolute, there is no such concept. What will happen to the self which you protect so carefully? It will surely go away. Therefore, love each other sincerely. After Self-realization, the five elements and three gunas become quiet and the mind retires. The support of all things is Parabrahman. Yet He does not do anything. The universe was created and dissolved thousands of times. The Absolute had no part in it.

The negation of consciousness is vijnana – where jnana and *ajnana* (ignorance) both disappear. In every word in Guru Ramdas's writings (Dasabodh), there is the affirmation of Brahman, and in every word there is also the negation of Brahman. Nourishment and rituals are there only when there is consciousness. If one makes efforts for the well-being of consciousness, taking it to be the form of the body, it is in vain. The beingness has to become non-beingness in the end. There can be no witnessing of what does not move. Witnessing can be done only of that which moves.

Your consciousness has come uninvited. You feel you are awake as you sense light and space with the other four elements. There is no creator of the universe. Only some wakefulness has come over you. That is all.

Space means time, and time signifies the life span. This cannot be understood merely by listening. We know that 'we are'; was any effort required for that? Think very deeply about the state of wakefulness. Whatever is seen or felt is due to that. Find out what it is and you will be free from the trouble of birth and death. There is no such thing as liberation. You felt that 'you are'. Did you do anything for it? No. This is because it is self-luminous. You cannot recognize your wakefulness without the grace of the Sadguru. It comes to the one who is searching for it.

You may enjoy great pleasures, but only for a while. Afterwards, what remains out of that joy? You may do japa and penance, but what makes you free of all experiences is your consciousness. When meditating on the idol, you project your consciousness on it indirectly. Then the image of the idol descends into the one who meditates. Then it takes the form of the deity. It is created in the consciousness. One has a vision. The Source of consciousness has to be found. It must be known while there is a body and prana. In order to understand consciousness, devotion to the Guru is required.

How much does a man have to do for satisfying his thirst? What is born is wakefulness, sleep, hunger, thirst; not the Atman. Nothing is true. From beginning to end it is all a play. Discriminate. Do not fall into delusion. You are true, eternal, and beyond all states of being.

Nirupana 125
Sunday, August 12, 1979

When witnessing of consciousness happens for all twenty-four hours, one is called a jnani. He is not visible. He is unknown and unmanifested. The unknown cannot be understood by the known. When the known (consciousness) becomes unknown, the ignorant says it is death. Time is created along with the known. It is the life span.

The known can be described in infinite ways. The knower cannot be described in words.

When someone says that he knows the Truth, it means he does not know it. The Truth is silent. How can one know That which is prior to wakefulness and sleep?

Being born implies wakefulness and sleep. What you are experiencing presently is consciousness that has come over you. Is it dark or fair? Is it male or female? How can it be stopped? How can you catch it knowingly when it has come over you unknowingly? All the names of beings – right from insects up to the highest deities – are the names of consciousness.

From consciousness, the five elements, three gunas, etc., are created. When consciousness goes, everything goes. Nobody dies. You may say that witnessing happens to the knower, but He does not say it! It is said that consciousness has arisen out of the body and prana, but this is not completely true. They were formed after consciousness arose. If there is no consciousness, what can be said? All experience that comes through consciousness is temporary. Truth cannot be realized through consciousness. Consciousness is only momentary. Yet it may experience a life of thousands of years. A little knowingness has come and it exists for some time and goes away. That duration is called time. It is neither male nor female, nor Brahman – it is nothing. But, because there is consciousness, all this is.

Why are people going from place to place (searching)? Because they cannot bear the bite of consciousness. It is compared to the bite of a scorpion. In order to negate all the experiences, just observe the consciousness.

Where is the Truth? It's all in a manner of speaking. You may say that someone is a great sage. I would say that he is much greater than what you understand him to be. This is because I know that he was never born. All this has come to be created just as entertainment. It has no rules. After listening to this you will say, 'We went about all over this vast world, but we have never met a fool like him!' But no one will give me a status which is between a fool and a realized person.

From the moment of waking up until sleep comes, there is continuous self-awareness. But is one aware of this fact? Because you have taken yourself as the body, you are not aware of consciousness.

There are so many religions. Even if people lose their lives, they will not accept anyone else's religion. The basis of it is loyalty to a concept. Consensus means identification with concepts. But are wakefulness, sleep, hunger and thirst different for different religions?

The mother and father created the body of the child and gave the body a name. You should understand your true nature and give it whatever name you choose. Jiva means consciousness; the name given to consciousness because of its worthiness is God.

The body is an idol of accumulated food. The mind is the same as the qualities and characteristics of the food. Consciousness within the body is unbroken like space.

'Atman should be in communion with Atman' means one should watch consciousness with consciousness. Only the needy will have a rebirth – not the one who is satisfied. A body can be called a human body, but not consciousness in the body. When one understands and recognizes the consciousness as consciousness, one becomes liberated while still in the body. Atman is the non-doer; prana does all the work under Its presence.

One should observe what it is that gives experience and who it is that gets experience.

All sufferings come to an end to the one who has forgotten himself by observing his consciousness. One becomes holy with the holy sight of his own true nature. He naturally becomes helpful to others. He knows that he is no different from others. The holy sight of the Self is the manifestation of the Self. Who will have ill will and for whom? One who is the devotee of his own Self becomes the soul of all. Live as consciousness. Do not look at others as individuals. With whatever worthiness you look at your Self, will be your true worthiness. Look at others with the worthiness of the Self.

One who comes here, has come here because he was inspired by the inner God. Only the one whose birth is the last one comes here (no rebirth for him). Look at all beings as if they are your own Self. Do not accept the concept that there is some deity other than the Self. Leave aside your beggarliness and worship your true nature by saying, 'I am Atman'.

Nirupana 126
Saturday, August 18, 1979

When one contemplates on Parabrahman, one merges into his blissful true nature. Before he reaches the Absolute, there is bliss. When he reaches that point all feelings get dissolved. The attainment of the Absolute is perfect bliss. It cannot even be described as a state of bliss.

Q. Maharaj, is there a way to reach Parabrahman?
A. Yes. With complete love, become one with your consciousness.

I do not talk in the traditional language. I only ask you to observe yourself. Being human indicates having a body. It is not the form of the Self. When you sit alone and observe your consciousness, you will come to know that consciousness is the world. It is the feeling 'I am'. For one who knows that, his form is the universe. However, you identify yourself only as one limited to the body. The universe has blossomed in your consciousness. You know your consciousness, but you have taken it up as something different from you. Therefore you have not achieved Self-realization.

You must see what the relationship is between you and the world. So long as you have the concept that you are an individual, you will not get perfect bliss. You are not created by anyone. You have no parents. You are self-luminous. The entire panorama, which is the cosmos, is your own visible form. Concepts like

'I will die', 'I practiced devotion', 'I am going to heaven', etc., are all false concepts. How can one whose form consists of the universe have parents? Your very life is keeping the cosmos alive. You have no responsibilities either as an individual or as the totality. You mistake your ego as your Self. That is the reason for delusion. You create responsibility with your own concept. Actually, you have no responsibility. Your body-consciousness creates the sense of responsibility. One who has realized himself need not come here. People should go to him!

Concept is like an ornament. The one who wears the ornament is not the ornament. The feeling 'I am' is root duality. The correct state is prior to that. Consciousness is a quality. Does the One who knows consciousness have quality? You speak words like Brahman, God, etc., but what meaning do you draw from them? Your words may mislead you. Mere intellectual understanding is not enough.

Just listen. If you take yourself as a jnani, you will definitely suffer. Do not take any stance.

Nirupana 127
Thursday, August 23, 1979

Birth implies the states of wakefulness and sleep. They are states of being. Am I these states? Is the Atman born? One who understands this is without birth. The universal phenomenon is full of life, but nothing is everlasting. When one dies, the body decays into countless organisms. How many lives are created out of one life? That shows that life is continuous. How long is the Atman (consciousness) there? So long as the vital force is there, the Atman is there. The name given by the word to the word, vanishes along with the word. You dwell on what others say. Do you think about your Self? You cannot *think* about your true nature. How to search for consciousness? Is it not the medium through which the search is made? Consciousness cannot search for itself because it is ever-present.

Poets and writers write intellectually about the joy of consciousness. The universal consciousness sprouts within your heart. The knower of that is Parabrahman, but He has no knowingness. All this is the sport of self-luminous consciousness. It has come unasked for. It is neither male nor female. They are concepts. The world lives in a nest of words. Is there no attachment, greed, or love at all? Yes they are there, but all are untrue – just an appearance. They are true only for that moment. They are thoughts hanging in the sky. They act through the vital force of beings created from earth. They are not *your* thoughts. Where science ends, spiritual meaning – the deepest meaning of what IS – begins. Words coming out of consciousness may seem to contradict each other. Feel free to still ask questions, otherwise there is no dialog. How will you recognize the enlightened person? He has no form. Even the word of a baby in the cradle achieves some mission, then why not the word of a sage? But what is there ultimately? Void? No, not even that.

Where there is no delusion of beingness or non-beingness, there is Parabrahman – the Absolute. It is not a void. It is beyond qualities. *Brahmananda* – the bliss of being Brahman (the manifest) – is also temporary. We give so much importance to the world. It is for our own beingness. Things you like in your ignorance will be disliked by you after Self-realization.

Truth must be properly understood. Whatever is done through the mind becomes untrue. The knower of the mind here, is called discrimination. The concept that the mind takes care of our affairs is wrong. The beingness is prior to the mind. The mind has separated itself from its true nature. Is pain known through the mind, or is mind itself the pain? There is no pain when the mind is dissolved. So long as you understand the mind as a form of the body, it is misery.

You worry whether you can function without the mind. Until you were three years old, did the mind give you the sense of having a form? Did you have an experience of the mind during the nine months inside the womb? Who nourished you there? One who has recognized the mind is not concerned about how to deal with the world without the mind. The mind has great importance because you have not gone beyond it. When you become the knower of the mind through discrimination, you will understand this. Where there is mind, there is a lot of misery and occasionally a little pleasure. Sorrow does not require a major cause. A little sorrow can last a lifetime!

The mind must be controlled with right discrimination. When you recognize that you are not even the vital force in the body, you will be deathless. It is possible only when you meet the Sadguru and hold onto His words. The names of Brahman are innumerable. You are Brahman! Just take the word of the Guru.

Where you are, God is. The universe is His visible form. Where there is God, there is the Self. Where there is no Atman, there is no Brahman, maya, jiva, or God. There is nothing. Your 'livingness' is without name or form. But the impressions collected by the mind take it as the body. Your consciousness is the experience of the existence of God. You are first and then comes God. The word 'God' has no individual form. The whole universe is God. You may have a long life. At the end of that tenure, absolutely nothing will remain. If you live for a hundred and twenty-five years, you may suffer the misery of a year-old infant! Without knowing, you will wet and dirty the bed! Would you not become the subject of ridicule? The whole world was saluting you, but now how terrible is your worn out condition! They will all praise you in high terms – but only if your life term is limited! If this is the situation, then how should we die?

Maya means something that never really happens. It is a delusion of existence, but not true existence.

This is the story of the mind. Where there is no mind, there are no needs. So long as you think that you are the doer, the mind will not spare you.

Consciousness is not limited to an individual. It is the knowingness, which is the totality of manifestation. Does the 'I' in the body have any shape? When did you first feel that 'you are'? Will you learn that by reading books? What is our true nature? Is it the feeling 'I am' or is it prior to 'I am'? The knower is beyond knowingness. If you listen to this and imbibe it, you will get your perfection that is already there.

Nirupana 128
Thursday, August 30, 1979

The jnani has consciousness, but it is not of an individual nature. It is universal. You may give a name to what is all-pervading, but actually it has no name. The unmanifest principle became manifest as your consciousness. Whether you practice spirituality or not, it makes no difference to the Absolute. You have created a sense of duality by separating yourself from the totality.

What is seen, felt, or known has been created through consciousness. It is created from the knower. Once the universal consciousness is realized, there is no need of liberation. From the point of view of a jnani, no one is ignorant. He is not separate from the totality.

Whatever name you take, you will be that. The universal consciousness can never be caught. The names of the various deities are the names of the all-manifest, universal consciousness. What is the indication that someone is a jnani? Each one recognizes the jnani according to the worthiness of his mind, intellect and feeling. Scientists will discover what is created out of what already exists, but they can never invent That which is spontaneously there without having been created. They may have discovered many things but they will not be able to discover consciousness. If they realize consciousness, at that very moment they will lose their hopes, desires and passions, and they will do nothing. They will have no expectation at all for themselves. All this knowledge is quite ancient. You are just learning about it, therefore you feel it is new.

Someday you are going to die, are you not? Then why do you not finish it right now? Only then will you know the Truth. (Here, Maharaj is not asking us to die physically. He is asking us to get rid of the attachment to the world and remain in a thought-free state.)

One understands love or kindness particularly when he begets offspring. Then such feelings come spontaneously. It is the same with Self-realization. It will free you when you realize that you understand nothing. But if you feel that you have understood, it is only an itch. One who gets Self-realization has no use for himself. Words cannot describe that unmanifest stage. Scientists may create beings, but they will not be able to conceptualize the Atman.

When the concept 'I am the body' goes, the ego also goes. Then whatever remains is pure consciousness. You have your knowingness with you; you cannot stop it or throw it away. One who has devotion to the Guru will soon get liberation. Everyone has a strong desire to live. When one discovers his own nature the desire goes away. You cannot pass a single moment without thinking. It is the nature of the mind. Therefore think of your existence without the body. So long as the form is there, the ego is there.

Continue with daily bhajans because the meaning of those bhajans will manifest through you. Bhajans remove the impurities in one's own nature, transforming the impurity into Brahman. Those who are realized remain in its worthiness, but the ensuing devotion uplifts people. When you sing bhajans, say every word. Each word has its own importance. The whole meaning of bhajans descends into your true nature.

Each being has got a destiny. From where has it arisen? From thereon, you have buried yourself in relationship with others. It is dependent upon prana. Think of how honest this prana is. Without taking any support from anywhere, dwell upon your determination for realization of the Self.

Nirupana 129
Sunday, September 9, 1979

The experience of the world has come to you uninvited. Our speech happens in the consciousness. The knower is beyond it. He is beyond the individual consciousness. The world is in space, but *you* are prior to space. The source of your existence is the essence of food, without your knowing it. (As pure consciousness, you are the characteristic of the vital life force of the body, which is nourished by the food.) You will enjoy hearing this (type of talk), only if you have gained worthiness from the past. Otherwise, you will go mad. It could cause fear because it will kill your individuality. It is a sign of good fortune if you like to hear such talk.

A tree is also Brahman. It has no speech. It has consciousness but it has no sense of individuality (body-consciousness).

Brahman is acting through all the five elements. You are aware of this due to your sense 'I am'. Therefore meditate only on your consciousness. It is universal. Who witnesses it? Consciousness means love. Love means expectation. The knower looks with the help of consciousness. Witnessing by consciousness contains expectation. It is the very nature of consciousness. (Without consciousness, the knower cannot be mentioned. Once consciousness arises, it wants to continue. That is its nature.)

I will never feel angry at what you tell me, because I know (though you do not) that it is a tape recorder talking. Does it have any intelligence? That tape is the root-maya. I do not take part in its function. There is a sense of individuality in your consciousness. My consciousness is all-pervading. The three worlds are contained in it.

Consciousness is the essence of the five elements. First the food is absorbed, then consciousness arises. It is of the nature of love. It is the need to be and all that is required to fulfill the need. It is like the taste of sweetness. What happens to consciousness in the end? Will it go to heaven or somewhere else? The ignorant are reborn according to their concepts. The jnani knows that when prana leaves the body, consciousness disappears. No one has come, no one has gone. He knows that. The one who is basically unknown returns to the unknown.

The One who knows that 'He is' has neither name nor form. Consciousness and the feeling 'I am' are not different. What do you take yourself to be? You are consciousness only. Because it is in the body, you take it to be yours. Otherwise, it is universal. You take a pot full of water from the ocean and call it yours!

That which is known is untruth, and that which is unknown is the Truth. What sort of an explanation do you need? Only when you know what you are, the work is done. A poor coolie found a wallet of a rich man. It meant great wealth to him; he could use it for a lifetime. For the rich man it was his weekly spending money. Like that, a single moment of root-maya corresponds to infinite cycles of cosmic manifestations. Once maya is realized, are you going to hold onto it? Do not do anything. Just understand. Maya is the name you have given to phenomena. When a child is born, you can give it any name you like. Actually, it has no name. All experiences are temporary. No one can experience the Truth. Can you ever become the Truth? Can one put on an act of Truth?

We did not have consciousness earlier. It has now become luminous in us. It is the same as Sri Krishna. He told us how and why we experience ourselves. Just listen. Do not interfere with your mind. Do not do anything else. Do not lose sight of the feet of the Guru. (The feet of the Guru means your own consciousness.) It is a foot without a shape. It is the manifested consciousness, which is movement in itself. When you came to the stage of body-consciousness, did you come walking? When there was no walking done, was any information there of the path? Therefore there is no path that I can point to.

Maya means a flood of experiences on a stage of experience. The knower is the Absolute. He is not an individual. Maya is consciousness, the knowingness. It is there in all living beings. Your true nature and your consciousness are not the same. It acts during the waking stage and acts during sleep as well. This experience is called maya. Maya treats the ignorant jiva as if he is a slave. Consciousness is never steady. It is steady only when it forgets itself.

In spite of being gross, worldly experiences are subtle. The mind may appear to be subtle, yet it is gross. One understands that he knows but can he demonstrate that knowledge? It is subtle. Every being is enjoying the behavior of the five elements. The highest courage is to have the conviction that you are not the body. Catch hold of the feet of your consciousness and then act.

Nirupana 130
Thursday, September 13, 1979

Learn to forgive and forget. This is not possible without devotion to the Guru (non-dual devotion). Consciousness is love. The experience of beingness is the same as love for our beingness. They are not separate. The primordial sound 'Om' is the continuous expression of this courtship. It is nothing but love. Do not confuse attachment with love.

The fact that you know 'you are' is evidence of Brahman. Paramatman is at the root of your consciousness. You must remember this till you die. You are not the body. You are the one who is in the body. You degrade yourself because you take yourself as the body. In fact you are of a higher status. The indication of Brahman is consciousness. Yet, by believing it to be like the body, sinful behavior increases. The desires for objective pleasures grow. You will not get the bliss of the Self if you are busy fulfilling your desires and passions. The more you indulge in them, the more you will feed the fire. When your mind and intellect get dissolved into your consciousness, all desires will be fulfilled. Your consciousness has become hungry for the pleasures of the five elements. It has degraded itself. When your mind is steady on the knowledge of your beingness, all your desires will be fulfilled. You can meditate on consciousness only by the grace of the Guru.

Knowledge does not have any form. The good and bad experiences that come with the form will cease when you realize that you are formless. So long as you have plans and dreams, you have no time to meditate on your true nature. The duality will continue. One has to endure what comes out of such plans. Therefore do not make projections. You struggle hard with all your intelligence, yet your needs remain unfulfilled. They will be taken care of when you realize the Self. You will be convinced that the body is not your true nature. You will understand how the five elements were created and how the body was formed. Things happen by themselves but they are accepted through the intellect. While you are listening to this, keep your attention on That who is listening. With that, all your desires will be fulfilled. Fear arises within but manifests outside. A rare one lives with the conviction that he is the Paramatman. All others identify with the body.

When the visible becomes invisible, it does not mean that it is dead. When it becomes visible again, they call it rebirth. That is the nature of consciousness. Rebirth is not the result of someone's effort. This rising and setting does not affect consciousness. Create the simple faith in yourself: 'I am immortal, imperishable, I am neither visible nor invisible. It is because of me that this phenomenon becomes visible'. Give this understanding to your consciousness, with consciousness. Do not try rituals. We make plans to get happiness. What appears pleasing turns out to be painful in the end.

True happiness is spontaneous bliss. It is different from pleasure. Childhood and youth do not come from outside. They come with the body. In the same way, the joy of consciousness arises out of itself. Our consciousness is the joy of our being. Detachment implies that one has no expectations. It does not imply sitting down with a weary face.

Nirupana 131
Thursday, September 20, 1979

You have awareness and its witnessing happens to you. The five elements are contained in consciousness. Have you not taken yourself as something or somebody? What do you have to identify with except for your body? Happiness and misery, Brahman and maya are nothing but your consciousness. Your problems will come to an end when your body-consciousness goes. In the end, nothing will remain including the 'I'. When you understand this, I will bow to you! But the understanding has to be steadfast.

Your worldly dealings depend upon the meaning of words. Where the word does not convey any meaning, what would you understand? At this moment, what is your identity? You think you are very learned in wordy knowledge, that is why you use words. When you have no wordy self-image, you become of the nature of God.

Prior to each problem, an answer is always ready. If there is no answer, the problem will not arise. No attention is paid to the true state. Did you come to the world knowingly? Then how will you witness your departure? That is delusion. While coming, there was no step taken.

Then what would your steps be like while leaving? (Your consciousness came spontaneously and will leave in the same way it came.)

It will be clear to you later that what you have heard today is going to be of no use to you. Is the consciousness that you are experiencing at all honest? As a stick becomes a support to a blind man, the same way God with His many names have been given as a support. If you have achieved Self-realization, then all the names are of your own Self.

As long as you think that you are going to die, and believe that you are going to suffer after death, there will be talk of morality. Does the sun see darkness? A jnani sees no difference between a seeker and a sinner. The religions of the world are the games of the ignorant. You have a sense of self-identity that makes you anxious. You are creating pains while looking for pleasures. You may take it with any meaning.

You have to realize that your awareness and the world are one and the same. Then you will also understand that you have no use for the world, nor are you of any use to the world.

How is the duality between the knower and the knowingness? It is like duality between the sun and its light. The manifestation of consciousness is itself duality. If there is no knowingness, there is no duality. Wakefulness is the duality and vice-versa. If the sun goes to take a tour of its own light, will it ever be complete? Like that, if you go to see the end of the world with your consciousness, will it be ever found? Your knowingness is not an insignificant thing. It is the whole universe. But you are not that. You are the knower of that.

Devotion, consciousness and Brahman are one and the same. Someone worships it directly whereas the other may worship it indirectly. Krishna says: 'I see My own form. That form is the world. Therefore whatever is in the world, it is My own Self. One who sees and senses is not separate from what is seen. Those who know this and worship Me are the best seekers'.

You have heard enough, but what are you going to carry with you (at death)? The body has also come over you, but what is actually yours is consciousness. This knowledge is infinite. This means it cannot be categorized.

Who understands that the body is female or male? It is consciousness. Great aspirants such as Rama, Krishna, etc., worship consciousness by taking it up as 'I am That'. The rest of them, using the same knowingness, make their idols and worship them and hold onto them in meditation. You may perform enough worldly activities, but follow your Guru's word as if you have taken a vow. It is the same promise: 'I am Brahman'.

Consciousness is the entertainment. It needs no other means to entertain itself. Before death one ought to know that there is no going and coming for him. If the mirror is clean, it reflects all things. Like that, when consciousness becomes pure, the whole world is clearly seen sporting in it. One who practices devotion does not ever risk a downfall.

Nirupana 132
Thursday, September 27, 1979

When the quality of Sattva (the vital force) starts deteriorating and the intellect gets weaker, memory fades. Therefore one does not remember things in old age. So long as we do not realize who we are, all superimposition will have to be accepted. But what will happen when we realize that we are neither the Sattva nor its quality of knowingness. The body is a collection of the essence of food. The quality which is present in the food juice says, 'I am the body. I am male or female'. As there is fragrance in a flower, the body has consciousness. It is called Sattva. The source of that quality is food. There is also no prana without food. Can you catch hold of prana and consciousness?

Nirvana is where there is nothing left at the end. Some of your actions may leave an impression on space, but not to the One who is nirguna (without quality). The sense 'I am' is no longer there. The guna has birth or rise, tenure and setting or dissolution. One who knows this remains speechless.

In Nirvikalpa samadhi – without any mental construct – consciousness disappears. It is samadhi when there is no physical or mental pain. The gunas are on hold.

If there is no support of the body, who can know? Then they give It names like Brahma, Vishnu, etc. That is consciousness.

The body is not our true nature. In our true nature there is not even a trace of any characteristics. It has no concepts. One who realizes his true nature becomes God-like. One who knows the Self is the jnani. He is the Guru. Those who dwell in rituals have no knowledge of the nature of Self. To realize the true nature and live as the Self is the Self-religion. Our consciousness is spontaneously there. What is known is through the mind. Consciousness exists prior to the mind. The one who lives by the nature of the Self does not suffer the pangs of birth and death. He has no self-interest as he has no form. So long as there is body-consciousness, desires arise naturally. Whatever has to be looked after, is not of the nature of a jnani.

True listening is not done by the ears. It is done through consciousness. When there is no body, consciousness cannot be mentioned. To say, 'I am dying now', or 'I am going now' is an illusory concept. Even the concept 'there will be Self-realization' is wrong. If you go to meet the Self, it separates. It meets you without your trying to meet It.

To hold onto the word of the Guru is great service to the Guru. For this purpose, you have to give full attention to your true nature all the time.

Nirupana 133
Sunday, September 30, 1979

Can anything be known without the mind? Where there is consciousness, the mind must be there. It is the language of consciousness. However, the understanding that 'I am not the body' is within consciousness. It is prior to the mind. The feeling 'I am' is called consciousness. Hold onto that. The mind will not go away. Just keep on observing what you are. Do not consult the mind. The mind continues – let it be. You have to convince yourself that you are not the mind. You say you flow along with the mind, but have you ever seen consciousness flowing?

When in difficulty, if the incantation of the Guru-mantra is practiced, the difficulty passes away. But there should be the conviction that my Self is my closest friend, my Guru. Engage your mind in devotion to the Self. Let it be friends with the Self. The mind runs from here to there. In order to direct it towards the Self, the incantation of the mantra is prescribed. Only when the mind and the Self mingle into one does samadhi ensue.

Mind is the language for worldly dealings. Mind is action. The more we seek Self-knowledge, the purer the mind will be. One should forget body-consciousness and keep the mind busy with the mantra. Focus attention on your true nature. So long as the mind recognizes you as a body, it will not be controlled.

Your sense 'I am' is the Self that you have. Who tells the mind what to do? It is the Self. Slowly you will realize that you have no form, no shape. Only then the mind will come under control. While meditating, a shining white light like a diamond may be seen. In the scriptures it is called the subtle body. Only the fortunate have a vision of it. It is a sign of Self-realization. It is with the power of this light that the body operates. To remain without body-consciousness is the greatest fortune. If you are sleepless, as long as you are thought-free you will get the same rest. Contemplation of the Self is exclusion of any other activity. You may not be able to contemplate on the Self while doing your daily work. When working, pay attention to the work. As soon as you get a free moment, embrace your Self. When you are quiet, do not give attention to other thoughts; just to your Self. Consciousness has to concentrate on consciousness. While meditating, if you come to know someone's past, present or future, do not talk about it. When the knowledge of the Self is established, It will know how to conduct Itself in the world.

One has to be anxious about Self-realization just as one is with regards to the wife, children or occupation. The seeker of the Self has no rule, no law. Rules are for those who are anxious for objective pleasures. The mind is difficult to control. Therefore do not give attention to the mind. Give attention to your true nature.

Leave aside the name given to you by your parents. Now tell me your name! Can you say something now about your own Self? There is no answer to this question. There is only silence. This state is prior to consciousness. While meditating, do not project any form or an idol. Do not take support of any form at all.

If you watch your body, you will find that it is a machine that manufactures dirt. Yet the sages say:

'The human body is the best of all. Without a human body no one has achieved the Parabrahman state, nor can it be achieved'. Having forgotten the self-luminous God, you say, 'I am like the body'. Therefore you are marked for death. Carry on with your various dealings, but do not forget your true nature. Body-consciousness gives no time for recitation of the mantra or meditation. While forgetting the most beloved Paramatman, you are busy entertaining yourself. But whatever you entertain passes away. Give up identification with the body. Then, verily, you will see that you are the Paramatman. Out of millions how many have got the eagerness for finding the Truth?

To remember the Self without words is to mingle the self with the Self. There should only be the conviction that you are not the body. Then body-consciousness (ego-self) will go away. Can the Self, which operates with the vital life force of all the five elements, ever be destroyed? The power of Self-realization is such that millions of people fall at the feet of a jnani.

As far as possible do not commit suicide. Consciousness in the human body is very difficult to get – extremely rare. There is no knowing when the Inner Self will be pleased. One who gets knowledge is forever aware that 'I am not the body, I am of the form of light'. If this is recognized, your body-consciousness becomes like that of Brahman. Your conviction should be for attaining your true nature. There is only the Self. Because He is, we are the shining light. After getting Self-realization, there will not remain even an idea of death. Be aware of this before the body falls.

Nirupana 134
Saturday, October 6, 1979

When one becomes free of body-consciousness, the affection of relations becomes immaterial. Once you realize your own identity, you can love everyone. The whole world is your form, your manifestation. As long as you do not give up body-consciousness, there will be no progress. One must meditate like this: 'That which (eventually) leaves the body and is invisible, is my true nature. The body is not my identity'.

After transcending body-consciousness, one does not neglect his nourishment. However, one does not have desires and passions. A sense of detachment is created. One is content. A man goes on entertaining various concepts during the whole day. The rest of the beings (animals) use their mind for survival. Attention, when diverted from other objects, comes back to one's own Self. When the mind detaches itself from other things, it establishes in the Self.

Is there really any duality? You believe in it so it is there. Does the sun consider its rays separate from it? In order to become a jnani, become pure awareness. Then maya, Brahman, God, etc., will prove to be untrue. Only a jnani can recognize a jnani. Where there is consciousness, there is sorrow. Is there any difference between consciousness and sorrow? Is there any pain to the body at all? The pain lasts only as long as there is consciousness. One must realize that consciousness with its pain is not one's true nature.

Birth means wakefulness and sleep. These are the two states. A jnani knows this. Consciousness cannot be understood objectively. In samadhi there is unity of sleep and wakefulness. There is no samadhi for the nature of the Self. Intellect is the play of the concept, 'I am'. It is the string that flies the kite. The jnani notices how consciousness gets extinguished (at the last moment). He is not affected. He has seen God, whose voice this is. He also sees that God vanishes – He is also transient. Other people, however, worship God so that their well-being is achieved. This is the difference. It is only a rare jnani that knows that the incarnation of God is finished, but he is not finished. The rest entertain the concept of heaven and hell.

The Guru always asks the Self from you as his sacred fees; some may offer the body, but not the Self. If you want to become a jnani you will have to give your Self to the Guru. A jnani is not consciousness. He is never born. Whatever is, is consciousness. The jnani as the Absolute is not even a witness. You will know in time when and how the manifestation takes place. For the present, just introduce consciousness to consciousness. It is not necessary to bring Paramatman into the picture. Once this marriage is consummated you may do what you like. Once you know consciousness, you will not have any anxiety.

Think only of how, why and when you came to know that 'you are'. Leave aside all the rest. What is unsteady may become steady. As the Absolute, you are already steady.

Nirupana 135
Sunday, October 7, 1979

I do not talk on the basis of scriptures. I only talk about the One who is listening. I do not talk about managing your life as a householder. Only see who you are. If you understand this, the pains and pleasures of household life will not affect you.

Any work you undertake will always be imperfect, because your beingness itself is imperfect. One who has realized Himself knows that the joys and sorrows of life are of the nature of the mind. They happen spontaneously.

Birth is a nuisance. When there is no birth, nothing at all matters. Birth means the manifestation of consciousness – the Sattva. That itself is the nuisance. Even if one increases the duration of consciousness, it still has to be cast off one day. Even a person like Krishna had to leave consciousness. Jnaneshwar left this nuisance at the age of twenty-one. (He wrote the commentary on Gita in verse form. He also wrote 'The Experience of Immortality'. He took samadhi. He closeted himself in a cellar and asked his elder brother and Guru to put a slab over the opening of the cellar.)

Consciousness is felt and even cherished, but it cannot be tolerated. In order to bear it, various activities have to be undertaken. Whatever you compare consciousness to, and whichever way you worship it, will manifest itself in the same form. Yet it does not last. Krishna said: 'All this indeed I am'. Many a sage used to lay prostrate before Him. Yet, He also had to leave His consciousness.

The self-sensation that was felt unknowingly, is it a joy or a nuisance? Man is suffering anxiety throughout his life, such as anxiety for children, anxiety for grandchildren, or the anxiety that each one should keep well.

The calf is the reason for the cow's oozing milk from its udders. Similarly, the sage is inspired to talk about Self-knowledge when he meets the devotee. You may know how to recognize the quality of gems, but you will not be able to recognize the root-maya. That only comes from a Guru who is very rare.

Is consciousness without pain even for a single day? Does this nuisance arise from outside, or is consciousness itself the nuisance? There were fewer anxieties when people were ignorant. There are more anxieties when they are more knowledgeable. The reason for this is that they have not understood the root of sorrow. You had no knowledge whatsoever until such time as you came to know the body.

You were told that there is fear, there is death, there is time, and there is God. They are there if you believe in them. What if you do not believe? If you deny all of it, there is nothing. Is there any design to the Absolute? Even great people have been puzzled by it. Some people have passed away after saying, 'I shall come after so many years'. Is this realization? As long as maya is there as the subtle consciousness, there is no Self-realization. There is no darkness at all from the point of view of the sun. So from the jnani's point of view, no one has any birth. Whatever appears or is sensed is a staged drama.

Find out the cause of birth. Does anyone think of

the nature of consciousness? What is it made of? People do penance for hundreds of years. Only understand your true nature. You have no identity, 'I am like this', etc. Just recognize this fact. This talk is not for the common people. The way consciousness makes them behave is correct. One does not have to cast off consciousness, but it has to be properly understood. Your true nature is beyond consciousness.

Consciousness is going to go away. The jnani understands this. Therefore the jnani has no fear. The sense 'I am' is called Brahman. After realizing Brahman, one goes beyond destiny. The name Brahman is given for practical purposes. From pure knowingness, the mind, intellect and consciousness have arisen. When there is no consciousness, the need for happiness is not felt. Why is it felt when consciousness is there? The reason is that consciousness itself is a nuisance. If you call it happiness, it is happiness; if you call it misery, it is misery. It is whatever you call it. Just see what you are at this moment. You are different from whatever is known to you. Consciousness is by nature fickle. Its movement causes fear. In order to make consciousness steady, faith in the Guru is necessary.

If your devotion to the Guru is firm, you will enjoy liberation while you are alive. What is known creates fear. What transcends fear is everlasting. You do not pay attention to your perfection. That is why you are afraid. Have full faith in the Guru, and then the fear will be completely uprooted.

Nirupana 136
Thursday, October 11, 1979

Everyone wants liberation. It is because no one can bear this consciousness. It has no identity.

Whatever exists in the world is only the tradition of words. All religions are mere concepts. Traditions of words are based upon these concepts.

The knowingness in the body is unique. It has no shape, no form. No one can tell when liberation will come to you. Therefore you should never commit suicide, no matter what the situation is. The human body is difficult to get, even for gods.

The jnani is stabilized in his true nature. He does not need God. The jnani does not suffer from his memory, whatever it may be. The ignorant one suffers due to the pain of attachment. If you do not feed them, will all your relations die? Is it not that the body has taken its shape automatically?

Had you not come to this *ashram* (residence of the Guru and spiritual community), you would have eventually died hoping, expecting something. As you have come here, your hopes will disappear. If you have understood me thoroughly and have embraced that understanding, you can go wherever you want. If you remember my word, that word will do everything that I would do for you. Then you will have nothing left to be done.

Once you know a person, only then can you either be a friend to him or an enemy. But if you do not know the person at all, then all is Brahman.

First, the aspirant has to be a seeker. He becomes of the nature of God. Then he has to let go of his godliness. It happens spontaneously. Whatever is seen without effort is true Brahman. That is the natural state of a jnani. He has no use of words for his own Self.

The other day a western lady came here. A yogi from the Himalayas who is ten thousand years old had given her a vision and asked her to see me. He told her that she should meet him after she meets Maharaj. Babaji Yogi is like space. I accuse him like this: 'You have sustained your form, but can you interfere in the affairs of the world? Then why are you sucking on your consciousness as a child would on a candy? Do you not know how the life-tenure takes place? Then why would you keep guarding it?'

Great incarnations have come and gone. Could they affect creation, sustenance and dissolution? Where were they when the great calamities and tyrannies took place?

One who has stabilized in the Brahma-randhra (cerebral aperture) can say, 'the world is unreal'. The one who has put an end to himself (his body-consciousness) will understand it. Everyone is identified with concepts, traditions of words, and flow of feelings. One in a million will think about it. Only a rare one will pay attention to his Self and go to the Source.

Is there a greater light than the one by which you know 'you are'? You blindly identify with the body, but you are self-luminous. Who knows the mind, whether it is quiet or restless? Catch hold of the knower. If you believe in your thoughts you will be disappointed. Become the witness of thoughts. That 'principle' is observing all. No one can look at that 'principle'. Remain as the seer. The sense of doership is false. You are a witness, so stay like that only. That is the only penance you should perform.

Consciousness has come unknowingly. It is called birth. The experiences you are getting now are coming from the stage of sleep (ignorance, which is body-consciousness). In deep sleep, a king dreams that he is a beggar and so he goes about begging. The dream state makes him beg even though he is a king. When the false wakefulness goes, he is again the king. Then what is true in all this? You have no body. You are not consciousness. You are only a witness. Just hold on only to that. Then it is not even necessary to meditate.

Just remember That by which you know that 'you are' is the manifestation of God. Then you need not go to the temple. The spiritual seeker should not disclose this secret in his heart to anyone. Be a loyal friend to God with the conviction that He is the One who hears, and He is the One who talks. It is not your ego. Make it a habit.

The moon, the sun, the stars are millions of miles away. They are seen through the light of your own consciousness. It shows how far the light of your consciousness has spread. The light belongs to the Self who is in your heart. Can consciousness belong to an individual (who through ignorance considers himself as the body)? It only belongs to God who is Infinite. So it is best to keep quiet.

Bliss is of the nature of God. One who has no trust will not get happiness with all his wealth. As a disciple of the Guru, do not speak of this secret in your heart to anyone. One who is the offspring of the Guru, tells him whatever he wants from within. As a disciple, do not believe what people say. They will make you wallow in their own concepts. This secret remains between you and the Guru (this implies the mantra at the time of initiation).

God says to the devotee, 'You will not die, as your death would bring on My death. I am immortal and imperishable Atman'. Your problems will be the problems of God. If there are troubles, just recite 'Jai Guru'. Paramatman, the Absolute, holds the banner of your consciousness. Who can snatch it away? Remember that He is present; therefore you are present. Consciousness is your beingness, 'I am'. That is God. That is the Guru, purest of the pure. This should be the simple pure faith. You should first speak to the God within. If you tell people, they will destroy it with their concepts. Your conviction should be pure and clean. This is the secret essence of all this.

Nirupana 137
Thursday, October 25, 1979

Ordinary men do not understand this subject. Still they come here and listen. They think that the world is real. As a result they feel they have some duty to perform. They wish for the life-experience to continue. For me the world is untrue and there is nothing to be done. I have no desire to live longer. Consciousness is very small, but the manifestation is so vast! The human body is very precious, hard to get and rare. Take full advantage of the same. Do not commit suicide.

The intellect created by maya is selfish, but there is no selfishness in God. Consciousness that has come without asking cannot be eradicated. Just witness it.

When someone talks about the greatness of a sage, I say it is truly because he was never born. Prior to any other concepts, what is the primary concept? It is the feeling 'I am'. To whom did this concept come? Since you cannot label That, you give it the name – God. It is like naming a newborn child. These questions and answers are a conversation between God and maya for putting it to practical use. The true position remains as it is. Some devotees get various visions, etc., in dreams. But who understands them? And through what medium?

How can the transient experience be the eternal? You know 'you are', and it is a transient experience. The knower is eternal. Consciousness becomes bearable because it remains busy. It is true that the world is a visible evidence of love. However, it is also a conflagration of three kinds of miseries i.e. body, mind and spirit. What is the use of love? Is it not for the removal of misery? The true meaning is beyond the understanding based upon the word. The sense 'I am' itself, is a falsehood. Then how can one talk about the ego, etc.?

We do not show any path or give any discipline here. If you like the talk, you can call it a following of the path. Who knows the Truth? Does any single one claim that he knows the Truth? Who has any power that he can call his own? In fact, it was only after the rise of consciousness that you came to know 'you are'. Prior to what your parents taught you, what did you know about yourself? Tell us from where have you come without mentioning your parents. Childhood means ignorance. The same ignorance shows often as knowledge in youth and old age. That means, is it not ignorance that is showing off as knowledge today, after all?

Nirupana 138
Thursday, November 1, 1979

The concept 'I am the body' must go. Then your condition will be like that of mine. In order to let go of body-consciousness, hold on tight to That by virtue of which you know. When you are not there, the mind is absent. When there is consciousness, there is everything. If there is no consciousness, there is nothing. There is nothing prior to consciousness and there is nothing beyond consciousness. Consciousness is eternal and infinite. But it has no individuality, no personality. It may appear as God, Brahman, or even as an insect or a worm. The world shines in the light of consciousness. The creations of the vital force are moving about. Do not identify them as individuals. The knowingness and the knower arise simultaneously. One is not created without the other. No one has an individual form as his own property.

Even the greatest deities do not have an existence of their own. So with which particular identity do you see yourself? All identities will vanish.

No one can claim that he, by performing some actions, has earned this form. All rituals are for the sake of those who believe that the body is their form. No one desires to realize his true nature directly. This is the power of maya. Suddenly, a stirring happened in the original state. It is the consciousness of living beings. You have taken yourself as the body. It is a delusion. When there is no such belief, it is the true state. When we are all and everything, will there be any sorrow?

Nirupana 139
Thursday, November 8, 1979

The body is made of matter, hence the consciousness in it is a material thing. Consciousness takes itself up as the body and entertains various concepts and experiences, pain and pleasure. Therefore understand that the body is not your true nature, it is not your form. Keep this in mind and meditate upon it.

Actually, no one was born. Why is it so? To understand that, you must meditate. Meditation means holding onto the knowledge 'I am'. To think that the birth of the body is 'my' birth or the death of the body is 'my' death is an illusion. That which is in the body is a reflection and proof of the Atman. As a matter of fact, the Atman or the Self is never born. Only consciousness in the form of the vital life force is created. The collected bulk of the essence of food has turned into a form that is the body. Believing 'the body is me' gives rise to all misery through hopes, desires and passions.

No one has an experience of birth. Deliberate on this point: 'my birth has not taken place in my presence'. If you identify with the body, you see yourself as male or female. When there is no body, there is no such experience. When there is no body, there is no Sattva (vital life force) and when there is no Sattva, its characteristic – consciousness – is not there. When someone starts his search according to the Guru-word, all the identities taken up by him will prove to be untrue. Further, it will be clear that he is not of the nature of the vital force in the body (Sattva). After realizing that he is not even the consciousness in the body, he will be detached from the body. He will be liberated. He will understand in an instant that he was never born.

Liberation means to be constantly aware that you are consciousness and not the body. This is the sagehood of sages. It is the liberation of the liberated. Actions of the mind are not the actions of the knower of the mind. Birth is the pain you feel as a result of a dream. Teach this to the mind. All your understanding is through the mind. However, you are not the mind. Continue the chanting of the mantra. It brings purity to the mind. Then whatever you tell the mind, it will obey. Become the Guru of your mind, and as you have heard, gently lead it to the nature of Self.

Nirupana 140
Sunday, November 11, 1979

A sage, when he is alive, has to undergo suffering. When he dies, memorials are built in his honor. People express great devotion to him. Why is it so? It is because people worship fame.

After Self-realization, there remains no individuality with the consciousness. Prior to birth, and after death, the jnani's real state remains as it always is. The true nature stays the same. What has arisen will surely end. The knower does not have any use of it, whether good or bad. Whether you like it or not, whatever is going to happen, you will have to experience it. Yet, a being desires everlasting happiness.

If an important person were introduced to an ordinary man, the latter would have some expectations of him. A jnani has no such desire for anything from anyone. What is a jnani? He is nothingness. He has no name, no form, nothing at all.

Consciousness is the characteristic of the five elements. Hence, it is intimately related to them. Consciousness has a need for itself, but a jnani has no use of it.

Someone earns a lot of money (in the city), goes back to his village and builds a house. He dies after the ritual of entering the new house. He has no heir, so it goes to the Government. Maya is like that. It does not mean that one should not act at all. But what is the future of that action, and what is the future of such a person? This has to be understood properly. We cannot be of any use to ourselves. The jnani knows this.

This is your natural state – rarely will anyone tell you about this. Most teachers will ask you to do something. They will not tell you that whatever effort one makes is meaningless. In the physical world if there is competition, a man gets some inspiration to live by. With this kind of talk, there will be no charm in living. A jnani does not usually talk because he takes away people's ambitions. Detachment means understanding that everything is in vain. Charity and love are naturally there. It is the nature of consciousness. It is not that you *do* it.

Glossary

Many Sanskrit words have multiple meanings. Here, we have attempted to provide the pertinent meaning in the context of the dialog.

aarti: Ritual of worship accompanied with singing of devotional songs

ahimsa: Non-violence, principle of not hurting other living beings

ajnana: Ignorance

ananda: Joy, bliss

ashram: Residence of a Guru and his disciples; where spiritual association and teaching takes place

Atman: The Self, the pure being

avatars: Divine incarnations

Bhagavan: God, the Luminous One

bhajans: Devotional songs sung during worship

Bhakti yoga: Yoga of devotion

Brahma: Brahman – the manifest reality. Also when pronounced as Brahmaa, it means God as creator

Brahma, Vishnu, Shiva: God as creator, sustainer and destroyer

Brahman: The manifest reality, also called Brahma

Brahmananda: Bliss of pure consciousness

Brahma-randhra: Cerebral aperture, the yogic energy center at the crown of the head

Brahmastra: The legendary ultimate weapon

brahmin: One belonging to the priestly caste

chaitanya: Consciousness

chidakash: The space of consciousness

chidananda: Bliss of pure consciousness

chit: Consciousness

chit-ananda: Bliss of consciousness

chitta: Inner mind

darshan: The holy sight

dharma: Code of conduct, to hold or sustain the original

guna-maya: Delusion due to attributes of consciousness

gunas: Quality, characteristics, attributes of nature. The three gunas are Sattva, Rajas, Tamas

hatha yogis: Practitioners of yogic exercises

Hiranya Garbha: The golden womb, the Source (singularity) where the unmanifest Absolute becomes manifest

Iswara: God

jagat: World

Jai Ganga: Glory to Ganges

Jai Guru: Glory to the Guru

japa: Incantation, repetition of the holy name

jiva: Individual self

Jnana yoga: Yoga of spiritual realization

jnana: Knowledge, spiritual awareness

jnani: Knower

Karma yoga: Yoga of righteous action

karma: In Hindu philosophy, karma refers to action and the fruits thereof

Kundalini: The primordial energy at the base of the spine

madhyama: Word unspoken

maha-akash: The great space (of the universe)

Mahakali: The great mother Kali – God in the form of the divine mother, destroyer of evil

maha-maya: The grand illusion

mahatma: Great soul

maha-yoga: The great union

mantra: Secret set of words given by a Guru; a sacred aphorism

Maruti: Hanuman, the monkey god of Hindu mythology

maya: Illusive and projecting power of Brahman, the manifestation, the 'reality' as we know it

mul-maya: The root-maya

mumukshus: Aspirant

Narayana: God, Lord

nirguna: Unmanifest

Nirupana: Stating, searching, investigation, examination, defining

nirvana: The great death (when a realized Self exits the body)

Nirvikalpa samadhi: Silent state of awareness without any thoughts, a state of pure being

Om: The primordial sound, one may call it the first vibration when the unmanifested Absolute becomes manifested

para: Intuition

Parabrahman: The Absolute, the unmanifest

Paramatman: The Supreme, beyond manifestation

pashyanti: Thought-form

prakriti: The phenomenal existence, nature

prana: The vital force, the life force

pranava: The primodial sound Om; the root of prana, the life force

Purusha: The Self

Rajas: The aspect of rajas, manifests as endless craving, passion for life, thirst for action, restlessness, lust, haste, impatience, anger

Rajo guna: Activity, passion; one of the aspects of nature

Sadguru: The Self as the Guru

sadhaka: Spiritual practitioner, a seeker

sadhana: Spiritual practice

sadhus: Mendicants, monks

saguna: That which has qualities – characteristics

Sahaja samadhi: Effortless state of samadhi

samadhi: A state of awareness where the mind is silent; oneness with pure being

samsara: The worldly life

Sat: That which exists forever

Sat-chit-ananda: Existence-consciousness-bliss

satsang: Association with the holy

Sattva guna: Pure being; existence as one of the three qualities

Savikalpa samadhi: The state of a realized being who is in samadhi – a state of Oneness – while he may have the necessary thoughts needed for the moment

shakti: Vital energy

Shiva: God in the aspect of the destroyer (also called Mahesh)

siddha: Realized person

Sri Hari: God

Tamas: The aspect of tamas, manifests as inertia, darkness of ignorance, sleep, slow motion, indolence, immobility, resistance to change, decay, dullness, stupidity, and stagnation

Tamo guna: Inertia, darkness; the negative aspect of nature

vaikari: Word spoken

vijnana: Pure knowledge or spiritual awareness

Vishnu: God as sustainer of the universe

vrutta: Knowingness

yoga: Union; processes and practices for spiritual search (in the applicable context); also a unique set of physical exercises

yogi: One who practices yoga

For further details, contact:
Yogi Impressions Books Pvt. Ltd.
1711, Centre 1, World Trade Centre,
Cuffe Parade, Mumbai 400 005, India.

Fill in the Mailing List form on our website
and receive, via email, information on
books, authors, events and more.
Visit: www.yogiimpressions.com

Telephone: (022) 61541500, 61541541
E-mail: yogi@yogiimpressions.com

 Join us on Facebook:
www.facebook.com/yogiimpressions

Sri
nisargadatta
maharaj

a tribute

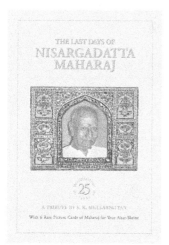

THE LAST DAYS OF
NISARGADATTA
MAHARAJ

25

A TRIBUTE BY S. K. MULLARPATTAN

With 6 Rare Picture Cards of Maharaj for Your Altar-Shrine

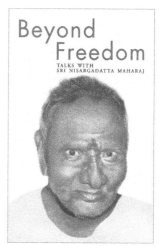

Beyond
Freedom

TALKS WITH
SRI NISARGADATTA MAHARAJ

The Sacred India Tarot
Inspired by Indian Mythology and Epics
78 cards + 4 bonus cards + 350 page handbook
The Sacred India Tarot is truly an offering from India to the world.
It is the first and only Tarot deck that works solely within the
parameters of sacred Indian mythology – almost the world's only
living mythology today.